When the King Took Flight

Arrest of the King and His Family Deserting the Kingdom. Townspeople and national guardsmen in Varennes have halted the king's carriage below the archway of the upper town, as hussar and dragoon cavalrymen arrive to defend the royal family. Events occurring at different times during the night have been collapsed into a single scene.

WHEN THE KING
TOOK FLIGHT

Timothy Tackett

HARVARD UNIVERSITY PRESS

CAMBRIDGE, MASSACHUSETTS, AND LONDON, ENGLAND

2003

Copyright © 2003 by the President and Fellows of Harvard College

Printed in the United States of America

Library of Congress Cataloging-in-Publication Data

Tackett, Timothy, 1945–
When the King took flight / Timothy Tackett.
p. cm.
Includes bibliographical references and index.
ISBN 0-674-01054-X (alk. paper)
1. Louis XVI, King of France, 1754–1973 —Flight to Varennes, 1791.
2. France—History—Revolution, 1789–1799.
3. Varennes-en-Argonne (France—History.
4. France—Kings and rulers—Biography.
I. Title.

DC137.05 .T33 2003   2002027334
944'.035'092—dc21

For Jean Miller Tackett
and Earl McClellan Tackett

Contents

Maps and Illustrations

MAPS

ILLUSTRATIONS

Acknowledgments

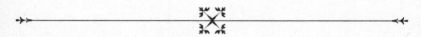

INITIAL RESEARCH in France was carried out with the support of a President's Fellowship from the University of California. Much of the book itself was written while I was a fellow at the National Center for the Humanities in North Carolina. The welcoming atmosphere and able assistance of the entire staff at this extraordinary center contributed greatly to the completion of the manuscript. It would be impossible to thank all those friends, colleagues, archivists, and librarians who have assisted me in the conception, research, and writing of this book. But I would like to offer a special word of appreciation to Jack Censer, Helen Chenut, Maria Chenut, David Garrioch, Carla Hesse, Jeff Horn, Marilee Jaquess, David Jordan, Thomas Kaiser, Jo B. Margadant, Ted Margadant, Jeremy Popkin, Joyce Seltzer, Donald Sutherland, Jean Tackett, and all the students in my undergraduate seminar on the French Revolution at the University of California, Irvine. For assistance with the illustrations, I thank Philippe de Carbonnière, Alain Chevalier, and Luc Passion. Earlier versions of Chapters 6, 7, and 8 were first presented at the annual meeting of French Historical Studies in March 1999, in the seminars of André Burguière and Patrice Gueniffey at the Ecole des Hautes Etudes en Sciences Sociales in February 2001, and at the international conference on "Violence and the French Revolution" held at the University of Maryland in October 2001. Finally, my thanks to Nicolas Tackett for making the index.

When the King Took Flight

Prologue

In the summer of 1789 a revolution began in France that is widely considered one of the turning points in the history of Western civilization. Although the origins of that revolution are complex, once it had begun, it was rapidly linked to the lofty humanitarian ideals of the Enlightenment, including religious tolerance, equal justice before the law, freedom of speech, freedom of the press, and control of the government by the governed. Most revolutionaries were also committed to political change through nonviolent means, "through no other force than the force of reason, justice, and public opinion," as one early leader put it.[1] These ideals, similar in many respects to those promulgated by the founding fathers of the United States, were soon embodied in a "Declaration of the Rights of Man and the Citizen," which became a model for liberal reform throughout the world.

Yet despite its idealistic beginnings, the Revolution of 1789 was transformed in a period of only a few years into a veritable "Reign of Terror." By the summer of 1793 a totalitarian and eminently intolerant regime had emerged that regularly employed fear and violence as instruments of power. Searches without warrant, arrests without indictment, the repression of free speech: all were pursued more systematically and more efficiently than in any previous period of French history. Justice before the law and "due process" were often abandoned in favor of guilt by association. A "law of suspects" attacked individuals on the basis of unverified denunciations. By the summer of 1794 thousands of people had been sent to the guillotine—some of them through travesties of the judicial system—or had been executed summarily without trial.

Any explanation of how the liberal, humanitarian revolution of 1789 was transformed into the Terror of 1793–94 would have to take into account a variety of factors: the state of war existing between France and much of Europe; the organized efforts of dissident opponents to launch a counterrevolution; the terrible factionalism that beset the revolutionary leaders themselves; and the emergence of an obsessive fear of conspiracy—real or imagined—that helped fuel the factionalism and justify popular violence. But a full explanation of the origins of the Terror must also reflect on the impact of a single event: the attempted flight of the reigning king of France on June 21, 1791. The dramatic effort of Louis XVI and his family to escape the capital and abandon the new government established in his name set in motion an extraordinary chain of actions and reactions with profound effects on all elements of society and virtually every corner of the nation.

This is the story of that event, the king's flight to Varennes and how it changed the history of France.

CHAPTER I

Sire, You May Not Pass

IT WAS NOT a particularly distinctive town. Astride the small river Aire, between two ridges of the Argonne Forest in northeastern France, it was a minor community where some fifteen hundred souls pursued their works and days as shopkeepers or artisans or farmers in the wheat fields and orchards of the surrounding countryside. Like so many other small municipalities scattered across the kingdom, it was a backwater.[1] The one road of any importance entered Varennes from the south and squeezed through an archway under the chateau chapel before curving down through the town and crossing the river on a narrow wooden bridge. North from the town a road led on toward the fortresses of Sedan and Montmédy some thirty or forty miles away, on the border of what is today Belgium but was then a part of the Austrian empire. Yet the roadbed was rough and poorly maintained and frequented primarily by local peasants and military personnel. For a great many residents the town of Varennes must have seemed a commercial and cultural dead end, where relatively little ever happened.

But on the night of June 21, 1791, something quite extraordinary did happen.[2] At eleven o'clock most of the inhabitants lay fast asleep, and with the moon not yet risen the town was very dark and very quiet. The only lights still visible were in a small inn called the Golden Arm, on the main street of the old quarter just below the archway. Here a number of young men were still drinking and chatting. There were a couple of out-of-town visitors spending the night in upstairs rooms; a group of German-speaking cavalrymen recently arrived in town and billeted in a nearby convent; and four local friends, all members of the volunteer national guard company of grenadiers. Among the latter were the innkeeper himself, Jean Le Blanc, Le Blanc's younger brother Paul, the schoolteacher's son Joseph Ponsin, and Justin George, son of the mayor. George's father was currently away in Paris, sitting as a deputy to the National Assembly, and the four men may well have been discussing the latest news of the Revolution. Very likely they were also questioning the Germans, trying to determine why they were in town and why there had recently been so many troop movements in the region.

At this moment two strangers rushed into the inn. The speaker for the two, an exceptionally tall and self-confident man who called himself Drouet, immediately asked the innkeeper and his friends if they were good patriots. When they assured him that they were, he told them an amazing story. He was manager of the relay stables in Sainte-Menehould, a small town about thirty kilometers to the southwest, and a few hours before he had seen the king and queen of France and the whole royal family traveling in two carriages, changing horses at his relay. After consulting with the town leaders, he and his friend Guillaume, both former cavalrymen, had pursued the royal party on horseback, and they had just passed them parked by the side of the road at the top of Varennes a few hundred paces away. He was sure that it was the monarch and that he was heading for the Austrian frontier. For the sake of the nation and the Revolution, he said, the king and his family must be stopped.

Such a tale might well have met with disbelief. But these were very special times, and Drouet's intensity and self-assurance carried conviction and stirred the men to action. The Le Blanc brothers rushed to awaken several other members of the national guard and a couple of town councilmen who lived nearby and then went home to fetch their muskets. At the same time Drouet and Guillaume and some of the others hurried down to the river and blocked the bridge with a wagon loaded with furniture.

The first council member to arrive on the scene was Jean-Baptiste Sauce, the town manager, or *procureur*, who had taken over the day-to-day operations of the municipal government while mayor George was away in Paris. A grocer and candlemaker by profession, he was thirty-six years old, tall, somewhat stoop-shouldered, and balding. Although he had only a limited education and wrote awkwardly with an improvised phonetic spelling, he was a dedicated patriot and carried himself with a quiet distinction that had won the respect of the townspeople. Flabbergasted by Le Blanc's wake-up call, he nevertheless dressed as best he could, grabbed a lantern, and sent his two sons to rouse the rest of the town with the traditional cry of "fire, fire!" By about twenty minutes past eleven Sauce, George, Ponsin, the Le Blanc brothers, and the two men from Sainte-Menehould had assembled with perhaps a half-dozen others in the street near the inn. Just then the two carriages described by Drouet, accompanied by two riders on horseback, clattered under the archway.

While some of the guardsmen held torches, others raised their muskets and forced the drivers to stop and get down. Sauce approached the first carriage, a two-horse cabriolet, and found in it two startled and trembling women who told him that their identity papers were being carried by those traveling behind them. The grocer then moved to the second, much larger carriage, pulled by six horses and heaped high with baggage. He held his lantern to the window and cautiously peered in. The carriage seemed to contain six people. There were two children—he could not tell at first if they were boys or girls; three women in middle-class dress, one about twenty and rather pretty, and two others somewhat older and distinguished in bearing; and a heavyset man with a large nose and a double chin, dressed in the clothes of a merchant or a legal agent. Sauce had never before laid eyes on the king, but he felt there might be a resemblance to the royal portraits he had seen.

Despite their protests, he took the travelers' passport into the inn for a closer look. As several city officials gathered around, he read the papers of a Russian baroness, Madame de Korff, and her suite, bound for Frankfurt, signed by the foreign minister and by

Jean-Baptiste Drouet.

Jean-Baptiste Sauce.

"Louis," the king himself. Although the document was somewhat vague about the number of people traveling, and although Varennes hardly seemed on the most direct road from Paris to Germany, the papers appeared to be in order, and Sauce and his colleagues were inclined to let them pass. But Drouet, who had already invested a great deal of his time and his honor, was adamant. He knew he had recognized the king. He had also seen a noble cavalry captain in Sainte-Menehould salute the carriage and take orders as though he were obeying a commanding officer. If the officials were to let the royal family escape to foreign territory, they would be accomplices to treason. In addition, Drouet asserted, the passport was not valid, since it had not been cosigned by the president of the National Assembly. In fact the president's signature was not legally required, but no one knew this for certain, and in the end the town fathers decided to play for time.

The occupants of the carriage were told that it was too late for their documents to be properly examined, that in any case the road ahead was in poor condition and dangerous at night, and that it was better to wait for daylight. Despite their angry objections, the party of eight travelers and three other men in yellow uniforms who accompanied them were forced to descend and were offered hospitality in the grocer's home. They were led several paces down the cobblestone street from the inn to Sauce's store and then crowded up a wooden stairway and into his small two-room apartment. At first the group studiously stuck to their story. One of the older women announced herself to be the baroness de Korff, insisting that they were in a great hurry and must be allowed to leave for Germany. But still intrigued by the man's resemblance to the king, Sauce remembered that a local judge, Jacques Destez, had married a woman from Versailles and that he had seen the royal family on several occasions. He went up the street to the magistrate's house, woke him, and led him back to his home. Destez had scarcely entered the upstairs quarters when he fell on one knee, bowing and trembling with emotion. "Ah! Your Highness!" he said.

It was the stuff of fairy tales: the king of France, Louis XVI, here in their town, in the storekeeper's bedroom. There, too, were the queen, Marie-Antoinette, their twelve-year-old daughter and five-year-old son—the dauphin, heir to the throne—the king's sister, Elizabeth, and the children's aristocratic governess, Madame de Tourzel. Everyone stood in wonder. Sauce's elderly mother came in soon afterward and fell to her knees sobbing, never having imagined that she might one day see the king and the little crown prince. Realizing that his incognito was broken, Louis XVI now spoke to them. "Yes, I am your king," he said. "I have come to live among you, my faithful children, whom I will never abandon."[3] And then he did a remarkable thing. He took the members of the municipal council in his arms, one by one, and embraced them. And he appealed to them and told them his story. He had been forced to flee his palace in Paris. A few fanatical revolutionaries, the Jacobins, had taken over the city. Worse, these agitators had repeatedly put the life of his whole family in danger. In fact, he now told them, he had no intention of fleeing to Germany, but only of traveling to the citadel of Montmédy near the frontier. There, far from the mobs of Paris, he could retake control of his kingdom and end the chaos and anarchy that, he said, were increasingly rampant. "After having been forced to live in the capital in the midst of daggers and bayonets, I have journeyed into the country to seek the same freedom and tranquility which you yourselves enjoy. If I remain in Paris, both I and my family will die."[4] The townspeople must prepare his horses and allow him to complete his journey.

And overcome by the emotion of the moment, awed and overwhelmed by the religious mystique of the monarchy and the aura of the king there in their presence, the town leaders agreed to help. If necessary, they said, they would accompany him themselves to Montmédy. As soon as dawn came, they would organize members of their own national guard and escort him. Their heads still swimming, they returned to the town hall to make arrangements. How could they not obey a command from Louis XVI himself, from the successor of a line who had ruled France for more than eight hundred years?

Yet after they had left the presence of the king, after they had talked to others and had come to realize the implications of the situation in which they found themselves, they began to have second thoughts.

The Third Summer of the Revolution

For the people of Varennes were no longer the same as they had been just two years earlier. Over the previous months, the town had been swept up in an extraordinary series of developments that had touched every corner of the kingdom and irrevocably changed the way in which the inhabitants viewed themselves and their place in the world. In March 1789, following a complex conjunction of events over which they had no influence whatsoever, all townsmen over twenty-four years of age who paid any taxes—the overwhelming majority—had been invited to participate in a national election, a process that would designate deputies to the representative assembly of the Estates General, which had not met for 175 years.[5] Varennes had been the site of both a municipal election and a secondary regional election leading to the choice of their own mayor, a former lawyer, first as an alternate deputy and then as a deputy in full standing. Perhaps equally important, the electoral assemblies in March had been asked to draw up statements of grievances that the citizens wished to bring before the king. Although the grievance list of the people of Varennes has been lost, it probably was not unlike the one preserved for the small town of Montfaucon, only six miles away.[6] As in communities all over France, the citizens began with a passage of extravagant praise for King Louis, who had convoked the elections. Then, scattered among demands for changes in a miscellany of local institutions, they asked that many burdensome taxes be lowered or suppressed; that all citizens, including nobles and clergymen, pay taxes in equal proportion to their revenues; that administrative authority be decentralized and shared with local provincial assemblies; and that more money be spent for the education of children. But whatever the specific demands made, the very act by which the citizens in Varennes and throughout the kingdom had systematically reflected on their lives and debated the institutions and practices that might best be changed or improved or abolished altogether had been a revolutionary event in itself. It had enormously raised expectations for a general transformation of a whole range of political, economic, social, and ecclesiastical institutions.

In the following weeks and months, the people of Varennes had watched in amazement as the Estates General they had helped to elect converted itself into a National "Constituent" Assembly. The new Assembly not only set to work drawing up France's first constitution, but engineered a wholesale transformation of French political and social structures that went far beyond anything most of them had requested in their grievance lists. At the beginning of August 1789, the news of the fall of the Bastille in Paris and the victory over an apparent plot to overthrow the Revolution had led to a great townwide celebration.[7] There were cannon salvos, festive bonfires, a public ball in the town square, even a distribution of bread to the poor—as might have occurred during a major religious festival. There was also a rare "illumination" of the town, in which every household was expected to place candles or lanterns in its windows at night. For a society unaccustomed to public lighting, such a display of concentrated candlepower would have made for a stunning spectacle indeed.

But it was not only a question of cheering from afar. Soon the citizens of Varennes had been asked to elect their own municipal and regional governments and to participate directly in the day-to-day implementation of the new laws. They entered into regular communication with the National Assembly, seeking advice and information, corresponding with their deputies, sending off a "lobbiest," and sometimes even offering their own suggestions for the drafting of the constitution. After centuries of domination by others—by nobles and churchmen and royal administrators—in everything but their most immediate family and local concerns, they had now been invited, indeed compelled, to participate in their own government, their own destiny. Such a process had imparted an exhilarating sentiment of involvement and local initiative. It had also instilled a new feeling of national identity, French identity, replacing the narrow world of the Aire Valley and the Argonne Forest, which had previously served as the inhabitants' principal points of reference. The great movement of the Enlightenment, the surge of intellectual emancipation and reevaluation that had blossomed among the cultural elites of the major cities of eighteenth-century Europe, had been very distant indeed for the people of Varennes. Perhaps it was only with the institutional transformations of the Revolution itself that Immanuel Kant's "motto of the Enlightenment," *sapere aude*—dare to know and to understand for oneself— came to have any real meaning for the great mass of small townspeople and villagers of provincial France. It is only in the light of this accrued sense of self-confidence and of identity with the nation as a whole that we can understand the actions of men like Drouet and Sauce and the various municipal leaders throughout the region during the crisis of June 21–22.

But two other institutional creations also played an important role in forming the Revolutionary psychology of the people of Varennes in the summer of 1791. In August 1789, confronted by the threat of anarchy and of possible counterrevolution after the collapse of the Old Regime, the town had formed its first citizens' militia.[8] Two companies of a local "national guard" were formed, the "chasseurs" and the "grenadiers," each with its distinctive uniforms, flags, and drummers, commanded by officers elected by the members themselves. One can scarcely exaggerate the feelings of pride with which the men of Varennes, some three hundred strong, aged sixteen to fifty, practiced marching through the streets and around the town square, accompanied by an improvised corps of local musicians. At first they carried only a few real weapons, hunting muskets or antique guns preserved by their families. But decked out in their new uniforms, the bright green of the chasseurs and the royal blue and white of the grenadiers, they felt an extraordinary sense of purpose and importance.[9] The status of uniformed officer, once the near-exclusive privilege of the nobility, was now within the reach of anyone—even the innkeeper Jean Le Blanc or the lawyer's son Justin George. Indeed, another of the officers leading the guardsmen of Varennes on June 21, the young Etienne Radet, would make a rapid wartime transition to the regular military, eventually emerging as a general in Napoleon's army.

In the spring and summer of 1790 the guardsmen from Varennes had joined with their fellows from throughout the region to march in a series of unity or "federation" celebrations.[10] One of these events, on July 1, 1790, brought some three thousand guardsmen to Varennes itself, where they socialized, paraded, and swore oaths of allegiance to the nation. Two weeks later, on the first anniversary of the fall of the Bastille, Justin George, Etienne Radet, and several other Varennes guardsmen had marched all the way to Paris to participate in the great national Federation Festival on the Champ de Mars parade grounds to the west of the capital, at the site of today's Eiffel Tower. There they had seen Louis XVI—only from a great distance no doubt—taking his own oath to the constitution. One can well imagine that they recalled this scene when the same king appeared in their town one year later, fleeing the very constitution he had sworn to defend.

A second institution of considerable importance in the new Revolutionary ethos, not only for Varennes but for other towns throughout France, was the local popular society or "club." Perhaps under the influence of his deputy father, Justin George had helped establish a local chapter of the Friends of the Constitution on March 25, 1791. With an initial membership of forty-four, the club was one of the first such associations in the new administrative department of Meuse to which Varennes had been attached.[11] It soon affiliated itself directly with the "Jacobins" of Paris, the popular name for the mother society of the Friends of the Constitution. The club's ostensible purpose was to support and propagate the decrees passed by the National Assembly. But in Varennes, as in much of the kingdom, the Jacobins rapidly revealed a special calling as watchdogs for the Revolution against all its known or suspected enemies.

In the months preceding the June crisis, the club had focused particular scrutiny on the local clergy. A year earlier the National Assembly had passed a sweeping reorganization of the Catholic church known as the Civil Constitution of the Clergy, and at the beginning of 1791 the representatives had required all priests with cure of souls to take a formal oath of allegiance to the constitution in general and to the clerical transformations in particular. In April the parish priest of Varennes, the abbé Méthains, was formally removed from his functions by regional Revolutionary officials after he had refused to swear such an oath. Adamant that the state had no authority to remove him, the abbé had attempted to celebrate mass on Good Friday, and the Jacobins and the national guard had entered the church and ousted him by force. While there is no evidence that the leaders of Varennes were particularly anticlerical or antireligious, they were clearly disturbed that a man who refused to adhere to the constitution should be allowed to teach local children and control the confessional. The refusal of nearly half the parish priests in the surrounding district to take the prescribed oath helped to intensify suspicions that concerted counterrevolutionary plots were afoot in their region.[12]

Indeed, almost from the beginning of the Revolution, the near-millenarian optimism engendered by the events in Paris had been mixed with fear and anxiety. From the perspective of the twenty-first century, we sometimes forget how frightening and unsettling the first experience in democracy must have seemed, even to those who fervently supported it. It was difficult to believe that the great aristocrats and clerics of the former regime were not manipulating events and that they might not still attempt to seize power once again or seek revenge for all they had lost. In fact three waves of near-panic apprehension had swept through Varennes before June 1791, all related to the fear of imagined enemies, perhaps in the pay of the former privileged classes. In August 1789 townspeople had been terrified by news that a band of brigands was approaching from the north. Even though the brigands in question never materialized, the defensive reaction that ensued had been fundamental in the formation of the town's first national guard units. Just one year later rumors spread wildly that Austrian imperial troops had invaded, and some five hundred guardsmen from the surrounding villages converged on Varennes to assist in its defense. A third surge of fear occurred in February 1791, with the rumor of yet another troop of brigands arriving from across the northern frontier. Although the alarm again proved unfounded, the town's desperate appeals for help had led the departmental administration to send substantial supplies of guns and ammunition, and even four small cannons, for the defense of Varennes.[13] The successive periods of panic had provided a series of practice mobilizations that would serve the local citizens well when a real danger materialized. Perhaps more important, the Varennes city hall now had one of the largest stockpiles of arms of any community in the region, arms in readiness when the crisis of June 21 arrived.

Beyond the fears of encroaching brigands or Austrians, a much more visible threat was posed by the large number of royal troops garrisoned in Varennes and in nearby towns, many of them mercenaries from Germany or Switzerland. Relations between civilians and soldiers had always been tense, even in the best of times. Local inhabitants were often expected to feed and house the soldiers at their own expense, and young military men were notoriously unruly, given to carousing and flirting with local women. The billeting of troops in individual villages had also been used on occasion to coerce communities into paying overdue taxes. Since October 1789 the municipal government had protested the placement of a detachment of German-speaking cavalry in Varennes.[14] These had been removed the following February, but six months later General Bouillé, the regional commander, had sent in some six hundred infantry troops. These troops had only recently been involved in the brutal repression of a protest movement of common soldiers against their aristocratic officers in the nearby city of Nancy, a protest with which many civilian patriots had openly sympathized. The appearance of these soldiers in Varennes had led to enormous tensions. The situation was defused only after municipal leaders found a way of housing the troops at the edge of town in an abandoned Franciscan convent.

The infantry troops had been removed in February 1791. But in early June General Bouillé announced he was sending yet another contingent of sixty German-speaking hussars. We now know that this action was part of the general movement of troops intended to protect the king's escape, a conspiracy in which Bouillé was intimately involved. Although this small detachment, again housed in the convent, caused relatively little immediate concern to the people of Varennes, many citizens had watched with growing skepticism as numerous couriers and wagons of military materiel passed through town and as they heard word of soldiers on the march throughout the region. Indeed, officials in the department of Meuse were mystified and intensely concerned by such movements in a period of peace: "marching and countermarching of infantry and cavalry, arriving one day, departing the next, advancing, retreating, and changing their quarters without any apparent necessity or utility."[15] On June 20 forty of Varennes' hussars set off to the west, supposedly to receive a "treasure" or strong box of money from Paris to pay the troops. The next day General Bouillé's youngest son and another officer arrived to spend the night at the Grand Monarch Inn, just east of the river, claiming they had come to prepare for the arrival of the general himself on an unexplained visit.

It is unclear how widespread local fears may have been. Sauce himself wrote a letter early in the day on June 21, welcoming the arrival of the hussars as a sign of his town's significance. He had spoken to the commander and had been assured that war was unlikely. But other citizens in Varennes, especially members of the Jacobin club, were far more mistrustful. A growing anti-aristocratic bias had made the noble officers who commanded the troops objects of general suspicion. One unknown club member wrote a series of letters to the department administrators in Bar-le-Duc on the very eve of the June 21 crisis. He detailed all the military activity in the town, extraordinary in a time of peace. He also described the visit of a certain François de Goguelat—another of the principal conspirators organizing the king's flight—who had interviewed Sauce about the national guard and the political views of the municipal leaders. In a wildly suspicious comment—which was only too close to the mark—he even speculated that the mysterious "treasure" the military was talking about might be the king himself, soon to be abducted from Paris by unspecified evildoers.[16]

It is not impossible that these various rumors and fears about the army were being discussed by George and his friends at the Golden Arm on the very evening of Drouet's appearance. In any case, the small, undistinctive town of Varennes, on the fringe of northeastern France, was far better prepared—institutionally, militarily, and psychologically—to meet the crisis of June 21 than any of the conspirators of the king's flight might have imagined.

The Army and the People

In the early morning of June 22, even as the town fathers debated what to do with the king of France who had arrived in their midst, the whole of Varennes had begun mobilizing. The exact chronology of that night is somewhat uncertain. Everyone noted the confusion, the rushing about, the numerous events happening at once. But it was hardly a moment for taking notes, and the account of the night's activities must be based on the sometimes discordant memories of the individuals present, written several days, even several months or years later. In any case, soon after Sauce's two sons had run through the town crying "fire!" someone had apparently begun ringing the bells in the parish church across the river. The church bells spoke a whole language of their own, with different rhythms or timbres calling people to mass or announcing a wedding or lamenting a death. But the rapid, repetitive tintinnabulation of the tocsin, as it was called, could only mean danger and emergency, and soon everyone was out in the streets asking what was wrong. Within minutes the national guard commanders had roused their drummers, who began beating the equally pressing cadences of the "call to arms," and, dressing as they went, men rushed to the center of town with their own muskets or to the town hall, where guns were distributed.

Once they learned of the king's arrival, their curiosity and amazement were matched by anxiety. Suddenly the meaning of all the troop movements and the talk of treasures became clear. Those who had not experienced the magic of the monarch's immediate presence were quick to see the danger of reprisal against those who would halt the king's flight and the imminent possibility of attack from the soldiers known to have been moved into the region. Fortunately, the most immediate danger, the German cavalrymen still quartered in Varennes itself, never posed a threat. Most seemed either asleep or well into their cups at the inn and watching harmlessly. But someone had seen their commander mount, ford the river, and flee northward, soon followed by the younger Bouillé and his companion. Everyone knew that the officers would inform the general himself and that they might soon find Bouillé's whole army on their backs.[17] The guard commanders sent detachments of men to the key entries of the town to set up barricades with wagons or logs or plows or whatever they found at their disposal. They also sent out couriers with desperate appeals for help from the surrounding villages.

Their worst fears seemed to materialize about one in the morning, when a group of forty hussars, followed soon afterward by a handful of dragoons, appeared at the southern entrance of Varennes. The commanders of the hussars, whom townsmen soon learned to be Goguelat and the duke de Choiseul, spoke to the cavalry in German, and the latter responded with surprise, "Der König! die Königin!" They then charged over the barricade, swinging the flat sides of their sabers to push the guardsmen out of the way, and rode into the center of town, ultimately positioning themselves in battle formation in front of Sauce's house.[18] The moments that followed were tense and uncertain, causing "the most fearful agitation" for everyone. The hussars, high on horseback with their plumed helmets, pistols, and sabers, were invariably intimidating to the population. Sauce came out and gave a brave patriotic speech in front of his grocery, protesting that he knew the cavalrymen "were too worthy as citizens and too brave as soldiers ever to participate in an operation which could only lead to bloodshed."[19] But no one knew how much French the soldiers understood, and the face-off between guardsmen and cavalry continued. Finally, first one and then two other officers asked to speak with the king. When Goguelat returned sometime later and seemed to be organizing a breakout, the guardsmen had prepared their defense. They had maneuvered their four small cannons into position on the street above and below the hussars and shouted for all house owners to open their doors, allowing citizens still in the street to escape and leaving the cavalry alone in a firing field. Seeing the danger, Goguelat himself charged at the guardsmen, ordering them to turn their cannons aside. But one of the citizen militiamen fired his pistol, shooting the baron off his horse. As the baron was carried wounded into the Golden Arm, followed closely by the guardsman who had just shot him—apologizing and almost in tears—other men and women went to work on the officerless cavalry. After more tense moments and offers of free drink, the Germans were persuaded to dismount, and soon they were embracing the townspeople and vowing obedience to the local guard commanders.[20]

For the citizens of Varennes, the appearance of Goguelat and the hussars marked a turning point in more ways than one. Through this threat of violent action, the inhabitants were more convinced than ever that the king's flight represented not simply the monarch's effort to find refuge from Paris for himself and his family, but a vast and dangerous conspiracy involving foreign soldiers and perhaps foreign armies. Moreover, the effect on the town leader Sauce must have been particularly strong. Only a few days earlier the baron had lured him with vigorous professions of patriotism into presenting a general report on the town and the national guard, even while other citizens had been far more suspicious. Now it dawned on the grocer that he had been manipulated by a noble, that he had been made a fool. "Under the veil of patriotism," as he wrote later, "Goguelat concealed from me his black treachery. I can only express my deepest resentment."[21] The experience may well have been crucial in Sauce's change of position toward the king.

In any case, not long thereafter reinforcements began arriving from every direction. About a half hour after midnight someone had dispatched three or four mounted constables, who were soon shouting "To arms, to arms!" from village to village. Shortly afterward Sauce sent messages for armed assistance from Verdun, the largest military center in the region: "Quick! Come with your national guards and with cannons. The king and the royal family are here. Quick, quick! Come to our aid!"[22] Even before the couriers arrived, some neighboring villages had heard the Varennes church bells ringing, and people were out in the streets; and in short order, peasant militias were marching to Varennes, drums beating, flags unfurled. In Montblainville, just two miles to the north, the first messenger arrived about one o'clock. Although there was some confusion as to the exact meaning of the emergency—the courier had galloped off to warn other villagers before the message had been clearly understood—the men sounded the call to arms and a hundred or so marched off on foot, arriving in Varennes a little after half past one. Once they had learned the true nature of the crisis, they took up positions ready for battle. As in previous mobilizations, the women with children in tow followed soon afterward, bringing wagons of food and supplies.[23]

Montfaucon, on a nearby hill in the Argonne, received word toward three in the morning. Villagers later remembered how calm everything had seemed the evening before and how stunned they had been by "this message, as unbelievable as it was unexpected." But they, too, set off immediately with whatever weapons they could muster, arriving in Varennes about dawn. By a quarter past five the news had arrived in Verdun, and the district leaders relayed it on before dispatching some four hundred guardsmen and regular French soldiers. Triaucourt, twenty miles to the south, received couriers about the same time; Autry, on the west side of the Argonne, got word an hour or so later, both directly from Varennes and indirectly via two other villages. Indeed, as soon as they learned of the emergency, many communities set their own church bells ringing and sent out additional messengers to warn friends and family in other farms and hamlets, so that a chain reaction was set in motion, passing the news with amazing speed. By morning militia were arriving in Varennes from Cuisy, Septsarges, and Béthincourt, just beyond Montfaucon; from Dannevoux and Sivry, on the Meuse River; and from Damvillers, well beyond the Meuse. That same morning, the word had spread to Saint-Dizier, some forty-five miles to the south, and to Châlons-sur-Marne and Reims, over seventy miles to the west. By afternoon Metz and Thionville, an equal distance to the east, had also received the news. All these towns rapidly dispatched armed contingents to Varennes.[24]

By the morning of June 22 several thousand people had converged on the small town in the Argonne: guardsmen with muskets, peasants armed with whatever they could find, women doing their best to prepare food and bake bread for the men. Although a few less-disciplined citizens began breaking into the homes of local inhabitants, looking for food and drink, most of the arrivals maintained themselves in good order, waiting for the attack they were sure would come. An elderly patriot nobleman, a former officer in the king's army, appeared on the scene and set to work organizing a systematic defense. Barricades were placed around most of the town's perimeter, and the wooden bridge at the center of Varennes was partly dismantled. Shortly after dawn another sixty-five hussars had arrived from the north, but the people were now prepared with a line of loaded muskets, and the cavalry was forced to wait outside the town, with only the commander, Captain Deslon, allowed to enter and speak with the king.[25]

The Fate of the Nation

In the meantime the municipal council, meeting in emergency session with other town notables and the judges of the local tribunal, was agonizing over what should be done with the king. The little group of men, shopkeepers, merchants, and small-town lawyers by profession, found themselves weighed down with the responsibilities of a veritable supreme court, with the fate of the nation perhaps in their hands. Soon after reconvening at about two in the morning, they had sent off a messenger—the master barber Mangin—to notify the National Assembly of the king's presence and to ask its advice. But they knew it might be days before they received a response from Paris, and they could not postpone their decision indefinitely. They had initially promised to help the monarch and his family travel on. But the arrival of the cavalry and the aggressive threats of their officers to carry off the king by force had substantially diminished the spirit of cooperation and goodwill—especially after they spotted Goguelat as one of the commanders and realized the extent of his trickery and deceit.

Moreover, through their own reflection and through the insistent advice of the Jacobins and other patriots present in the town hall, the council members came to reflect on the full portent of the king's flight. Louis had told them he would not leave the kingdom and would remain in Montmédy, but was the king really in control of the situation? They were surprised by the king's version of the atmosphere in Paris, which did not match their own understanding, garnered from newspapers and from the correspondence of their mayor. Most of them had heard reports of Louis' unreliable councilors and of the ease with which he could be influenced, however worthy his intentions might be. What would be the consequences for their town if it were subsequently determined that the king had been misled? Could they themselves be accused of treason, as Drouet claimed? And even if the king were not to cross the frontier, what would his absence from Paris mean for the survival of the National Assembly and the new constitution, which most of them supported as fervently as they supported the king? The potentials for civil war and perhaps foreign invasion were only too obvious, particularly for a town like Varennes, obsessed by its proximity to the frontier.

How long they grappled with these questions, agonizing over the dilemma of divided loyalties, we do not really know. At some point, however—probably about the time Sauce sent out his call for help from Verdun—they clearly ceased thinking of accompanying the king to Montmédy and sought rather to play for time and wait for the arrival of sufficient forces to defend the town. At any rate, toward the end of the night, Sauce and a portion of the council felt obliged to return to Louis and explain their change of heart. It was an extraordinary scene. A grocer and a tanner and a small-town judge informed the king of France that they must reject his orders, that they could not allow him to continue his journey. Struggling to express themselves in the royal presence, they told Louis of "their tender but anxious feelings, as members of a great family who had just found their father, but who now feared they might lose him again." They assured him "that he was adored by his people, that the strength of his throne was in everyone's heart and his name on everyone's lips; but that his residence was in Paris, and that even those living in the provinces eagerly and anxiously called him to return there." They also expressed their fears of "the bloody events which his departure might cause" and their conviction "that the salvation of the state depended on the completion of the constitution, and that the constitution depended on his return." The council's conclusions were reduced to their essence by the persistent cries of the ever-greater crowds of men, women, and children gathering outside Sauce's house: "Long live the king! Long live the nation! To Paris, to Paris!"[26]

At first the king and the queen seemed not to understand, not even to listen, and they continued to ask that the horses and escort be prepared so they could pursue their journey. Marie-Antoinette even appealed to Sauce's wife to influence her husband, telling her of the great benefits that the town would reap from its support of the king. Madame Sauce replied, as the townspeople remembered it, that she truly loved her king, but that she also loved her husband, and that he was responsible, and that she was afraid he might be punished if he let the party pass. Another story—perhaps true, perhaps apocryphal—told of Louis' appeal to old Géraudel, one of the guardsmen present and a simple woodcutter by profession. The king vowed once again that he would never leave the country and that he only wanted the good of the nation. But Géraudel was said to have replied, "Sire, we're not certain we can trust you."[27] Two years of Revolution had changed everything.

When Captain Deslon arrived at the Sauce house about five in the morning, he immediately asked the king what he should do. But Louis now seemed resigned and fatalistic: "I have no orders to give you," he replied; "I am a prisoner." Deslon then tried to speak with the queen and one of the other officers in German—the queen's native tongue—broaching once again a possible military action to extricate the royal family. But the townsmen in the room immediately shouted out "No German!" and Deslon returned to wait with his troops outside town for orders that never came.[28] In any case, the situation was entirely transformed about an hour later, when two couriers, dispatched by the National Assembly and General Lafayette the previous morning, arrived in Varennes. Bayon, an officer in the Paris national guard, and Romeuf, one of the general's assistants, had been traveling day and night in pursuit of the king and his family—still uncertain whether they had left on their own accord or had been abducted. Their orders were formal and addressed "to all public officials and members of the national guard or the line army." If the couriers succeeded in reaching the royal family, "officials would be held to take all necessary measures to halt any abduction, to prevent the royal family from pursuing its route, and to notify the legislature immediately."[29] Confronted with contradictory orders from the two central authorities of the new Revolutionary state—the will of the king and the will of the National Assembly—the people of Varennes opted without hesitation for the Assembly. The couriers then climbed to the second floor of Sauce's home and presented the decree to the king and queen. Marie-Antoinette appeared outraged. "What insolence!" she sneered, and she threw the decree to the floor. Louis, more phlegmatic but saddened nevertheless, said only: "There is no longer a king in France."[30]

In fact the National Assembly only specified that the king and queen must be stopped and the Assembly notified. But the people of

Varennes had no doubts on the matter: the family must be sent back to Paris immediately. Beyond the constitutional requirement that king and Assembly remain in close proximity, everyone was anxious about the local military situation. They were still expecting an attack from General Bouillé, and they could only hope that their town might be spared if the king were sent elsewhere. And so at half past seven, the sun already high and becoming hot, the municipal leaders and the royal party approaching exhaustion from their night without sleep, the two carriages were turned about and driven through the archway and back up the hill out of town. Accompanied now by thousands of national guardsmen, the king, the queen, and the royal children began the long trek back to Paris.

THE NIGHT the king suddenly appeared in a small town in northeastern France is arguably one of the most dramatic and poignant moments in the entire French Revolution. For the local inhabitants the experience was unforgettable, and in some cases it would entirely reshape their lives. Drouet would soon find himself elected to the National Convention, largely on the basis of his actions that night. Sauce would be tracked for years by fanatical royalists for whom he became the embodiment of evil. His wife would fall to her death as she attempted to hide in a well to escape the invading foreign armies in 1792. Indeed, the whole town would be periodically threatened with annihilation by various counterrevolutionary groups. "Varennes, unhappy Varennes," wrote one prophet of doom: "your ruins will soon be plowed into the earth."[31] By contrast, patriots from all over France flooded the town with letters of gratitude. An enormous sum of close to 200,000 French pounds was offered by the National Assembly as a reward to be divided among various local citizens. Engravings and flags and handpainted dishes would hail the town and its people, "from the nation, in grateful recognition," and the state would erect a memorial tower at the site of the Inn of the Golden Arm, where the royal family had been stopped by the national guard. Novelists and historians would make pilgrimages to Sauce's small upstairs apartment throughout the nineteenth century, until it and the whole center of town were destroyed by the German invasion in August 1914—and battered once again by the Americans four years later in the Battle of the Argonne.[32]

Yet beyond their effect on the inhabitants of Varennes, the events of that night would prove a turning point in the history of the Revolution and of the French monarchy, with an enormous immediate impact on Paris, on the National Assembly, and indeed on the whole of France and of Europe. It is to this broader context of the flight to Varennes, how it came about and how it affected the lives of various social and political groups throughout the kingdom, that we turn in the following chapters.

The King of the French

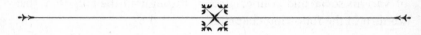

AT THE CENTER of the drama was king Louis himself, fifth monarch in the Bourbon line, thirty-six years old at the time of Varennes. He was a curious, enigmatic man, in many respects quite
unlike any of the kings of his family who preceded or followed
him. Even those contemporaries who knew him well found him
difficult to assess, uncommunicative, unpredictable. Whether from
timidity and uncertainty or from political strategy, he spoke very
little, remaining silent and somewhat inscrutable.

By all accounts he had been a diffident, taciturn child, lacking in
self-esteem and never really comfortable in the world of parade and
flattery and wit that were the essence of court life at the palace of
Versailles, the great royal residence about fifteen miles southwest of
Paris. He had been the second of four boys born to the son of the
previous king, Louis XV, and he invariably came out last in comparisons with his brothers. Contemporaries mistook his shyness and
sluggish manner for a lack of intelligence, and this negative image
was reinforced by his physical appearance. Although he had the
blue eyes and blond hair of his German mother, he inherited a ten-
dency toward corpulence from his father—a trait compounded over
time by a passionate love of food and drink. Even as a young man
he seemed little concerned with his personal appearance, and he
walked slowly in an awkward, tottering gait that seemed the very

Louis XVI at the End of the Old Regime. Heavyset, with his double chin, stooped posture, and somewhat sleepy look, Louis appeared the very opposite of the elegant Versailles courtier.

antithesis of courtly grace. The description of Madame de Campan, one of the queen's ladies in waiting, was not untypical: "His step was heavy and without noble bearing. He quite neglected his clothes, and despite the daily efforts of his hairdresser, his hair was promptly in disorder from the utter carelessness of his manner."[1]

Contemporaries were also nonplussed by his fascination with physical activities like locksmithing and masonry, hobbies that "shocked the common prejudices as to the proper pastimes for a monarch"—as even his locksmith instructor was reported to have told him.[2] The one such practice that fully matched both general expectations and the image of his royal predecessors was his passion for hunting. As an adolescent, he went out almost daily, roaming the several great royal forests surrounding Paris and learning by heart every alley and byway. As king, he was prepared to cancel a meeting with foreign ambassadors, even in time of war, whenever a fine day for the hunt presented itself.[3] And he maintained a precise journal of every expedition, listing each stag, boar, rabbit, and swallow shot or run down by his dogs, in an animal hecatomb of nearly 200,000 "pieces" spanning fourteen years.[4]

Yet despite the snide remarks of courtiers and ambassadors and despite his own misgivings, Louis was not unintelligent. Considerable care had been taken with his education, especially after the deaths of his father and older brother made him the dauphin, the direct heir to the throne. He applied himself methodically, perhaps even taking refuge in his studies from the demands of a court for which he had so little natural grace and predilection. And his accomplishments were not unimpressive. Eventually he learned English, German, and Italian. With an excellent memory for detail, he excelled in astronomy, geography, and history, and with the help of his tutor he undertook a translation of the English historian Gibbon. He read all his life, occasionally commenting on the newspapers he had perused, even purchasing a copy of Diderot's celebrated *Encyclopedia* in 1777. He also adored maps, knew French geography exceptionally well, and sometimes plotted out the trips he hoped one day to make through his kingdom.[5] Indeed, he had an almost obsessive fascination with facts and figures, as demonstrated by his immense hunting logs and by the endless lists and summary tables drawn up with all the precision of an accountant or a Benedictine monk: of the names and careers over time of all the palace servants and the keepers of his hounds; of the names and descriptions of every horse he had ridden since age eleven (a total of 128); of the animals sighted in the various royal parks; and of every detail in his daily household budget. He maintained a personal diary as well, but this, too, was essentially a factual recapitulation of activities, in which hunting again took pride of place. Nowhere were there any indications of personal sentiments or ideas.[6]

Perhaps more than any of his Bourbon predecessors, Louis also received careful instruction in what his tutors conceived to be the duties and obligations of kingship, instructions that while still a boy he dutifully copied down as a kind of royal catechism.[7] There can be no doubt that he was deeply influenced by his religious training, and that he took Christian piety and morality as seriously as any French monarch of the early modern period. His tutor had him vow "to imprint the precepts of my religion deeply into my heart," and throughout his life he attended mass daily and performed his "Easter duties" year after year, as carefully noted in his diary. His divine right to rule was clear and unquestioned: "I know that I owe it to God for having chosen me to reign," he wrote on the first page of his "catechism." And it was probably from the lessons of his tutors and from his sense of Christian duty and paternalism that he acquired a firm belief in a king's responsibility to his people. "My people should know that my first care and desire will be to relieve and improve their condition . . . The charity of the prince must be modeled on the charity of God," a sentiment he reiterated both before and during the Revolution.[8] At the same time, he seemed to feel a psychological need to be appreciated by his people and to receive their adulation for his efforts on their behalf. He was particularly affected by the popular reception he received at the time of his coronation in Reims in 1775—one year after his ascension to the throne—and he described his 1786 trip from Paris to the port city of Cherbourg, a paradelike carriage ride among the cheering masses, as one of the happiest moments of his reign. To the end of his life, he felt deeply pained if crowds failed to shout the traditional "Long live the king!" or if they did so with insufficient vigor.[9]

If he had picked up from his tutors and from his own readings the Enlightenment emphasis on "utility" and the "general will," it was clear that he understood such concepts in distinctly paternalistic terms. The king must consider the "general will" in making his decisions, but it was the monarch's will that was the final arbiter, the very "substance of the law."[10] And coexisting with his belief in the king's responsibility for the welfare of the people, he retained a keen sense of a hierarchical, aristocratic society of status and caste that was far removed from the ethos of the Enlightenment. He was clearly possessed of the same dual vision, the contradictory goals— of popular welfare on the one hand, and the maintenance of privilege and royal authority on the other—that bedeviled a whole generation if monarchs in the late eighteenth century, monarchs sometimes referred to as "enlightened despots." The intrinsic difficulties of this divided objective were compounded by Louis' personality, by a lack of self-confidence that seemed even to increase as time went on. Torn both by a pathological uncertainty of his own judgment and by disagreements among his advisers—toward reform on the one hand, and the preservation of authority and tradition on the other—he frequently found decisionmaking an excruciating process. According to Madame de Tourzel, his children's governess, who would accompany him to Varennes, he had "an exaggerated lack of self-confidence, always persuaded that others understood things better than he." "His heart," wrote Madame de Campan after his death, "led him to see the truth, but his principles, his prejudices, his fears, the clamoring demands of the privileged and the pious, intimidated him and brought him to abandon the ideas that his love for his people had led him initially to adopt."[11]

His sense of identity had been further complicated in 1770, when state policy and the international system of alliances found him a wife and a future queen. Marie-Antoinette was the second youngest of Austrian archduchess Maria-Theresa's sixteen children, and a year younger than Louis himself. Graceful and attractive if not beautiful, with her blond hair, her aquiline Hapsburg nose, and her thick lower lip, she had received only the rudiments of an education. She spoke French well enough, with a slight German accent, but she long had difficulty writing correctly and knew next to nothing of history, geography, or literature. The tutor sent to Vienna to prepare the fourteen-year-old girl for her future role as French princess described her as intelligent but extremely willful and with a short attention span for anything that smacked of study or serious conversation. One could scarcely conceive of a more complete mismatch: the heavy, introverted, insecure Louis and the elegant, vivacious, self-assured young princess.[12] The potential for discord was compounded by the sexual dysfunction that plagued the couple for the first seven years of their marriage, a genital malformation making it painful and nearly impossible for Louis to consummate his union. As time went by without a pregnancy, and as word leaked out that Marie found her husband boring and physically repulsive, tongues began wagging about the queen's reputed dalliances and Louis' lack of male competence. It was a humiliation that could have only further lowered the self-esteem of a man whose royal predecessors had been celebrated for their sexual prowess.[13]

The near-disastrous marriage took a turn for the better in 1777, three years after Louis had ascended to the throne, when Joseph II, the Austrian emperor and Marie's oldest brother, traveled to Versailles in an effort to patch things up. The king was persuaded to undergo a small operation to facilitate his conjugal performance. At the same time the young queen was berated by her brother into accepting her responsibilities as a wife and mother for the sake of her family's international strategies.[14] The success of Joseph's marriage counseling was impressive indeed: five pregnancies ensued over the next eight years, with a daughter and two sons surviving infancy. When his first child was born, Louis was overwhelmed with joy and with gratitude to his wife, and he proudly announced at court that he was hard at work conceiving more progeny.[15]

Especially after Louis began to sire heirs, always an important concern for the French population, the king acquired remarkably high favor in public opinion. Following their disillusionment with the reign of the previous monarch, Louis XV—with his endless mistresses and his broad failures in international affairs—many people seemed to seize on the young king, widely praised for his perceived sincerity and his hardworking application to duty, his faithfulness to his wife, and even his religious piety. His very bonhomie, his unpretentiousness, his distance from the court, his absence of concern for his physical appearance—all seemed to endear him to the public. The gossip pages of the *Mémoires secrets* described him in 1778: "No one could be more natural and amiable than Louis XVI." And there were stories of his kindness and familiarity with the palace servants, and of his return from the hunt "neither shaven nor powdered, his clothes in disarray."[16] This strongly positive popular image would persist and even intensify into the early years of the Revolution.

The queen, on the other hand, had never overcome, nor made much effort to overcome, the decidedly negative image acquired early in her reign. Pregnancy and the overseeing of her children's education had slowed her style somewhat, attenuating the perpetual carnival atmosphere of her first years in the French palace. Yet she had never felt entirely comfortable in France and always disliked the endless rounds of public ceremony associated with Versailles. She became ever more private and cliquish in her socializing, gathering around her a small group of attractive young women and men, notably the count of Artois (the king's youngest brother), the princess de Lamballe, and the beautiful duchess de Polignac. The "Austrian woman," as she was called dismissively, became the subject of endless rumors and innuendoes. She was even featured in pornographic accounts of alleged incestuous and lesbian activities. The tawdry Diamond Necklace Affair, in which the queen was accused of complicity in an expensive court swindle, further tarnished her public image.[17] Given the king's limited interest in the court and the queen's exclusiveness, many of the older aristocratic families found themselves marginalized or ostracized. Several of the younger members of these families would soon embrace the reforms of the Revolution.[18]

Although most of the rumors about Marie's sex life were certainly false, one of her male favorites did in fact assume a very special relationship with the queen. She first met the Swedish count and military officer Axel von Fersen when they were still adolescents, she a princess and he on his grand tour of Europe. He was away for several years, fighting under General Rochambeau in the American Revolutionary War, but he returned to Versailles periodically thereafter, whenever his military duties permitted. Never enthralled by the French, the queen was immediately attracted to this handsome foreigner, with his quiet dignity and reserve, so unlike the other young men at court. Through her help, Fersen acquired a French regiment of his own and a residence in Paris. After the birth of her last child in 1786, Marie and the king began living separately once again, and it was probably during this period that she and the Swedish count became particularly close. We will probably never know if they were lovers. Fersen always maintained a remarkably discreet position at court. But they had numerous encounters alone in the Petit Trianon palace in the forests near Versailles. The count de Saint-Priest, a minister who knew the royal couple well, believed there was no doubt about the matter, describing Fersen as the queen's "titular lover"—as Madame de Pompadour was once called the "titular mistress" of Louis XV. Whatever the extent of their physical relationship, the two maintained a deep and close attachment—as was made amply clear in Fersen's private correspondence with his sister—an attachment that would play a central role in the flight of the royal family in 1791.[19]

The King and the Revolution

By the late 1780s the king and the queen and all of France had been swept up in a period of state instability and crisis. The country's ever-increasing fiscal difficulties were driven by France's successful but enormously expensive involvement in the War of the American

Count Axel von Fersen in 1785.

Revolution and by an inefficient and inequitable tax structure that left the state struggling to pay its bills. The role of the king in the crisis of the Old Regime and in the coming of the French Revolution can be argued endlessly. But Louis' most pervasive impact on the train of events probably came less from what he did than from what he did not do: from his very lack of leadership, his indecision and inconsistency.

In the early days of his reign, following the death of his grandfather Louis XV in 1774, the young monarch seems to have applied himself to the kingship with a considerable effort of will and a sense of duty. He spent long hours reading reports and communicating with councilors. His correspondence with his foreign minister, awkward and a bit clumsy at times, revealed nevertheless an able grasp of the complexities of international relations. He carefully followed the revolutionary events in the American colonies, and he measurably contributed in developing a policy of French intervention, in part to "support an oppressed people who have come to ask my help," but above all to direct a blow at England, "the rival and natural enemy of my house," for its past "insults to the honor of France."[20] Yet he had always relied heavily on the advice and decisions of the two elder councilors who had directed and tutored him since he first became king, the counts Maurepas and Vergennes. With the successive deaths of his two mentors in 1781 and 1787, with the fiscal crisis of the 1780s becoming ever more intractable, with the intrigues and infighting among his remaining ministers intensifying, the king turned nervously from one adviser to another and seemed increasingly overwhelmed by the tasks at hand. Year after year he spent more time hunting, and the number of "kills" listed in his logs rose sharply.[21] He continued, in principle, to want the best for "his people," but he remained uncertain and divided as to how that aim might be achieved. Those who observed him at close hand in the late 1780s found him growing almost lethargic. Always taciturn and uncommunicative, he now seemed even more inarticulate and silent, even sleeping—and snoring—in the midst of critical debates.[22] Much of his later reign oscillated between progressive ministers and caretaker ministers, between efforts for dramatic, radical reforms from above and reactionary retrenchment. Finally, in mid-1788, under the ascendancy first of Archbishop Loménie de Brienne and then of the Swiss banker Jacques Necker, Louis was persuaded to take the momentous step of convoking the Estates General for consultations on the deteriorating situation. But the continual fluctuations in policy not only created a deep sense of uncertainty and instability in the nation, but also—through the inconsistent fits of reform—helped educate and accustom the population to the possibility of massive change.

The later 1780s also saw a progressive rise of the queen's political influence. In the first years of his reign, Louis had systematically excluded Marie from policy decisions and council meetings—following the advice of the king's anti-Austrian tutors, or so the queen believed. Yet she had long exercised an indirect influence through her ability to make or break individual ministers. Her involvement in court intrigue undoubtedly played a role in the fall of the reforming minister Turgot in 1775 and of Necker's first ministry in 1781. At the time, her brother the emperor had been outraged by her "meddling," particularly as it did not necessarily advance the Austrian position. But Joseph II and his able ambassador, the count de Mercy-Argenteuil, regularly coached the young queen on Hapsburg policy, initiating her into the workings of international politics and grooming her to be a veritable Austrian agent at the heart of the French regime.[23] As the Revolution approached, as Louis lost his most trusted mentors, and as he became more perplexed and uncertain through the failure of the various reforms, he came to rely on Marie for advice of all kinds. By 1788 he had begun inviting her to attend certain council meetings. Even when she was not present, he would sometimes leave the room in the midst of discussions to consult with her—much to the consternation and bewilderment of the royal ministers. And unlike Louis, the queen was not plagued by indecision and uncertainty. She never doubted for a moment that the reforms being proposed by "patriots" and liberal ministers were anathema to everything she believed in. Her steady and determined opposition to all reforms invariably came to influence the king as well.[24]

Throughout the first months of the Revolution, through the momentous events of the creation of a National Assembly, the popular uprisings in Paris against the Bastille, the suppression of noble and clerical privilege, and the dismantling of the "feudal system," the king remained remarkably popular among almost every element of the French population. The patriot deputies were deeply disappointed by his speech on June 23, in which he adhered to the position of the conservative nobility and rejected the existence of a National Assembly. But he was soon forgiven in the rush of events that followed, events that turned clearly to the advantage of the Revolutionaries. Most patriots remained convinced that he was well meaning and genuinely seeking the best interests of the nation, that it was the classic case of a good king badly advised. Later developments seemed to present evidence that Louis had put aside once and for all the "prejudices" of his caste and embraced the Revolution. The positive perception of the monarch was further reinforced by the great Festival of Federation, on the first anniversary of the fall of the Bastille. It was here, in the presence of several hundred thousand cheering people, that Justin George, Etienne Radet, and the other national guardsmen from Varennes had seen Louis raise his hand before the "altar of the Fatherland" and swear an oath to uphold the new constitution. Since everyone knew that Louis was a devout man for whom such an oath must be a sacred act, there was widespread rejoicing that the Revolution had now been won and that the monarch was definitively on the side of the people, well deserving the title of "king of the French."

But in retrospect we know that this popular view was more a product of wishful thinking than of reality. Already in early June 1789 the king had been angered by the perceived insensitivity of the patriot deputies to the sad death of his oldest son. He was also deeply unhappy with the National Assembly's failure to grant him an absolute veto in September 1789. Yet for Louis and for the queen the pivotal event of that year was undoubtedly the terrible "October Days." On October 5–6 several hundred Parisian women, followed somewhat later by several thousand armed national guardsmen, marched on Versailles and coerced the king into moving his residence to Paris. No one in the royal entourage could ever forget the queen's early-morning race for safety down the corridors of the palace, clothed only in her dressing gown, followed closely by the nursemaids and the royal children.[25] We will never know whether the crowds who pursued her sought to do her harm or only wished to talk to her and appeal for bread. But Marie herself had no doubt that she had escaped murder by the slimmest of margins. The royal family's slow carriage drive back to Paris that afternoon, followed by the rough and boisterous crowds of men and women—some with the severed heads of royal guards held aloft on pikes—only further intensified the horror and revulsion of the experience.

Grim and sullen, the family had moved into their assigned residence in the Tuileries palace, at the western end of the great Louvre complex in the heart of the capital. For weeks thereafter they refused even to leave the buildings or to stroll in the adjacent gardens.[26] A few days after the event the king wrote to his cousin the king of Spain an extremely significant letter—discovered by historians only in the twentieth century. In it he openly and self-consciously repudiated virtually the entire Revolution and protested "all those acts contrary to royal authority that have been extorted from me by intimidation" since the attack on the Bastille. Whatever temptations he might once have felt to cooperate with a reform movement, he now fully embraced a traditional image of authoritarian kingship: "I owe it to myself, I owe it to my children, I owe it to my entire family to ensure that royal authority, confirmed in my dynastic line through the test of time, shall not be diminished in any respect." And he solemnly declared that his conservative declaration on June 23 was the only policy to which he would subscribe.[27] Both he and the queen had now come to believe that a small group of Parisian radicals, the Jacobins, had seized control of the state and that the great mass of the population outside the capital fully backed the king and only awaited the opportunity to show him their love and obedience. But for the time being, insofar as the king had a policy, it was a "politique du pire": to wait patiently and allow the evil to work its course until the Revolutionaries destroyed themselves through their unworkable schemes of democracy and social equality. "He had persuaded himself," wrote Saint-Priest, "that the Assembly would be discredited through its own errors. The king's weakness led him to take hold of this idea, thus relieving him of the need for a permanent day-to-day opposition, too difficult for his character to sustain."[28]

We now know that the king's oath and his various appearances before the National Assembly—when he seemingly supported their actions—had been largely choreographed by the patriot leadership and notably by the marquis de Lafayette, the young hero of the American Revolution and the single most influential revolutionary leader in 1790. To be sure, a steadfast consistency was never Louis' forte, and he may have wavered at times in his assessment of the situation. In the spring of 1790 the family had finally begun venturing out of the Tuileries palace into the gardens and even by carriage into the city. In June they were allowed to drive to the queen's chateau of Saint-Cloud just to the west of Paris, and the time spent in the country seems to have raised their spirits. The king was also greatly affected by his enthusiastic popular reception during the Festival of Federation and the weeklong celebration that accompanied it. He rode out daily to review troops and national guard units and their rousing cheers of "Long live the king," pronounced with such fervor and sincerity, helped fill his need to be loved and appreciated by his people.[29] For a time both he and the queen seem also to have come under the spell of the great orator and Revolutionary leader Count Mirabeau, who had now sold himself as secret adviser to the monarchy, and who held out the vision of a compromise that would return the king to power as a greatly strengthened constitutional monarch.[30]

But Mirabeau died suddenly in April 1791, and long before that the queen, if not the king, had entirely lost confidence in him.[31] As the months passed, moreover, and as the situation became ever more complex and uncertain, Louis increasingly fell back on his wife for advice and guidance. And it is doubtful whether Marie ever seriously considered a compromise with the evil that was Revolution. Throughout most of the period she had complained in letters to her brothers in Vienna and to her Austrian confidant Mercy-Argenteuil that she considered herself and her family the captives of a "rebellious mob"—or of unruly "vassals," as she sometimes said, using the medieval phrase. She was beside herself with fury at the audacity of such people, at their pretensions to equality with the nobility and even the royalty. "These monsters," she wrote to Mercy in June 1790, "are becoming more insolent by the day. I am in utter despair." The words *monsters* and *monstrous* recurred con-

Louis XVI Taking His Oath to the Constitution at the Champ de Mars, July 14, 1790. The king appears at the top of the steps (far right), facing Lafayette and surrounded by the president of the National Assembly, Mayor Bailly, and the queen holding the dauphin. Among the deputies (seated below at right) are Barnave (pointing), Alexandre Lameth and Duport (to Barnave's right), and Robespierre sitting next to Pétion (eleventh and twelfth to Barnave's right).

tinually in her descriptions of the Revolutionaries. When the Spanish ambassador spoke to her in January 1791, he felt that he "stood in the presence of a woman at the extreme limits of her endurance." "Louis," she had told him, trembling with emotion, "will fail in his obligations to himself, to his subjects, and to all of Europe, if he does not cast out the evil that besets us, no matter what the price."[32] Under the influence of his queen and in his own fumbling and self-deceptive manner, Louis was increasingly playing a double game, a game that would be not only exceptionally dangerous for the king but catastrophic for the Revolution and for France.

The Decision to Flee

We will probably never know for certain how and when Louis made the momentous decision to take flight from Paris. The night he actually escaped from the palace he left behind on his desk a declaration written in his own hand containing a whole litany of grievances, justifying his decision to flee the capital and to cease cooperating with the Revolutionary leaders. He complained bitterly of all the royal powers that had been stripped from the throne by the National Assembly: direct control over the army, over diplomacy, over provincial administrators; the right to issue pardons; and indeed the power to reject outright any law of which he disapproved. He was angry with the Assembly's drastic reduction of his personal revenues, reductions that greatly reduced his lifestyle and diminished, he felt, the prestige of the monarchy. He was also rankled by slights to his honor, as when he had been forced to sit next to the president of the Assembly during the Federation ceremonies and had been separated from his family. And then there was the Assembly's sweeping reorganization of the French Catholic church and the subsequent requirement that clergymen take an oath of allegiance to the constitution, measures that he felt he had been compelled to accept. The latter decrees, in particular, tore at the conscience of the pious and orthodox monarch—especially after they were formally condemned by the pope in the spring of 1791.[33]

For a Bourbon king, heir to an absolute monarchy tightly linked to Catholic orthodoxy and a millennium-long tradition of rule, these were no doubt all good reasons. Whether they were the real reasons pushing the king to flight is not certain. In fact many of the laws that Louis opposed had been decreed more than a year before the escape plan began to take shape. Since at least July 1789, and on numerous occasions thereafter, courtiers and ministers and eventually the queen herself had encouraged Louis to retire to a safe distance from the dangerous crowds of the capital and to surround himself with loyal troops. But Louis had always declined such schemes. During the October Days, he had rejected Saint-Priest's carefully organized evacuation to Rambouillet, some twenty miles to the west of Versailles. So, too, in the spring of 1790, while he and his family were in Saint-Cloud, he had refused proposals of escape to Compiègne or elsewhere.[34] In part, it was the old problem of making up his mind. Yet he also seems to have worried about the consequences of flight for the other members of his family. His youngest brother, the count of Artois, had gone into exile shortly after the fall of the Bastille, and his two elderly aunts, the daughters of Louis XV, had managed to leave on a "pilgrimage" to Rome in early 1791. But his sister, Elizabeth, and his brother the count of Provence—the future Louis XVIII—remained in Paris. In any case, two dramatic and violent events in early 1791, both directly affecting the king and his family in the Tuileries palace, seem to have been critical in steeling Louis' resolution to attempt an escape.

The complex and often confusing events of February 28 were sparked by a popular attack on the great royal prison of Vincennes, to the east of the capital, rumored to have become a new Bastille where patriots were secretly imprisoned. When General Lafayette led a large contingent of national guardsmen to halt the riot, new rumors spread that the king had now been left unprotected and that his life was in danger. With threats of violence rising rapidly, some three hundred fanatical young nobles living in Paris, many of them members of the now disbanded royal bodyguard or of the conservative Monarchy Club, rushed to the Tuileries to protect their king.

Brawl in the Tuileries palace, February 28, 1791. In this patriot depiction, Louis XVI is shown speaking with Lafayette (background left) and approving the order to the national guard to disarm the counterrevolutionary nobles who had come to protect the king. In reality, Louis was deeply angered by the manner in which his defenders were treated.

Once inside they began baiting and insulting the patriot guards whom they found in the palace. Fearing a bloody confrontation, the king stepped in and asked his "defenders" to lay down their arms and leave peacefully. But as soon as they had complied, many were roughed up and arrested by the angry guardsmen. The king was outraged by what he felt was the betrayal of a mutual agreement and an affront to his honor. "My faithful servants," as he would write on the eve of his flight, "had been violently dragged from the palace," and he himself had been forced to "drain his cup to the last dregs."[35]

Even more threatening to the king and his family were the events of April 18, 1791. It had all begun with the royal family's plan to return to the chateau of Saint-Cloud to celebrate the Easter festivities. Huge crowds formed outside the eastern gates of the Tuileries to prevent his departure, crowds that soon received support from many of the national guardsmen who were supposed to help clear the way. The people rightly assumed that the king was leaving to avoid Easter services with the pro-Revolutionary "constitutional" clergy, and they refused to disband, and the guard refused to obey, despite the pleas of Lafayette himself. In the process, several of the king's servants and courtiers were seized and threatened with hanging, and for the first time the king heard himself directly mocked and even threatened with being deposed. Once again Louis was beside himself with frustration and anger. "It is amazing," he was reported to remark, "that after having given freedom to the nation, I myself am deprived of all freedom." In the end, the family was forced to descend from the coach and walk back into the palace, thus "compelled to return to their prison." Several close observers felt that the events of April 18, in particular, were crucial in convincing the king of the imminent danger to his family and of the necessity of flight. He would allude directly to the incident when he explained his departure to the grocer Sauce in Varennes and later to the National Assembly.[36]

But the two violent events at the palace of that late winter and early spring had another effect. After February 28, the national guard was given orders to forbid the entry of nobles into the Tuileries, whatever their traditional honorific titles, unless they had specific personal or administrative reasons for consulting the king. April 18 saw the imposition of even tighter restrictions, banishing most of the king's closest noble confidants, as well as the family's retinue of bishops and other clergymen, all of whom had refused the oath of allegiance. Although Louis and Marie had never been as tightly linked to court ceremonial as their predecessors, the trials of the Revolution had pushed them closer than ever before to the support and company of their aristocratic followers. And now, suddenly, the palace seemed a very empty place. Where once the "great" of the kingdom, men and women, had surrounded the two monarchs and basked in their presence, now there were only the Revolutionary guards and the teams of simple servants scurrying about their duties. To the royal couple, the dismantling of the court in the spring of 1791 seemed an especially cruel and unnecessary blow, conceived primarily, as they believed, to humiliate and isolate them, "denying His Majesty the gentle consolation of being surrounded by those who were devoted to him." "Not content with holding the monarch captive," wrote the noble deputy Irland de Bazôges, "they now want to banish from his presence those very individuals whose continuing devotion might bring him some comfort." Indeed, in the declaration left at the time of his departure, Louis would complain specifically of being stripped of "almost all his principal palace dignitaries."[37]

Whether these violent events pushed the king to a final decision to flee or merely reinforced a previous determination, by the middle of April 1791 there seems to have been no turning back. "It is now all the more evident to the king," wrote Axel von Fersen on April 18, "that it is time to act and to act with all due haste."[38]

Planning for Flight

The plan used by the royal couple in June 1791 had been conceived some nine months earlier by the bishop of Pamiers and the baron de Breteuil, the king's conservative ex-minister now living in exile in Switzerland. The proposal was different from earlier versions in that the goal was not just to move the king to a safe distance away from Paris—to Rambouillet or Rouen, for example—but to ensure his escape all the way to a frontier, where he could receive support or at least the threat of support from foreign troops. The basic assumption was that once he had distanced himself from the capital, from the Paris Jacobins, and from the radicals of the National Assembly, the king would find a massive popular following. Surrounded by his loyal soldiers and backed by the foreign deterrent—

so the idea went—other Frenchmen from around the country would rally to his support. In this new position of strength the monarch would be able to renegotiate the entire constitution and bring the Revolution to an end.[39]

By late October 1790 the king had agreed to consider such a scheme, at least as a contingency plan, and the conspirators set about devising detailed arrangements. From the beginning, the marquis de Bouillé—general of the army of northeastern France, headquartered in Metz—was given full charge of preparing the king's reception at the frontier. The actual escape from Paris and the overland journey were to be planned by the queen and, above all, by von Fersen. The long relationship between Marie and her Swedish companion now acquired a new dimension, and the plot that the two organized would be as sophisticated and deceptive as anything spawned during the entire Revolution.

Night after night, through the winter and spring of 1791—even before the king had definitively accepted the idea—Fersen and Marie met secretly in the palace to assemble a plan for what was surely the single most daunting element of the entire undertaking: the escape from the Tuileries and from the great, teeming, and suspicious capital itself. Although Louis was also consulted on key decisions and undoubtedly maintained a kind of veto power, on this as on so many other issues he now increasingly delegated his authority to the queen. In the process, and in the midst of such extraordinary circumstances, Fersen became a kind of de facto prime minister for the royal household. Several evenings a week, he arrived at the palace, disguised in a commoner's dress with a frock coat and the round-brimmed hat worn by some elements of the popular classes. His account of his relationship to the royal family was probably not exaggerated: "Without me," he wrote to the baron Taube, his closest friend in Sweden, "their escape would be impossible. I alone have their confidence. There is no one else whose discretion they can count on to carry out such plans."[40]

From the beginning it was clear to Fersen that the success of the project would depend on foreign support. The king's personal budget was limited, and he would need substantial amounts of money to pay mercenary troops and to maintain his family's requisite lifestyle until the situation could be "normalized." The plan also called for Austrian troops to be massed at the border "in large enough numbers to serve as a rallying point for all those well-intentioned parties, dissatisfied with events, who will come to join us."[41] But the long negotiations with foreign regimes, pursued primarily by the queen, proved enormously frustrating. Many of the neighboring monarchs, though sympathetic to the plight of the royal family, were wary of committing themselves unless the other great powers agreed as well. The queen was particularly disappointed by the caution of her own brother Leopold, who had become emperor of Austria after Joseph's death in 1790. It was only in early June 1791 that Leopold directly promised full support of money and troops. But even then the emperor specified that assistance could be provided only *after* the king had escaped and was in a position to act independently. Such a position added another powerful incentive for flight, but it made advance planning all the more difficult.[42]

As for the course of the escape, both Bouillé and Fersen had originally urged the royal family to travel in separate groups and in small, unpretentious vehicles in order to make a rapid dash for the border. This would be the strategy followed by "Monsieur," the king's brother, who escaped without a hitch to Brussels, disguised as an English gentleman, on the same night that the royal couple left.[43] But the king and queen adamantly refused to journey apart, or without their two children and the king's sister, Elizabeth. Making matters more complicated, the queen insisted on taking along two of the children's nurses. Soon they also added the marquis d'Agoult, a family confidant, to act as "guide" and spokesman if difficulties arose, as well as three other nobles, disguised as coachmen, to serve as bodyguards. With a total of eleven individuals, the party had now grown too large for a single coach.[44]

Presented with such requirements, Fersen set to work on the complex travel arrangements that had to be worked out if this small troop of people were to be transported in secret to the frontier. In order to establish a fictitious front, the Swede obtained the support of a Russian baroness de Korff, who was planning to leave France with her daughter in June. The baroness would claim that she had "accidentally destroyed" her passport and would then ask the authorities for a duplicate copy, the document to be used by the royal family. It was also de Korff who ordered the construction of a "berline"—the coach with large wheels and great coiled suspension springs, which was to take the royal party to safety. Supervised by a "friend" of the baroness—none other than Fersen himself—the specially designed vehicle took nearly three months to build and cost close to 6,000 French pounds, a huge sum for the day, beyond the budget of all but the wealthiest individuals. Exceptionally large, painted black with a bright yellow frame, it was a true luxury model, fit for a king, though poorly conceived for inconspicuous travel. It came complete with leather and taffeta interior, padded seats, numerous built-in luggage compartments, picnic apparatus, bottle racks, an emergency repair kit, and a leather-covered chamber pot. A smaller, two-wheeled cabriolet was also prepared to carry the two nurses.[45]

To transfer all eleven people out of the Tuileries and onto the post road outside the city, Fersen devised a sophisticated movement of people, carriages, and horses with all the method and meticulousness of a military order of battle. Plans were made to employ an array of little-known corridors and empty rooms within the palace, the most important being a ground-floor chamber with a small door opening directly onto an exterior courtyard—a chamber vacated since April 18 by one of the king's gentlemen and designated as the family's secret assembly room for escape to the outside. The queen had an interior door opened up between this room and a stairway leading to the royal suites, supposedly to provide access for her first lady-in-waiting. Several of the royal chambers had also been remodeled to secure easier access to rear passages and to insulate the family's rooms further from the servants and guards who slept just outside.[46]

In the meantime, the queen and a few trusted servingwomen set about devising disguises appropriate to the "de Korff family," including a small girl's dress for the five-year-old dauphin and the outfit of a financial agent for the king. Other than this special costume, the king seems to have taken only the magnificent red and gold suit worn during the trip to Cherbourg in 1786, which he planned to don when he took command of his loyal military on the frontier. A queen of France, however, could hardly be expected to live like a commoner, and Marie took great pains to smuggle out in advance not only an entire wardrobe, but most of her diamonds and jewelry, several items of furniture, and a specially constructed and fully stocked cosmetics case. Care was taken to cover these diverse arrangements with a variety of ploys and explanations. Unfortunately, however, the construction and shipping of the "necessary" for the queen's cosmetics was discovered and aroused the suspicions of one of her servants, a woman who was not only a patriot but also the mistress of an officer in the national guard. In the end, the family would make the fateful decision to postpone the escape by one day so that this woman would be off duty.[47]

Indeed, if they were ever to hope to slip out unobserved, it was essential to catch the Revolutionaries off guard and unsuspecting. Through the first half of 1791, and especially after April 18, the royal couple consciously pursued a policy of deceit. While they denounced the Revolution at every opportunity in secret messages to foreign leaders, they did everything in their power to lull the patriots into thinking they now fully supported the National Assembly. On April 19 Louis went to the Assembly in person for the first time in over a year and reiterated his acceptance of the constitution, and four days later he sent a similar well-publicized message to all his ambassadors. Shortly thereafter the king and queen attended Easter mass with the constitutional clergy, despite the king's revulsion for the "schismatic" church. As Fersen explained to Breteuil, the king had resolved to "sacrifice everything for the execution of his plans and to lull the factious parties [the Revolutionaries] to sleep concerning his true intentions. Henceforth, he will give the appearance of recognizing and entirely embracing the revolution and the revolutionary leaders. He will appear to rely entirely on their counsel and will anticipate the will of the mobs in order to keep them quiet and create the sense of confidence necessary for his escape from Paris."[48]

During the same period, General Bouillé was following a similar campaign of deception with the local patriots in his headquarters of Metz, some 180 miles to the east of Paris. François-Claude-Amour, marquis de Bouillé, fifty-two years old, had already won considerable notoriety in France as veteran of the Seven Years' War and the American Revolution, and the hero—or archvillain, depending on one's point of view—in quelling the recent military mutiny in Nancy. Indeed, several Revolutionary political leaders had recently approached him as a potential ally. But since the bishop of Pamiers first brought him a letter from the king, requesting his assistance, he had, by his own account, entirely devoted his services to the monarch. After a visit by Fersen to Metz and after having sent his oldest son and aide-de-camp to Paris, he had developed an elaborate plan for the king's journey to the frontier.[49]

The first and most pressing task had been to choose a fortified position to which the king could retreat. Although Bouillé at first considered both Besançon and Valenciennes, he ultimately recommended the small citadel town of Montmédy, to the south and west of Luxembourg. Not only was this fortress under Bouillé's direct command, but it had the advantage of strong fortifications directed toward the southwest, in the direction of Paris, as well as toward the northern frontier. However, the king would not be kept in the fortress itself, for fear he might be trapped by a siege, but in the chateau of Thonnelle, just north of Montmédy and less than two miles from the Austrian frontier. In all, the monarch would be protected by some ten thousand troops, both inside the fortifications and in adjacent positions.[50]

As for the escape itinerary of the king and his family, Bouillé had initially proposed the most direct road through Reims, Vouziers, and Stenay—to the north of the route actually taken. Not only was it the most direct road, but it passed primarily through poor

Marquis François-Claude-Amour de Bouillé.

and sparsely inhabited countryside, largely avoiding the major radical strongholds. But Louis had traveled a portion of this route for his coronation in Reims, and he seemed obsessively frightened that he might be recognized by local Revolutionaries. In the end, a more southerly road was chosen: through Montmirail, Châlons-sur-Marne, Sainte-Menehould, and Clermont, though carefully avoiding the town of Verdun, reputed to be particularly "extremist."[51] Once the itinerary had been selected, Bouillé enlisted François de Goguelat to reconnoiter the 150-mile journey by making the trip with watch in hand in one of the regular postal coaches. Forty-five years old and trained as an army engineer and mapmaker, Goguelat was an exalted monarchist who had once been personal secretary to the queen. Since the king's party would have to travel as rapidly as possible and change horses frequently, Goguelat also took note of each of the relay posts along the way. After Clermont, however, the travelers would turn north to avoid Verdun and leave the royal post road. So plans had to be made to prepare fresh horses from the army itself for the last leg of the journey, positioning them in a secluded spot just outside the town of Varennes. Since the conspirators had little knowledge of the political atmosphere in Varennes, Goguelat quietly—but awkwardly, as we have seen—interviewed several citizens there, including the deputy mayor Sauce, and concluded that the town was entirely "safe." Bouillé himself would be waiting with horses and a large escort at the final relay near Dun, about fifteen miles beyond Varennes and an equal distance south of Montmédy.[52]

The issue of a military escort for the king posed a particular problem for the planners. They all wished to provide Louis with protection as soon as possible after he left Paris, but it was dangerous to send troops too close to the capital. Moreover, if a military escort were positioned too long in advance, it might actually attract attention to the royal family's carriage. Ultimately, in agreement with the king and queen, it was decided to dispatch a relatively small number of cavalrymen a few hours before the family's arrival. If need be, they would explain to the local population that the troops had been sent to escort a shipment of money for the pay of the soldiers. But in general, all such detachments would be instructed to watch from afar and to follow well behind the royal carriages, intervening directly only if the king were recognized and appeared to be in trouble.[53] The extent to which soldiers should intervene or not was perhaps the most delicate question of the entire operation. And here Bouillé was forced to rely on the discretion of his younger field officers, many of them to be informed of the king's arrival only at the last moment.

After some debate, it was decided to establish the most advanced escort brigade near the relay post of Somme-Vesle, a village just east of Châlons. Among his other duties, the commander of this brigade was to send a courier notifying detachments farther along the route as soon as the royal party had passed. Perhaps equally important, he must post a rear guard across the road after the king had gone by, blocking any messengers from Paris who might attempt to spread the alarm.[54] As commander of this key position, Bouillé made the curious choice of duke Claude-Antoine-Gabriel de Choiseul-Stainville, only thirty years old and relatively inexperienced. Although everyone recognized Choiseul's loyalty and honored his aristocratic pedigree, both Fersen and the queen were wary of his reputation for flightiness and urged the general to find someone else. Fersen referred to him in one letter as "a muddleheaded young man."[55]

Yet Bouillé worried far less about his officers than about the loyalty of the troops they would be asked to lead. Throughout the winter and spring of 1791 local patriotic clubs had been vigorously recruiting the French soldiers garrisoned in their localities and casting doubt on the loyalty and motivation of their commanding officers—officers who, almost without exception, were members of an increasingly mistrusted nobility. Commanders everywhere watched helplessly as their subordinates became more unruly and undisciplined, sometimes announcing their intention of following only orders that they themselves had approved. Under such conditions, Bouillé felt no choice but to make plans based entirely on the use of foreign mercenaries.[56] He appealed to the Tuileries for funds to ensure that his Swiss and German troops were all well paid and that extra money would be available for the day of reckoning. Fersen and the queen managed to scrape together nearly a million French pounds—much of it from Fersen's own fortune—which they audaciously shipped to Metz wrapped in bolts of white taffeta. Plans were further jeopardized in the spring, however, when the new pro-Revolutionary minister of war moved some of the general's best foreign troops to another province.[57]

But Bouillé was also concerned about the reliability of the king himself. The inclusion of the marquis d'Agoult in the escape party had been conceived to compensate the monarch's lack of experience in traveling by himself. Then, at the last minute, the royal family removed d'Agoult to make room for the royal governess Madame de Tourzel, who had insisted on traveling with her charges as soon as she learned of the escape plan. Bouillé was also haunted by the fear that the monarch would never summon the determination and constancy to go through with such a bold plan, that he would back out at the last minute, leaving the conspirators unprotected and vulnerable to arrest for treason.[58] Such fears were only increased by the king's repeated postponement of his departure date. First scheduled for late May, then early June, the flight was put off successively to June 12, 15, and 19.[59] More unfortunate still, Bouillé learned only on June 15 that the royal family had rescheduled its departure yet again to the twentieth. By this time all the general's instructions had been issued, and his troops were moving into position. The necessary changes in orders, cobbled together at the last moment, would cause several minor mistakes and inconsistencies that measurably affected the success of the enterprise. Perhaps most serious of all, a number of cavalry contingents would be forced to bivouac an extra day in towns along the way, arousing great nervousness and suspicion among the local inhabitants.[60]

Despite the elaborate plans developed for the king's escape, remarkably little attention seems to have been given to what the king would do when he actually arrived in Montmédy. Bouillé claimed that he was never informed of the king's intentions. Louis may have planned to establish a provisional government with his conservative ex-minister, the baron Breteuil, as prime minister. Breteuil was asked to draft a policy paper from his exile in Switzerland and to join the king in Montmédy as soon as possible. But the draft, sent ahead to Luxembourg for delivery to the monarch, was never opened and was apparently destroyed.[61] To judge from the declaration left on his desk at the time of his departure—and from his speech of June 23, 1789, to which the declaration referred—Louis would probably have maintained the National Assembly. But he continued to refer to the Assembly as the "Estates General," and he suggested that the nobles would play a dominant role within that body and regain most of their former privileges. And in other ways he indicated his intention of dismantling most of the Revolution, reclaiming the greater part of his former royal powers, abrogating the Civil Constitution of the Clergy, returning the church property seized by the Revolutionaries, and generally repudiating all laws passed since October 1789. In Louis' mind, this sweeping "counter-revolution" would be peacefully "negotiated" between the father-king in Montmédy and his recalcitrant subjects, whom he graciously promised to forgive for all the humiliations he had suffered. When the situation had calmed, he would return from his frontier fortress and choose a residence a safe distance from Paris—perhaps in the palace of Compiègne, some seventy-five miles north of the "former" capital.[62]

The Stakes

But would the king's subjects docilely accept the settlement that Louis proposed? Given their reactions in the days following the flight, it seems certain that a large segment of the population would not. It is difficult to imagine that the king's successful escape would not have led to a civil war. Both the queen and General Bouillé presumed this would be the case. Moreover, Marie and the general also assumed that Louis would soon have to retire into Austrian territory for his own safety, and they were already making plans to persuade him to do so.[63] Despite his long-stated intention of remaining within his kingdom, the king would almost certainly have crossed into foreign territory, only a short distance away, once it was evident that his family was in danger—and once those around him, who knew so well how to manipulate him, began exerting pressure. Although Louis may have imagined he was acting only for the good of his people, it is more than likely that a successful escape would have ignited a full-scale civil war and probably an international war as well—with the prospect of untold suffering for the very people the king called "his children."

The Austrian ambassador, Mercy-Argenteuil, had no doubts on this score. In a long series of letters written through the winter and spring, Mercy had begged the queen to reflect on the consequences of flight, and on what would transpire if the escape were to fail.

The king and queen, Mercy argued, had greatly underestimated the extent of popular support for the Revolution: "escape has become impossible at this time. Every village could be an insurmountable barrier to your passage. And I tremble to think of the catastrophe that would arise if the enterprise fails." He understood that the situation was frustrating and unhappy and that the king had lost much of his former power. But the family would do far better, the Austrian diplomat argued, to wait out the storm. "If only you persist where you are, you can be certain that sooner or later the mad creations of the Revolutionaries will collapse by themselves"; in contrast, choosing "the extreme solution [of flight] will inevitably decide, for better or for worse, the fate of the king and the kingship."[64]

These, then, were the stakes, if Louis should attempt an escape. And the stakes were high indeed. Success could well mean civil war. Failure might bring "catastrophe" and perhaps the end of the monarchy.

CHAPTER 3

The King Takes Flight

THE ROYAL COUPLE'S CHALLENGE on that last day before their flight was clear and sobering: to extricate themselves and their entire family undetected from a palace staffed by no less than two thousand people—national guardsmen, domestics, and government workers—whose lives centered entirely on the presence of the king and queen. The task was all the more daunting in that rumors of just such an escape plan had been circulating in Paris for some time. Following the denunciation by the queen's servingwoman, extra guards had been established in and around the Tuileries. Indeed, with suspicion in the air, it was particularly important that the royal family maintain their systematic deception to the final moment. Thus the queen scrupulously maintained her usual schedule throughout the day. She attended mass; she had her hair done; she went out for a drive with her children and several courtiers to the Tivoli palace; she dined with the family, including the king's brother and sister, before retiring for the night. Yet her daughter, the twelve-year-old "Madame Royale"—as she was called—sensed that her parents were unusually tense. She was especially mystified when all her attendants, with the exception of the chief nurse, Madame Brunier, were sent away for the day on the pretense that the princess was sick.[1]

In fact her parents were preoccupied with the myriad of last-minute arrangements that had to be made if the escape was actually to come off. One of their most pressing concerns was to brief the three professional soldiers who were to accompany the flight, take charge of the practical details, and provide some limited measure of protection. For this task the count d'Agoult, former commander of the now disbanded royal bodyguards, had recruited three of his best men. François-Florent de Valory, François-Melchoir de Moustier, and Jean-François Malden were obscure provincial nobles who had served in the same company of the king's guard for almost twenty years. All three had seen their regiment humiliated by the Paris crowds during the October Days, and they had since frequented the circle of reactionary nobles in Paris who had rushed to the king's defense on February 28—though they claimed not to have participated themselves. All had taken oaths of submission to the king, and they would maintain their loyalty to "their master" even under the harsh questioning of the Revolutionary interrogators after their arrest. "Entirely dedicated to my king," as Valory would tell them, "I would never have questioned his orders, having sworn to him my loyalty, my obedience, my respect, and my love." Louis himself first called in Moustier on June 17 and asked him to obtain the disguise of a private courier for himself and for the two others: short coats, suede knee breeches, and round-brimmed hats. Just before dinner on the evening of the escape, the king and queen had the men secretly led into their chambers through the back corridors of the Louvre. Here the king gave them their instructions in detail, instructions that had been worked out by Fersen and Bouillé over the previous months. The three always claimed, and there is no reason to disbelieve them, that they knew nothing of the escape before that night.[2]

In the meantime, Fersen was a whirlwind of activity, setting into motion a complex choreography of men, coaches, and horses. During the day of June 20 he visited his banker and the Swedish ambassador; he secretly passed through the Tuileries to pick up more packages for the berline; he saw to the last-minute purchase of horses, saddles, and riding whips, and to the final movements of the various carriages—often in stages, to avoid arousing suspicion. About six that evening Fersen's German coachman, Balthasar Sapel, drove the large black escape coach from the carriagemaker's shop to the home of a wealthy Englishman on Rue de Clichy. Toward eight o'clock the two-wheeled cabriolet that was to carry the two nurses was parked on the Seine across the river from the palace. At about the same time an ordinary *fiacre*, or hackney cab, was left near the Tuileries gardens on the Champs-Elysées, where Fersen himself would pick it up later. At half past nine, Valory and Moustier met Sapel on Rue de Clichy, and they drove the berline together on a circuitous route through the western suburbs and then out around the new northern boulevards just beyond the city walls, positioning it near the Saint-Martin's customs gate at the northeast corner of Paris. Valory then rode off to the village of Bondy to prepare horses for the first relay stop.[3]

In the palace itself the first phase of the escape plan was launched at about three in the afternoon, when the duke de Choiseul, who had been sent to Paris with final messages from Bouillé, left by carriage for the relay post of Somme-Vesle, where he was to meet the advance detachment of cavalry sent out for the protection of the king. In his company was perhaps the most unlikely participant in the whole adventure, the queen's hairdresser, Jean-François Autié, known to all the world as "Monsieur Léonard." In the final days the queen had decided that it would be unthinkable to face the rigors of life in Montmédy without a proper coiffeur. Shortly before Choiseul's departure she had called in Léonard and asked him if he was ready to do anything she asked. When the hairdresser responded enthusiastically in the affirmative—and what else could one say to a queen?—she told him to leave with Monsieur de Choiseul and to follow his orders to the word. With no idea where he was going, with no change of clothes, without even the possibility of canceling his afternoon appointments, the thirty-three-year-old hairdresser, stunned and confused, left with Choiseul on the road east.[4]

At about half past ten the escape of the royal family itself was set into motion. When dinner was finished, Louis embraced his younger brother, the count of Provence, and sent him off on his own successful escape northward to Brussels—the last time the two brothers would ever see each other. Then Marie-Antoinette and Madame de Tourzel slipped away to awaken the two royal children and to inform their nurses of the departure set for that evening. The two royal caretakers, Madame Brunier and Madame de Neuville, were scarcely less surprised than Monsieur Léonard. But they were utterly devoted to the royal family and prepared to follow them anywhere—indeed, it was Neuville who had rushed through the halls of Versailles with the dauphin in her arms during the October Days. The queen, Tourzel, and the nurses leading or carrying their royal charges went quietly down the back stairway to the ground floor and into the dark apartment abandoned by the king's first gentleman. The nurses quickly helped the children change into their disguises, with the dauphin and his sister both dressed as young girls. Once they had prepared the children, the nurses were led by the guard Malden back upstairs, out the main palace entrance, and across the Seine to the waiting carriage. A hired coachman drove them to the village of Claye, the second relay stop on the planned escape route, where they would wait anxiously through the night.[5]

Back in the darkened ground-floor room, the queen quietly unlocked the exterior door of the apartment with a key she had obtained through a ruse some weeks earlier. A gibbous moon was low on the horizon and probably covered in clouds. The queen had carefully timed their exit to correspond with the moment when large numbers of servants left the palace to return to their homes.[6] In the considerable nightly exodus of men and women, the exterior guards seem never to have noticed the departure of the disguised escapees. Trembling, Madame de Tourzel gathered up the sleepy prince, took the older girl by the hand, and walked casually across the somber outside courtyard toward the line of carriages with their lanterns lit in the street just east of the palace—where they commonly waited at this time of night to pick up those leaving the Tuileries. Fersen himself, dressed as a common driver, was waiting in his hackney cab. They then took a short drive around the city until it was time for the rest of the family to leave, returning about eleven to the same spot. Tourzel was amazed at the Swede's imitation of a Parisian coachman, his whistling, his stopping to chat and exchange tobacco with the other drivers. The princess remembered only that "never had time seemed so long."[7]

Soon after Fersen had returned, the king's sister, Elizabeth, who had donned her own disguise and slipped out of her room through a secret door built into the apartment's woodwork, made her way out of the palace to the waiting hackney cab, where Fersen directed her to the correct door. The king was supposed to leave next, but at the last minute General Lafayette and Bailly, the mayor of Paris, arrived unannounced at the palace, and Louis was obliged to speak with them. Only at about half past eleven, when the two Parisian leaders had left, could he pretend to go to bed, dismiss his servants, and then get up, put on his own disguise, and walk cane in hand with Malden to the waiting carriage. With his usual phlegm, he even stopped to buckle his shoe as he crossed the courtyard. Last to depart was the queen herself. By some accounts she nearly collided with Lafayette who was also just leaving the palace. But dazzled by the torches held around him and preoccupied with other matters, the general took no notice of the lone woman walking in the shadows, and after an anxious moment she, too, climbed into the cab.[8]

It was now about half past twelve, an hour later than planned. As the family embraced one another and settled into the small carriage, Fersen drove across Paris, with Malden at the back as footman, advancing slowly for fear of attracting attention. Rather than taking the most direct route to the Saint-Martin's tollgate, he drove first to the northwest along Rue de Clichy, where he verified that the berline had been removed. He was also anxious to avoid the popular northeastern neighborhoods of Paris, where suspicions were always

Departure of Louis XVI from the Tuileries palace at 12:30 A.M. on June 21, 1791. The king, holding a lantern, leads the escape party across the Tuileries courtyard to meet Fersen and the waiting hackney cab. In reality, most of the party left one at a time.

high and where activity in the streets continued well into the night. When he finally arrived at the gate, he spent several anxious minutes looking for Moustier, Sapel, and the berline, which had been parked in the dark much farther away than he had expected. Once he had located it, Fersen and the two bodyguards quickly transferred the travelers into the larger coach, pushed the smaller cab into a ditch, and set off along the main eastbound road out of Paris. The various delays had put them two hours behind schedule. It was the shortest night of the year, and the first signs of dawn were already appearing. Fersen shouted to his coachman to drive at full speed: "Come now, Balthasar," he said, as Sapel himself remembered it; "be bold, be quick! Your horses can't be tired, push them faster!" Half an hour later the berline arrived at the first relay post of Bondy, where Valory was waiting with a change of horses.[9]

Here Fersen left the party. He had brought off his part of the conspiracy with aplomb and audacity, engineering an almost miraculous escape from the Tuileries and from Paris. He planned now to travel separately on horseback, northward into the Austrian Netherlands and then along the border just outside the kingdom, meeting the family again in Montmédy. "Goodbye, Madame Korff," he said simply, addressing the disguised queen. And he rode off toward Le Bourget as the family headed east.[10]

At their next relay stop, in Claye, the travelers completed their party, picking up the cabriolet containing the two nurses. As the sun rose—somewhat after four—the caravan headed across the rolling plains of Ile-de-France and Champagne. They were hardly an inconspicuous ensemble. The yellow cabriolet, the large black berline with its yellow frame, and the three bodyguards in bright yellow coats—Valory leading on horseback, Malden atop the larger coach, and Moustier on horseback bringing up the rear—attracted the attention of countrypeople and townsmen wherever they passed.[11] To be sure, this was the main road from Paris to Germany, and the passage of wealthy travelers in luxurious vehicles was by no means unprecedented. But as they advanced farther toward Lorraine, observers focused in particular on the three guards. Apparently Moustier had chosen yellow uniforms quite by accident. For the local people, however, they seemed remarkably similar to the livery of the prince de Condé, the detested emigrant leader of a counterrevolutionary army and seigneurial lord of numerous territories in this region of France.[12]

The route followed was one of the major highways of the kingdom, broad, straight and well maintained, lined with trees for the most part and with a roadbed—paved with stones for about half the journey and thereafter covered in gravel—raised well above

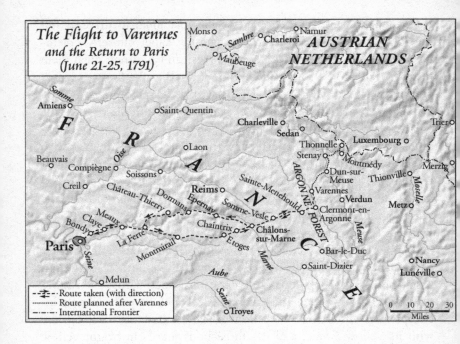

The Flight to Varennes
and the Return to Paris
(June 21-25, 1791)

AUSTRIAN
NETHERLANDS

Mons   Sambre   Charleroi   Namur
Maubeuge

Amiens   Somme   Saint-Quentin   Charleville   Sedan   Trier
F   Laon   Thonnelle   Luxembourg
Beauvais   Oise   Soissons   Stenay   Montmédy   Merzig
Compiègne   R   Dun-sur-   Thionville
Creil   Château-Thierry   Dormans   Reims   Sainte-Menehould   Meuse   Moselle
Meaux   Epernay   Somme-Vesle   Varennes   Verdun   Metz
Claye   A   Clermont-en-   Metz
Bondy   Chaintrix   Châlons-   Argonne
Paris   La Ferté   Etoges   sur-Marne   N   Meuse
Seine   Montmirail   Marne   Bar-le-Duc   Nancy
Melun   Aube   Saint-Dizier   Lunéville
Seine   C
Route taken (with direction)   E
Route planned after Varennes   Troyes   0 10 20 30
International Frontier   Miles

the fields. Portions of the road had been completed only in 1785.
Like many other wealthy long-distance travelers, the king's party
changed both horses and drivers at each of the royal relay posts
along the way. Valory generally rode well ahead of the others to
rouse the "post-master" at the next stop and have the horses prepared, ready to be hitched to the arriving carriages. At each post
they requested ten or eleven fresh horses—six for the berline, two
or three for the cabriolet, and two mounts for Valory and Moustier.
Each team was accompanied by one or two "drivers" or "guides,"
who usually rode astride one of the carriage horses, directing the
party to the next relay station and then returning the teams to their
home post. Louis carried a sack of gold coins that he periodically
distributed to Valory to pay and tip the drivers.[13] They normally
made about nine or ten miles per hour on the road, although if one
also takes into account the fifteen to twenty minutes spent at each of

the nineteen relay stops, the average for the trip was closer to seven miles per hour.[14]

As the day warmed and the carriages moved steadily across the countryside, the horses changed regularly and without difficulties, the travelers felt a sense of liberation and euphoria. The weather was hot and humid, but they encountered no rain. At one point, probably near Etoges, one of the berline's wheels hit a stone road marker, and four of the horses stumbled, breaking their traces. The thirty- or forty-five-minute repair job put the party even further behind schedule.[15] But otherwise the drive itself went without a hitch. The most dangerous part of the trip seemed to lie behind them, and now it was simply a question of arriving at Somme-Vesle, where they would be watched over and taken in care, if necessary, by Choiseul's cavalry.

Inside the coach, the family ate a pleasant picnic breakfast with their fingers, "like hunters or third-class travelers," as Moustier described it. They shared accounts of their experiences in leaving the Tuileries. The queen commented on how Lafayette must be embarrassed and squirming now that the royal departure had been discovered. The king took out his maps and the itinerary he had carefully prepared in advance, announcing each village or relay post as they passed by. It was only his third trip outside the region of Paris, the first since his glorious journey to Cherbourg in 1786, and he indulged his passion for geography and detailed lists. The queen took charge of assigning the roles they would all assume—as she had once delighted in doing with her courtiers in the Petit Trianon palace near Versailles. Madame de Tourzel would be the baroness de Korff, the dauphin and the princess would be the baroness' two children, and Madame Elizabeth and Marie-Antoinette would be her servingwomen. The queen and the king's sister were appropriately attired for such roles in simple "morning gowns," short capes, and matching hats. As for the king, dressed in his commoner's frock coat with a brown vest and a small round hat, he would be Monsieur Durand, the baroness' business agent.[16]

But the travelers soon tired of their role-playing and the rigors of guarding a strict incognito. Louis in particular had never been adept at pretending to be someone he was not. In any case, he was convinced that with Paris behind them, with its Jacobin club and fanatical newspapers and wild-eyed mobs, everything would be different; the king and queen would now be properly respected. As the heat increased, they lowered the blinds, took off their hats and veils, and watched the peasants laboring in the fields. And the peasants watched back, wondering at the identity of these wealthy aristocrats in their curious yellow and black caravan. At the long uphill grades, like the one ascending from the Marne Valley after La Ferté-sous-Jouarre, most of the party got out and walked along behind while the horses labored up the hill. Later in the day the king began stepping out at the relay stops, relieving himself at the "necessary shed," and even stopping to chat with the people gathered around, asking about the weather and the crops, as he had talked in his youth with the laborers outside Versailles. The bodyguards and the two nurses worried at first about the king's insouciance, and Moustier tried to shield him from a group of gaping countrypeople at one of the rest stops. However, Louis told the guard "not to worry; that he no longer felt that such precautions were necessary; and that the trip now seemed to be free of all uncertainty." In the end, the bodyguards concluded that the royal members knew what they were doing and that they themselves need not be concerned.[17]

And the king was in fact recognized. A wagon driver, François Picard, was convinced he had seen the monarch when the horses were changed outside the relay in Montmirail. Louis was recognized again three stops further, in Chaintrix, by the post-master, Jean-Baptiste de Lagny, and his son-in-law Gabriel Vallet, both of whom had attended the Festival of Federation in Paris in 1790. Here, as local memory would have it, the whole royal family got out and took refreshments at the inn attached to the relay, leaving two small silver bowls stamped with the royal insignia in appreciation. In any case, Lagny assigned Vallet to drive the berline on to Châlons-sur-Marne, and the son-in-law immediately whispered the news to the post-master there, a close friend of the family.[18]

As they drove into Châlons about four in the afternoon, the travelers might have had cause to be nervous. It was by far the largest town between Paris and Montmédy, and there were undoubtedly several local notables who had seen the royal couple in Versailles. Yet Louis seems to have taken no more care here than in the small rural posts he had just traversed. In addition to the post-master Viet, several other persons seem to have recognized them. "We were recognized by everybody," recalled Madame Royale. "Many people praised God to see the king and wished him well in his flight."[19] Whether people were really pleased to see the king leave Paris, or were simply too shocked to know what to do, Viet and his stable hands quietly changed the horses and watched the carriages drive out of town. The mayor was informed almost immediately, but he, too, was uncertain what to do. Only several hours later, when messengers began arriving from Paris, confirming the news of the king's escape and sending the Assembly's decree to stop him, did the municipal government swing into action.[20]

On leaving Châlons and heading east toward the border of Lorraine, the travelers were extremely optimistic, feeling they had crossed their last major obstacle and would soon be in the care of the duke de Choiseul and his loyal cavalry. With his detailed itinerary at hand, the king was aware that they had fallen nearly three hours behind, yet it probably never occurred to him that this could pose a problem. The mood shifted abruptly, however, as they came in sight of the small relay post at Somme-Vesle, isolated on the main road at some distance from the village. In the great expanse of openfield farmland surrounding them there were no troops in sight. Valory cautiously inquired and discovered that the cavalry had indeed been there, waiting across a small pond beyond the relay, but that the troops had been harassed by local peasants and had left an hour earlier. At first the travelers thought that Choiseul might simply have pulled back to a quieter spot farther down the road. Yet when they reached the next relay, he and his men were still nowhere to be seen. As the family drove in the early evening toward the town of Sainte-Menehould, framed against the dark band of the

Argonne Forest, they were beset, in Tourzel's words, by "terrible anxiety."[21]

The Debacle

Over the previous days, the organization of the king's escort had initially gone quite smoothly, despite the modifications caused by Louis' last-minute decision to delay his departure by one day. As Fersen and the royal family completed their preparations and launched the escape from Paris, General Bouillé had been activating a whole series of prearranged troop movements to prepare a reception for the king. The general himself had left his headquarters in Metz on June 16, informing local officials that he was off to inspect the frontiers for possible Austrian troop activities. Orders were given to begin concentrating soldiers and large quantities of food and supplies in Montmédy. On June 20 he had arrived in Stenay, the fortified town on the Meuse between Montmédy and Varennes. His youngest son and another officer, the count de Raigecourt, had been sent ahead to Varennes with a team of relay horses, joining some forty German troops already stationed there. To avoid suspicion, they were to keep the horses in the stables of an inn just east of the river, leading them to the southern edge of Varennes only when they were notified of the king's impending arrival. During the night of June 20–21 the elder Bouillé and a small group of officers had secretly ridden eight miles farther south to wait for the royal party in a secluded position just north of the small town of Dun. Meanwhile, other contingents of German cavalry were led from the south by commanders Damas and Andoins to take up positions in Clermont and Sainte-Menehould respectively. On the morning of June 21, François de Goguelat himself had led forty hussars from Sainte-Menehould to Somme-Vesle, arriving about noon to meet the duke de Choiseul—and the hairdresser Léonard—who were waiting at the relay post.[22]

All these well-laid plans, however, were evolving not in a vacuum but in full view of a civilian population that was anything but passive. The townspeople of Varennes were not alone in their growing apprehension about the unexplained troop movements throughout the region during the month of June. The pervasive suspicion of General Bouillé, the "butcher of Nancy," and of the aristocratic officers who commanded in the field was only intensified by the overwhelming presence of German-speaking mercenaries in all the contingents that people now saw passing. The tension was compounded by the army's failure to give ample advance warning of the arriving cavalrymen. Town leaders were notified at the last moment that the troops had been sent to protect money being shipped from Paris to pay the army guarding the frontier. But the story did little to allay local fears. Why were there so many cavalrymen, when a single escort from start to finish should have been sufficient? Why had the commanders dispatched only German-speaking troops? Was a war about to break out—always a critical question for this frontier region—and, if so, on which side would a German army led by aristocrats fight? Ironically, then, the very escorts sent to protect the king were arousing great suspicion among the population through which the king must travel.

In Montmédy the apparent preparation of a large military camp —and the order to bake 18,000 rations of bread—had also excited "mistrust and anxiety." "These extraordinary movements in a time of peace, aides-de-camp appearing on all the roads, sentinels positioned everywhere, had raised a general alarm among the population."[23] The people of Clermont, just south of Varennes, watched as 150 cavalry rode through one day and 180 more the next, the latter abruptly announcing their intention to stay the night. Few believed the story of the shipment of a strongbox, and rumors spread that the "treasure" in question was actually being smuggled out by the queen to her brother the Austrian emperor—or that maybe the treasure was the queen herself.[24] Likewise Sainte-Menehould, farther west, saw the sudden and unannounced appearance of two successive cavalry contingents. The second, a group of dragoons under the command of Andoins, dismounted at midmorning on June 21 in the town's large central square and waited there throughout the day while their nervous commander paced the street and periodically rode out of town to watch the horizon. Whenever the officers were away, townspeople attempted to communicate with the foreign-tongued cavalrymen, plying them with drink and asking them their "real" purpose in the region. Many of the soldiers, mystified themselves by their strange assignment, began to wonder whether their officers could be trusted. By the end of the afternoon, suspicions had reached such a level that elements of the national guard began arming and preparing for an unidentified calamity.[25]

In the meantime, even more disastrous events were unrolling at the critical forward position of Somme-Vesle, where the duke de Choiseul's hussars were waiting not in a town but in the open countryside. Here, as in so many rural regions of France after the Revolution began, the peasants had been recalcitrant about paying their seigneurial dues. When the cavalrymen arrived, splendid and frightening in their high plumed helmets, panic spread through the community that the men had come to seize the peasants' money or crops, and people arrived from every direction, pitchforks and sickles in hand, shouting and threatening the horsemen. In the mid-afternoon, having heard stories of the unrest from passing travelers, a delegation of national guardsmen came out from Châlons to investigate. Choiseul and Goguelat attempted to reason with everyone, telling them the story of the strongbox. Although the guardsmen were apparently pacified and returned home, the peasants remained unconvinced and continued to menace the detachment.[26]

At the same time, Choiseul grew increasingly uneasy about the long-overdue arrival of the king. Goguelat had carefully timed the trip, and by his calculations the royal party should have arrived by two o'clock. In a letter to Bouillé, Fersen had even promised that the king would be in Somme-Vesle by half past two: "you can count on it." Finally, late in the afternoon the young duke made a series of poorly conceived decisions heavy with consequences for the whole plan of escape. Unnerved by the presence of the crowds, worried that the king had somehow failed to leave Paris, fearful that even if the king did arrive, the near-riot conditions at the relay post might jeopardize his passage, Choiseul resolved to retreat, and to retreat not just a short way down the road, but all the way to Bouillé's headquarters in Stenay, some fifty miles distant. Perhaps even more fateful, he then sent word to the other contingents of cavalry waiting behind him: "It would appear that the treasure is not arriving today. I am leaving to rejoin General Bouillé. You will receive new orders tomorrow." Finally, to deliver the message he made the exceptionally strange choice of Monsieur Léonard, the queen's hairdresser.[27]

For the next eight hours the duke and his small force would disappear to the northeast, traveling across country rather than following the main road, raising pandemonium as they galloped unannounced through village after village, before storming into the Argonne Forest and losing their way. In contrast, Monsieur Léonard in his small carriage, rapidly taking to his role as military courier, performed his task perfectly. Driving in succession through Sainte-Menehould, Clermont, and Varennes, he passed along the message implying that the king was not coming. In the first two towns, Andoins and Damas welcomed an excuse to have their men unsaddle and retire to their lodgings, to some extent reducing the fears of the townspeople. Both nevertheless remained at their posts with a few officers and soldiers, waiting to see what would happen. In Varennes both commander and cavalry retired for the night. Only Raigecourt and the younger Bouillé stood in readiness at their hotel window, waiting to see if the relay horses, below in the stables, might still be necessary.[28]

As THE ROYAL CARAVAN drove down the long main street of Sainte-Menehould and into the central square, the anxieties aroused by the failure to find Choiseul were scarcely allayed. They did now see cavalry, but the men seemed to be relaxing, dismounted and disarmed, some of them drinking in an inn. Even more worrisome were the groups of national guardsmen, many carrying muskets, milling about on the opposite side of the Place Royale in front of the elegant brick and limestone town hall. The travelers must have felt as if they were stumbling by chance into a drama unrolling on the stage of the town square, where the entire citizenry seemed to be gathered. They must also have been aware that everyone had turned to watch them, staring in particular at the bodyguards, who looked for all the world like the men of the prince de Condé. A few buildings farther along, on a street that angled off to the right, the royal party found the relay post where Valory and the stable-hands were already preparing the horses. The change of teams went smoothly and rapidly. While they were waiting, the queen, anxious to learn what was happening, called Andoins over to the berline. The officer tried to look casual as he walked up, but when he saw the king he instinctively saluted. He then whispered, "Plans have not worked out; I must leave for fear of raising suspicion." And he quickly walked away. "These few words," as Tourzel recalled, "pierced us to the heart."[29]

The manager of the relay post, Jean-Baptiste Drouet, apparently arrived on the scene only after his stablehands had almost completed the change of horses. Twenty-eight years old, the younger of two brothers, he had served seven years in the cavalry before returning to his hometown to work in the family fields and operate the post owned by his widowed mother. He was ambitious and self-confident, but he found himself forced into the drudgery of farm work and manual labor, a considerable comedown from the glamorous career of his youth, and a source of much frustration.[30] Now, when he saw the berline and looked carefully at the passengers inside, he was stunned to recognize the queen of France, whom he had once seen while his company was stationed near Versailles. Although he had never before viewed the king, the face of the heavy-set man sitting next to her struck him as remarkably like the image of Louis XVI printed on the new paper money that had lately come into circulation. After watching the two carriages drive away, he began telling everyone around him that the king had just passed. At first, like the people in Chaintrix and in Châlons, no one knew what to do or what to think. But only a few minutes later Andoins had the bugle sounded, calling his dragoons to remount and prepare to

Drouet Recognizes the King in Sainte-Menehould. The royal family waits while Louis dines on pigs' feet, the culinary specialty of Sainte-Menehould, in an inn called Au Fuiard (The Runaway). Drouet identifies the monarch by comparing him with the portrait on a bill of paper money. In reality, the king never left the carriage while in Sainte-Menehould.

leave, and suddenly the scales fell from their eyes. It had all been a plot. The cavalry had come not to escort a strongbox, but to accompany the king, who either was fleeing or had been abducted.[31]

Thereafter the chronology of events in Sainte-Menehould is somewhat unclear. Almost immediately the local national guard, armed with muskets, drums beating, organized themselves and lined up across the street to block the passage of the cavalry. At the same time, other citizens began talking to the horsemen, encouraging them to disobey their officers. While Andoins tried to talk with the townspeople, one of his mounted officers fired a pistol into the air and made a run for it, breaking through the guardsmen and riding out of town, dodging the musket shots that were fired his way. With the church bells now ringing and riot conditions breaking out, Andoins and the remaining officers were disarmed and locked in the town jail for their own safety. Drouet was called into the municipal council, meeting in emergency session in their hall, directly adjoining the riot site. And after he had told his story, the town fathers, on their own initiative, made an extraordinary decision. If the king was leaving Paris, it could only mean that he was heading for the frontier, perhaps to return with a foreign army, to invade the country and end the Revolution. Other towns in the direction of the frontier must be warned and the king stopped. They asked Drouet himself, known as one of the best riders in town, to go after him. The postmaster quickly recruited his friend Jean Guillaume, another ex-cavalryman, and the two set off in pursuit of the royal family, by now a good hour and a half ahead of them. As they approached the town of Clermont, Drouet and Guillaume encountered the postmaster's driver bringing back the team, and he told them that the berline and the cabriolet had left the main road and turned north. The two horsemen then headed across country in the direction of Varennes.[32]

About an hour earlier, around half past nine, after a slow climb over the hills of the Argonne, the royal caravan had pulled into the relay stop at Clermont. It was almost dark, and the post was on the near edge of town, so few people saw the travelers arrive, and the change of horses went quickly. The count Damas, who had remained waiting nearby, cautiously spoke to the royal family and at greater length with Valory, warning them of the wide unrest in Clermont over the presence of troops, and promising to follow as soon as the two carriages had advanced some distance ahead—thus following Bouillé's orders to the letter. But the caravan was seen clearly as it passed through the middle of town and turned toward Varennes. The events that followed in Clermont were strangely similar to those in Sainte-Menehould. No one had recognized the royal couple, but everyone saw the prince de Condé's yellow livery and concluded there must be some connection with the soldiers who had been inexplicably billeted in their town the last two days. About an hour later, as national guardsmen put on their uniforms and assembled, the officer who had escaped Sainte-Menehould arrived and informed Damas that the king's party had been recognized and that a full-scale riot had broken out as soon as they had left. When the commander tried to rally his men, most of them, now drinking heavily and won over by the citizenry, refused to obey. He escaped with only a handful of cavalry, riding at full speed in an attempt to warn the king.[33]

In the meantime the occupants of the berline were advancing steadily down the long valley of the Aire, exhausted by their trek and dozing in the darkness "despite their tension and anxiety."[34] Their tension would have been still greater if they had been aware of the waves of panic and insurrection rapidly approaching from the rear. There was the smaller local surge generated by the events in Sainte-Menehould and Clermont and by the duke de Choiseul's wild ride through the villages of the Argonne. Not far behind was an even greater wave of emotion spreading over the whole kingdom, as official couriers and private citizens rushed down the roads of France announcing the news of the king's disappearance.

The arrival in Varennes about eleven brought yet another jolt of uncertainty and disappointment. Bouillé and Choiseul had promised to position a new team of horses in the trees near the road just before the first houses. But although Valory and Moustier searched everywhere, riding into the sleeping settlement as far as the river, they found no sign of the expected relay team. They even knocked on a few doors close to the entrance of the town, yet they could obtain no assistance. The travelers then asked the drivers to skip the relay and continue on to Dun, but the men from Clermont had strict instructions from their post-master to go no farther than Varennes unless the horses were first fed and rested. A half-hour, perhaps forty minutes passed as they searched the town and argued with the drivers. And while they were still parked by the road, Drouet and Guillaume trotted past and into town.[35]

Finally the drivers agreed to proceed to the center of Varennes while the party looked for more horses. They advanced slowly through the darkness, the street illuminated only by the lanterns of the cabriolet. They began to hear voices, shouts, someone crying, "Fire! Fire!" Madame de Tourzel remembered the moment vividly: "We thought we had been betrayed, and we drove down the street with a feeling of sadness and distress that can scarcely be described." They passed under the archway by the Inn of the Golden Arm. And there they were stopped.[36]

Return to Paris

For the royal family and their supporters, the night in Varennes could only have been a prolonged agony, the stuff of their worst nightmares—those "eight deathly hours of waiting," as Madame de Tourzel described them. There were moments of hope: the seeming willingness of the town leaders to help them, the miraculous appearance first of Choiseul and Goguelat, and then of Damas and Deslon at the head of their cavalry units. To the last moment there was also the wishful assumption that General Bouillé was nearby, that he was on his way to deliver them. But Louis resolutely rejected his officers' proposals to extricate the family violently, lest harm befall his wife and children. The town council's change of heart soon thereafter, its refusal to allow them to continue their journey, was a bitter disappointment. The appearance of the couriers from Paris, ordering their return to the capital, brought final humiliation and defeat.

For a time they tried to stall. They requested that the children be allowed to sleep longer, that they themselves be given time to rest. One of the nursemaids even feigned a violent stomachache. In the end, they asked and were granted a moment alone to gather their thoughts, time which they spent preparing a common story and burning the incriminating documents in their possession. Finally, at about half past seven in the morning, the royal party was led from Sauce's store and taken to the two carriages, which had now been turned around. The family was frightened by the great sea of people filling the street and the square beyond the river, jostling for a view of the king and queen, shouting continuously, "Long live the nation! Long live the king! Back to Paris!" The duke de Choiseul, ever gallant, helped the queen into the berline. She turned and asked him, "Do you think Monsieur Fersen has escaped?" The duke said that he believed he had. Soon afterward he was pulled away into the crowd, badly beaten, and eventually led away to prison in Verdun, along with Damas and several other officers. Only the wily Goguelat with his bandaged pistol wound somehow managed to slip out of town, to be captured several days later on the Austrian border. As the carriages moved slowly up the hill along the road back toward Paris, the family looked across the river, still wondering what had happened to Bouillé.[37]

At that very moment, the general was a good hour and a half away. He had been told the disastrous news at a little after four that morning by his youngest son, who caught up with him as he and his officers had almost reached Stenay after abandoning their long wait outside Dun. It had taken another forty-five minutes to get the bulk of his royal German cavalry, three or four hundred strong, into the saddle and riding back toward Varennes. As they approached the town they encountered hundreds of peasants and guardsmen in full mobilization, marching in all directions with drums and flags, and on several occasions they were forced to draw their sabers and charge, threatening a fight before the crowds gave way. When they finally arrived on the hill above Varennes, it was nine or half past. And they went no further.

Bouillé would later argue that the bridge had been dismantled and that they were unable to ford the river. But the commander of the Varennes cavalry had waded the river on horseback a few hours earlier, and the road actually crossed to the right bank of the Aire only a couple of miles farther south. More likely, the general had been informed that the king was now two hours away and that he was surrounded by several thousand armed guardsmen. Menaced from all sides by the local population, concerned about the condition of the horses after their long ride south, and perhaps nursing doubts about the reliability of his own cavalry—who would in fact go over to the patriots a few hours later—the general now turned and retreated to Stenay. He had a quick cup of coffee in his inn, gathered together his two sons and about twenty officers, and rode into exile in Austrian Belgium, a few miles away.[38] Two days later the baron Klinglin, one of the officers who had worked most closely with Bouillé over the previous months, wrote a letter to his sister. He lamented the failure of "our sublime conspiracy." "How difficult it is to overcome fate! What a strange destiny that the leaders of an insignificant little town like Varennes should have halted the king. Oh my dear friend, how sweet it would have been to have died, if only we could have saved the king!"[39]

By the time Bouillé had begun his retreat the royal cortège was just entering Clermont. Those in the king's party would never forget the terrifying journey back to Paris. Compared with the race to Varennes on June 21, the return was ponderously tedious, dragging on for four long days. The hottest weather of the summer had now settled in, and the pace of the carriages was usually too slow to raise even a hint of a breeze. The enormous crowds of people tramping along outside raised great clouds of dust that only intensified the misery. Valory, who sat atop the berline with his hands tied, recalled the ordeal: "We were cooked by the sun and choked by the dust."[40]

When they first drove out of Varennes, they had been accompanied by some six thousand national guardsmen, marching in double

columns with some semblance of order, led by the Parisian guardsman and messenger Bayon. But as they made their way west, countrypeople converged from every direction: men, women, and children, often whole villages arriving en masse, in carts or on foot,
carrying every conceivable weapon. Observers were staggered by
the numbers of people, spilling off the road into the surrounding
fields and following like a great swarm: this "countless multitude,"
as the bodyguard Moustier remembered, "of every age and of both
sexes, armed with muskets, sabers, pitchforks, pikes, axes, or sickles." The deputy Pétion, who accompanied the family on the last
half of their journey, said much the same: in addition to the guardsmen, there were "old men and women and children, some carrying
sickles or long spits, others with clubs, swords or antique guns."[41]
Many came simply to gawk at the king and the queen, whom they
had never seen, never hoped to see. Others, members of their town
or village militias, rushed to the defense of both the nation and the
king—for at first there were rumors that the monarch had been kidnapped. Often it was their first chance to put to use their company
flags and colorful new uniforms, previously worn only in parades
around the town square. At times the crowds were in a celebratory
mood, especially when the royal cortège crossed the communities
touched by the previous night's panic. People exalted at their victory sang and danced and drank to the health of the nation and the
king. Mayors gave splendid speeches, patterned on the rhetoric they
had read in accounts of National Assembly debates. The faithful
Madame de Tourzel was shocked by the many harangues the king
had to endure from local dignitaries, anxious to lecture him on his
thoughtlessness in abandoning his people, in causing them such a
fright—even if he had only been heeding the advice of treacherous
councilors. Town officials, she felt, "had only one thought in mind:
to glory in their own triumph and to humiliate the royal family. It
was a joy for them to overwhelm the unfortunate monarchs with
bitter invectives."[42]

Yet there was also a strong element of fear. General Bouillé and
his four hundred cavalrymen, galloping down the road to Varennes,

had caused an enormous fright among the countrypeople, a fright that quickly spread from village to village and was magnified by the movement of other troops in the region. Soon reports began spreading of thousands of soldiers, perhaps the whole Austrian army, led by the villain general, arriving to punish the people of Lorraine and Champagne for capturing the king.[43] Among the crowds following the cortège, swept by ever-changing rumors, the festive mood could be rapidly transformed into anger and a desire for revenge. Usually the outrage was directed not toward the monarch—cries of "Long live the king!" could be heard throughout the journey—but toward those presumed to have influenced or kidnapped him. However, the crowds had few qualms about targeting the queen. There were the inevitable coarse references to Marie's sex life, and snide remarks about the dauphin's "real father." When Marie offered a piece of chicken to a guardsman who had been particularly kind and obliging, a great roar rose up that it was poison, that the young man should not touch it. But hatreds were focused above all on the three bodyguards, seated prominently above on the driver's seat, still dressed in their rich yellow livery coats, symbolic of all that was hateful under the Old Regime. Assumed by many to have been the instigators of the flight, they were continually threatened verbally and pelted with rocks or dung. On several occasions groups tried to approach the berline and attack them physically, before being pushed away by the national guardsmen.[44]

Sauce himself accompanied the coaches as far as Clermont, before turning back to see to the defense of his town against a possible attack by Bouillé. The cortège then moved along the main post road to Sainte-Menehould, where the mayor gave another formal speech and Drouet and Guillaume—who had returned home during the night—ostentatiously joined in the march. West of the town a local noble, the count Dampierre, who had witnessed the mayor's address in Sainte-Menehould, attempted to approach the berline on horseback and speak to the family. When the guards pushed him back, he shouted "Long live the king!," fired his musket in the air, and rode off toward his chateau. The count was already widely hated by the local population, and groups of people followed him, shot him off his horse, and killed him in the fields. It is unclear whether the king himself saw the massacre, but the bodyguards watched in horror from atop the carriage.[45]

By the time the procession reached Châlons-sur-Marne at the end of the day, the royal family had been almost forty hours without sleep. "It is almost impossible," as one witness put it, "to describe their state of exhaustion."[46] But here they would know a few hours of respite from the tension and fatigue. They were feted by the mayor and the departmental leaders, who arrived to meet them at the gates of the city, and they were given accommodations in the palace of the former intendant. It was the very building where the young Marie-Antoinette had once spent the night on her trip to France from Austria, some twenty-one years earlier. Authorities here were clearly more sympathetic to the plight of the monarch. That night a small group of individuals even offered to help him escape, though Louis refused to consider leaving without his family, and the plan came to nothing. The next morning the king and queen attended Corpus Christi mass, but before the service was completed they were hustled away by another company of national guards just arrived from Reims. New stories were coming in that Varennes and Sainte-Menehould had been sacked and burned by marauding armies, and the guardsmen insisted on moving the king rapidly back toward Paris.[47]

They set out once again in late morning, advancing painfully slowly with their great escort, now estimated at 15,000 to 30,000 people, following the Marne Valley rather than the shorter route through Montmirail that they had used for their flight. They stopped briefly for dinner in Epernay, but a riot broke out in the streets, and Madame de Tourzel was nearly pulled away into the crowds before they were rushed onto the road once again.[48] Then toward half past seven in the evening, as the route skirted the river in the open countryside, the cortège suddenly came to a halt, and the crowds hushed and pulled aside from the road ahead. Three deputies sent by the National Assembly in Paris had arrived and were approaching on foot, preceded by the Assembly's sergeant at arms. The representatives had learned that the king had been stopped in Varennes some twenty hours earlier, and they had immediately dispatched three of their members, carefully chosen to represent the diverse political groupings in the Assembly. Antoine Barnave led the way, a moderate Jacobin and gifted orator, only twenty-nine years old and looking even younger. He was followed by Jérôme Pétion, somewhat older, a fervent democrat and close associate of Maximilien Robespierre and the radical Jacobins; and by Marie-Charles de Latour-Maubourg, a monarchist and a friend of Lafayette. After the long hours of fear and uncertainty, the women in the carriage were overcome with emotion at the appearance of these men, men they had once so despised, but who now seemed to promise their safety. Madame Elizabeth took the deputies' hands and begged them to protect the three bodyguards, who had only recently been threatened with lynching. After a few words of comfort, Barnave formally read the decree of the Assembly, commissioning them to ensure the king's safe return to Paris. He then climbed atop the berline and, sharply illuminated by the setting sun, read out the decree a second time for the benefit of the crowd. It was another extraordinary moment in the Revolution, clearly marking the transfer of sovereignty from the king to the nation.[49]

The deputies had been accompanied by the military officer Mathieu Dumas, a moderate patriot and veteran of the War of the American Revolution, and Dumas now took charge of the national guard contingents, reestablishing some semblance of order in the immense procession. Barnave and Pétion squeezed their way into the larger coach with the two children moved to the laps of the women, and the much taller Maubourg found a place with the nurses in the cabriolet. They spent that night in the small town of Dormans, getting to bed well after midnight. The next day, as they passed through the town of Château-Thierry, Dumas managed a maneuver at the bridge that cut them off from most of their amorphous popular escort, and they were able to proceed rapidly to Meaux, where they passed the night of June 24 in the bishop's

The Royal Family Approaches Paris. The king's berline and the smaller diligence holding the nurses pass below the customs gate of Le Roule just north of the entrance to the Champs-Elysées. The hill of Montmartre, exaggerated in height, is visible in the background.

residence. But more masses of people, guardsmen and spectators, converged on the town during the night, and the final drive to the capital through the summer heat was as slow and encumbered as before. "I have never experienced," wrote Pétion, "a longer and more exhausting day."[50]

As the procession passed through the Paris suburbs, the mood grew decidedly more aggressive. There were several concerted attacks on the berline, probably aimed at the bodyguards. Barnave and Pétion began to fear for the safety of the passengers and shouted for protection from the guardsmen, some of whom had now arrived from Paris. Two officers were badly wounded, and

The Royal Family Returns to the Tuileries. The berline crosses the Place de Louis XV (today Place de la Concorde) and is about to enter the Tuileries gardens. Almost all the spectators have left on their hats and bonnets, an obvious snub to the king. Note the women confronting a man (right) who has taken off his hat.

Dumas was nearly pushed from his horse before they finally arrived at the city walls, where General Lafayette met them with a large contingent of cavalry.[51] The cortège was then directed around the perimeter of the city, again avoiding the working-class neighborhoods and entering from the northwest via the Champs-Elysées. The whole of Paris had kept abreast of the king's progress, and tens of thousands of men, women, and children pressed to watch the slow advance down the avenue, with hundreds more clinging to trees and rooftops. The occupants of the carriage appeared exhausted, dirty, ruffled. There were a few cheers for the deputies, and for Drouet and Guillaume and the guardsmen from Varennes who had made the long trek, and who were positioned prominently at the front of the march. But for the most part the crowd remained silent, refusing to remove their hats and their bonnets, in an obvious expression of disrespect for the monarch. As a similar sign of disapprobation, several companies of the national guardsmen lining the street held their muskets upside down, barrels pointed at the ground. In Paris, unlike in the provinces, the traditional salute of "Long live the king!" was not to be heard.[52] For Louis, always so sensitive to the acclamations of the crowds, it could only have been a moment of great sadness.

At the end of the avenue they crossed the great square—known today as the Place de la Concorde—and entered the Tuileries gardens, coming to a halt near the entrance to the palace. Discipline almost broke down now, as people in the crowds rushed toward the coach and attempted to seize the bodyguards. Only with great difficulty were Dumas and Pétion and several other officers able to carry the three battered and bleeding men to safety. In the meantime the royal family had quickly descended and walked untouched into the Tuileries, the palace they had hoped to escape forever just five days earlier.[53]

Postmortems

"What a strange destiny!" the baron Klinglin had exclaimed. Only fifteen more miles, one or two hours' drive to Dun through the dead of night, and the royal family could have been in the protective care of General Bouillé and his force of several hundred cavalry. From the very moment of the king's capture, participants in and witnesses of the flight to Varennes began asking themselves what had gone wrong, how they had failed, who was ultimately at fault. Even the patriots, for whom the flight's failure was a great victory, reflected at length on the strange workings of fate that had halted the king of France so close to his escape. Indeed, generations of historians have followed in their minds the divergent universes of "contrafactual history," meditating on how different everything might have been if Louis had succeeded in reaching Montmédy. What would have happened if the servingwoman in the palace had not become suspicious, compelling the royal family to postpone their departure; if Lafayette had not come by the Tuileries for a late-night chat; if the duke de Choiseul had waited one more hour in the meadow near Somme-Vesle; if Drouet had remained in his fields a few minutes longer before returning to his post; if the drivers from Clermont had been convinced or bribed or coerced to continue beyond Varennes without a change of horses? The string of "ifs" is almost endless. For indeed, the "event" of Varennes—like almost any event in history—is constructed of a nearly infinite series of subevents, any one of which might have changed the outcome of that day.

Yet if one steps back from this sequence of circumstances, from the minutiae of individual actions and reactions, one might argue that two major factors shaped the experience of Varennes. The first was the personality and behavior of the central figure of the whole adventure, Louis XVI himself. The king's chronic indecision and unreliability had profoundly affected the origins and course of the entire Revolution. In the case at hand, an early and steadfast decision for flight would almost certainly have increased the chances of success. Even after April 1791, when Louis seems finally to have opted for escape, the act itself was postponed time after time, even though all the plans were in place by early May, if not before. Every day that the flight was delayed made it more likely that the complex conspiracy would be found out—as it was in fact found out by the queen's servingwoman sometime in early June. Every day that the flight was delayed made it more likely that French soldiers—under the ever-greater influence of the patriotic clubs—would refuse to obey their aristocratic commanders, would act aggressively to halt any action whose goals they rejected. During the months before the departure, General Bouillé had grown progressively more pessimistic about the reliability of his troops and the feasibility of the whole plan.[54] In the end, his decision to rely on foreign-born, German-speaking cavalry enormously raised the suspicions of the villagers and townspeople who would observe their movements. But even then the flight might have succeeded, if only the king had not tempted fate by riding in his carriage with the window shades down and by stepping outside and openly presenting himself to all bystanders. Such actions were, of course, closely related to the king's failure to comprehend the real meaning and wide appeal of the Revolution, to his assumption that the Revolutionary changes he detested had been provoked by a few radicals in the National Assembly and their demagogic control of the Parisian "rabble."

But in this sense a second fundamental cause of the failure of Varennes was precisely the sweeping transformation in French attitudes and psychology engendered by the Revolution. A new sense of self-confidence, of self-reliance, of identity with the nation as a whole and not merely with the local community—the transformation that we observed in the small town of Varennes—had penetrated much of the French population. It was developments such as these that help explain the extraordinary initiatives taken by small-town officials in Sainte-Menehould and Varennes to halt the king. Although the individual actions of Drouet and Sauce should not be underestimated, those actions would scarcely have been possible without the support of the town councils and indeed of the whole citizenry. The readiness of support had been further activated by the unusual and unexplained movements of mercenary cavalrymen in the days before the escape and by the population's pervasive suspicion of the aristocratic officers who led those troops. Near-insurrectional conditions already existed in both Sainte-Menehould and Clermont before the arrival of the king's caravan. Mercy-Argenteuil had not been mistaken when he warned the royal couple that now, in the context of the new Revolutionary mentality, "Every village could be an insurmountable barrier to your passage."

Indeed, from one point of view, the real question is not why the flight failed, but how it came so close to succeeding. The family's spectacular achievements in exiting from the Tuileries palace undetected, escaping from the great wary and suspicious city of Paris, and traveling along the main post roads to within a few dozen miles of the Austrian border all underline the organizational talents of General Bouillé and, above all, of Axel von Fersen. Working together, they came close to pulling off what would certainly have ranked among the greatest escapes of all time.

CHAPTER 4

Our Good City of Paris

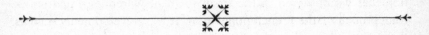

THE CITY to which Louis and his family returned on June 25, and in which they were to find themselves virtually imprisoned, was a universe unto itself, dramatically different from any other town or region in the kingdom. With some 700,000 souls, Paris was the second-largest city in all of Christendom and one of the ten largest in the world. If one had climbed a tower of Notre Dame, the great cathedral on an island in the Seine at the heart of the metropolis, one might have gained some sense of the extraordinary diversity of this teeming, vibrant, complex world.[1] From this vantage point an observer could easily make out many of Paris' architectural monuments, which eighteenth-century tourists already flocked to visit: the great Gothic hall of justice, just to the west, where the Parlement of Paris formerly met; the splendid Renaissance city hall across the river to the north; the Baroque dome of the French Academy farther west along the river; and, just opposite it, the massive Right Bank structure of the Louvre and its western extension of the Tuileries.

Besides the turrets and towers of these civil constructions, one could count no less than two hundred spires and belfries erected over the centuries by the Catholic church, many of them now confiscated by the Revolution, along with much of the clergy's property and revenues. To the west in general, and in pockets at several other points in the city, a visitor could also discern neighborhoods that were markedly whiter, with newer structures interspersed among greenery. These were the town houses and gardens of what was perhaps the greatest concentration of aristocratic families in all of Europe. Although the Revolution had swept away the distinct legal and political privileges formerly enjoyed by these families, they—unlike the clergy—retained most of their enormous wealth and much of their cultural influence.

Alongside these imposing monuments of wealth and power, much of the city would have appeared darker and rather tawdry, a jumble of smaller, multistory structures, some leaning precariously forward or holding one another up. Particular clusters of working-class abodes could be seen in the eastern suburbs: notably in the Saint-Antoine district, jutting eastward like a spur into the countryside from the square where the now-demolished Bastille had stood; and in the Saint-Marcel neighborhood, clustered along the smaller Bièvre River winding into the Seine from the southeast. Fersen had carefully avoided districts such as these when he drove the royal family out of the city in the early morning of June 21. But similar dwellings were visible in almost every part of the city, often directly abutting the palaces and churches. Here were the homes of the great mass of Parisian commoners, describing themselves until recently as the "Third Estate."

Many of the individuals in question, perhaps 100,000 scattered across the city, lived comfortable and stable lives in families of government workers and professional men, merchants and shop owners, or master craftsmen. A substantial proportion of this group had been born in the city, and virtually all the men and most of the women were literate. This critical mass of the "middle class," more numerous here than in the rest of the kingdom put together, was already providing the core of local Revolutionary leadership. But the bulk of the Parisian population lived more uncertain lives. There were journeymen and shop workers, laundrywomen and street hawkers, lackeys and day laborers and prostitutes (some 40,000 by one estimate): the precariously employed, the unem-

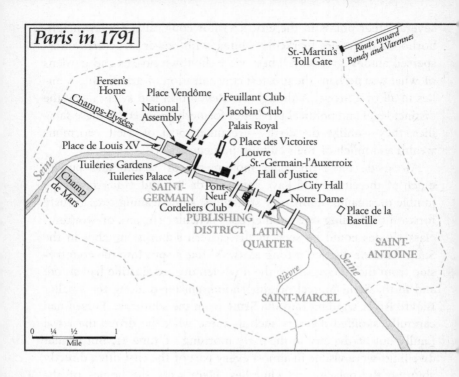

Paris in 1791

St.-Martin's Toll Gate

Route toward Bondy and Varennes

Fersen's Home

Place Vendôme

Feuillant Club

Champs-Élysées

National Assembly

Jacobin Club

Palais Royal

Place de Louis XV

O Place des Victoires

Louvre

St.-Germain-l'Auxerroix

Tuileries Gardens

Tuileries Palace

Hall of Justice

Seine

Champ de Mars

SAINT-GERMAIN

Pont-Neuf

City Hall

Notre Dame

Cordeliers Club

PUBLISHING DISTRICT

LATIN QUARTER

Place de la Bastille

SAINT-ANTOINE

Bièvre

Seine

SAINT-MARCEL

0   ¼   ½   1
Mile

ployed, the down-and-out. A great many were immigrants, arriving with a motley mixture of costumes and accents from many different regions of the kingdom and even from other countries: some with trades and talents immediately fitting into the workaday world; others illiterate and unskilled, floating on the margins, unstable and miserable. It was the juxtaposition of large numbers of both great and small, rich and impoverished, highly educated and illiterate—and of most everything in between—that gave the city its very particular character. Indeed, Sébastien Mercier, that inveterate observer of Paris in the late eighteenth century, aptly described the city as "a melting pot of the human race."[2]

Although the king liked to imagine that the unrest in Paris since 1789 was the work of a small minority of Jacobins and rabblerousers, there is ample evidence of the Revolution's impact on all levels of Parisian society. Foreign tourists passing through the city in 1790 and 1791 invariably commented on the outward signs of this transformation: the political discussions taking place in the streets, even among strangers; the tricolor patriot badges, or cockades, worn by virtually all men and women; the Revolutionary newspapers and brochures sold and distributed everywhere; and the patriotic songs intoned during intermission at the popular theaters and the opera.[3] This politicization of Parisian daily life was part of a Revolutionary process not unlike that which had affected the peasants and townsmen of Varennes over the previous two years. Almost everywhere, the National Assembly's onslaught against Old Regime institutions in the name of popular sovereignty and equality had encouraged men and women to question authority and injustice more generally. But in Paris the corrosive logic of democracy and equality had rapidly pushed some segments of the population toward near-millenarian expectations for a radical transformation of the world.

This exceptional radicalization was linked, first, to the city's eighteenth-century experience as a veritable cultural battleground. The political struggles of the French Parlements against the fiscal and religious policies of the monarchy, the dissident movement of Jansenism against the Catholic establishment, and the intellectual struggles of Enlightened philosophers against clericalism and obscurantism in any form had all been more intense in Paris than anywhere else in France or in Europe. Indeed, the city was the recognized capital of the Enlightenment, drawing intellectuals from throughout the Atlantic world to its salons and cafés and editorial houses. These complex and often contradictory movements affected many elements of the unusually literate, highly educated Parisian population, helping to create an atmosphere of critical and independent thought.

But the radicalization of Paris was also tied to more recent developments. By early 1791 Paris had been saturated with dozens of daily newspapers and numerous other sporadic publications. Such papers articulated almost every position on the political spectrum. In many sections of the city the tone and content of debate were increasingly influenced by a group of exceptionally talented radical writers—like Camille Desmoulin, Jean-Paul Marat, Nicolas de Bonneville, and Louise Kéralio and her husband, François Robert—who advocated ever more expansive democratic and egalitarian principles.[4] Throughout most of France newspapers, radical or otherwise, had little direct effect on the great majority of men and women, who had only minimal access to the printed word. In Paris, however, not only was functional literacy exceptionally high, but there were other means by which even the illiterate had access to the latest political commentary. Those who frequented any of the seven-hundred-odd cafés in the city might hear papers and brochures read aloud and commented on nightly by one of the self-appointed "head orators" who held sway in such establishments.[5] Others were informed—or misinformed—of the affairs of the day by the hundreds of pamphlet and newspaper hawkers roaming the streets. They continually shouted out the "headlines," or gave their own sensationalist interpretations of those headlines, the better to sell their copies. William Short, the protégé of Thomas Jefferson and the American representative in Paris, was amazed at the extraordinary influence of the popular newspapers: "These journals," he wrote to Jefferson, "are hawked about the streets, cried in every quarter of Paris and sold cheap or given to the people who devour them with astonishing avidity." Mercier was appalled by the potential influence of the paper sellers, many of them actually illiterate: "Simple legislative proposals are transformed into formal decrees, and whole neighborhoods are outraged by events that never took place. Misled a thousand times previously by the false announcements of these peddlers, the common people continue nevertheless to believe them."[6]

Finally, Parisian radicalism had been influenced since the beginning of the Revolution by an exceptional proliferation of political associations. We have already seen the influence of the local patriotic club in Varennes and in the surrounding towns. In Paris, at the moment of the king's flight, there were no less than fifty such societies.[7] A few of these groups—like the majority of clubs in the provinces—were relatively elitist, with elevated dues limiting the membership to the middle or upper classes. Such was the case of the celebrated Jacobin Club, which met on the Right Bank not far from the National Assembly and the Tuileries palace, and which was the mother society for a whole network of "Friends of the Constitution" throughout the kingdom. Yet many of the Parisian clubs had been created specifically to attract the more humble elements of society, those "passive citizens" whom the National Assembly had excluded from voting and officeholding by means of property qualifications.

No Parisian group was more active in recruiting the lower classes into political participation than the Society of Friends of the Rights of Man, best known to history as the Cordeliers Club. Meeting on the Left Bank, near the Latin Quarter and in the heart of the publishing district, its members consisted of a group of radical intellectuals—men like Desmoulins, Marat, Robert, and Georges Danton—and a substantial contingent of local merchants and artisans, both men and women. From the beginning the Cordeliers pursued a dual agenda: on the one hand, to promote the expansion of democracy and equality and to defend the rights of the common people; and on the other, to root out the plots and conspiracies that most members believed were threatening the Revolution.[8] But this club was only the oldest and best-known of thirty-odd "fraternal societies," popular democratic associations that had emerged in Paris in 1790 and 1791. Some of these had grown up around individuals with aspirations to leadership in particular neighborhoods of the city. Others—like the Fraternal Society of the Indigent— had been promoted by the Cordeliers themselves in early 1791, with the specific intention of mobilizing the masses in support of their brand of egalitarian politics. All the fraternal societies sought to obtain the right to vote and to hold office for all men, not just for those with property. Several also permitted participation by women, some of whom were urging an increasing role for female patriots more generally. By the spring of 1791 François Robert and the Cordeliers were attempting to coordinate the activities of all such societies around a "Central Committee." The Friends of the Rights of Man were thus well on the way to creating a Paris-based network of political clubs closely paralleling the national network of the Jacobins.[9]

A second set of urban associations had developed around the forty-eight "sections" of Paris. Created in the spring of 1790 to replace the older "districts," the sections had been designed as electoral units for the periodic selection of officeholders. But by early 1791 they were meeting almost continuously, assuming control over an array of neighborhood affairs, and frequently voicing opinions on the political issues of the day. Although membership was limited to "active" male citizens, the leadership cultivated close ties with the local communities, lending them a certain grassroots character. Indeed, many of the sections with large working-class constituencies adopted egalitarian and democratic positions not unlike those of the Cordeliers Club and the fraternal societies. Their power and influence grew even greater after they began communicating with one another and holding joint meetings to coordinate policies. By the spring of 1791 both the sections and the fraternal societies were becoming organs of influence increasingly independent from the National Assembly and the regular Paris municipal government.[10]

In the months preceding the king's flight, a series of developments had left the neighborhoods of Paris ever more nervous and suspicious. A great wave of strikes and other collective actions by workers kept the city in near-constant turmoil throughout the winter and spring. Working men and women were disturbed, in part, by the rapidly rising prices, triggered by the great quantities of paper money being printed by the government. Yet the unrest could also be linked to the Revolutionary process itself, as journeymen workers applied the same egalitarian logic to the labor system that others had used against the political and social systems. Many of these workers had been encouraged in their struggles in March 1791, when the National Assembly formally abolished the guild system, an institution that had given so much authority to the master craftsmen. Only a few days before the king's flight, however, the Assembly passed a decree far less favorable to the workers, the famous Le Chapelier law, which outlawed worker associations and collective bargaining.[11]

Lower class and middle class alike were also unsettled by continuing rumors of counterrevolutionary plots. Fears had been aroused by the blustering pronouncements of emigrant nobles, threatening to invade from across the Rhine, and by the very real and well-publicized conspiracies hatched during the first two years of the Revolution. Such tensions were exacerbated by the large numbers of aristocrats living in the city, many of them with their own reactionary clubs and publishing houses, closely attached to the conservative minority in the Assembly itself. The creation of a Monarchy Club at the end of 1790, with a membership drawn largely from the nobility and clergy, seemed tangible evidence of a conspiracy to reinstate all the abuses of the Old Regime. Perhaps even more disturbing was the religious schism set in motion by the Civil Constitution of the Clergy and the requirement of an ecclesiastical oath. Some 34 percent of the parish clergy in the capital and its suburbs had rejected the oath. For the Parisians, as for the people of Varennes, the "refractory" clergy became a visible symbol of the counterrevolutionary forces lurking in their midst. The fear of conspiracy hatched by refractories or aristocrats was a primary cause of numerous riots in Paris throughout the winter and spring.[12]

The responsibility for reining in and controlling this tense and turbulent city had fallen to two key figures in municipal politics, both chosen from the National Assembly itself in July 1789: the mayor, Jean-Sylvain Bailly; and the commander of the national guard, the marquis de Lafayette. Renowned astronomer, member of the prestigious French Academy, and onetime friend of Voltaire and Benjamin Franklin, Bailly had made his political reputation as the exceptionally able first president of the National Assembly. The much younger marquis—only thirty-three at the time of Varennes—was well known not only for his exploits in the American Revolution but also for his involvement in a variety of liberal causes in France on the eve of the Revolution. In 1791 Bailly and

Lafayette had at their disposal over 50,000 national guardsmen. Some 10,000 of these forces—most of them former military men—were on permanent duty, paid and living in barracks. The remainder were volunteer citizen soldiers, serving only by rotation or in moments of emergency. Because the volunteers were required to provide their own uniforms and to have enough free time for a smattering of drills, the majority came from the middle class.[13] Although the total force seemed imposing, and was vastly greater than anything existing under the Old Regime, it was not without its problems. The same suspicion of authority that had beset the regular army was having its effect on the national guard. The refusal of some contingents of the guard to allow the royal family to leave the Tuileries on April 18—despite Lafayette's formal order—was revealing in this respect. But in the aftermath of the April 18 incident, the general had been given a free hand to reform the corps, and stronger discipline had been imposed with the dismissal of the insubordinate guardsmen.[14]

Throughout the first half of 1791, the guard had been continually active, intervening almost daily in a variety of worker protests, market brawls, and insurrections against clergymen or nobles rumored to be plotting counterrevolution and civil war. Both Parisian observers and foreign visitors were obsessed by the incessant turmoil, the ever-present threat and reality of social violence besetting the city, violence of which February 28 and April 18 were only the most dramatic instances. "Tumults happen daily," wrote the British secret agent William Miles: Lafayette and his subordinates were "kept trotting about like so many penny-postmen." The English ambassador, the earl George Granville Gower, reported on "the absolute anarchy under which this country labours." William Short felt that the endless disturbances cast "a gloom and anxiety on the society of Paris that renders its residence painful in the extreme." The elderly Parisian Guittard de Floriban had much the same feeling: "Can't we ever be happy," he pleaded, "to simply live together in peace with one another? All this violence leaves me overwhelmed and depressed."[15] On the eve of Varennes Paris was already in danger of exploding from one day to the next.

For months rumors of plots to kidnap the king had been circulating in Paris. One of the deputies had reported such a threat as early as January, and similar reports were published in newspapers in February and throughout the spring. Although the details of the conspiracies were generally quite vague, the assumption was usually that someone else—a foreign power, the "aristocrats," perhaps even the queen—would forcibly abduct the monarch against his will.[16] On the eve of the flight, the radical journalist Stanislas Fréron reported rumors circulating through the city that Marie-Antoinette and the king's sister, Elizabeth, had actually attempted such an escape. Marat published a vaguer rendition of the story, colored by his standard prophecies of doom. Following accusations by one of the queen's servants, Lafayette and his lieutenants had increased the guard on the royal palace. Yet there had been so many rumors in the city over the previous months, none of which had materialized, that no one took the new denunciation very seriously.[17]

In any case, servants in the Tuileries were stunned at seven in the morning on June 21, when they pulled aside the king's curtain and found his bed empty. At first they hoped the monarch had simply gone to the queen's room, but when they found that her bed had not been slept in and that the royal children and Madame Elizabeth were also missing, pandemonium swept through the palace. Many of the servants quickly changed into street clothes and fled for their lives, fearing they would be accused of complicity.[18] By the time Lafayette and Bailly arrived, tipped off by yet another rumor that they had initially refused to believe, the news had spread outside the Tuileries and was coursing through the streets with amazing speed.[19] One Parisian remembered the experience: "I heard a roar approaching, similar to the sound made by waves in an approaching storm. It came closer, it grew louder, and it passed by with ever greater force." The young magistrate Félix Faulcon, deputy from Poitiers, was writing in his room when he noticed shouting in the streets and in the house next door and then caught the words that the king was gone. Another deputy, the lawyer and historian

Antoine Thibaudeau, was awakened by a cannon firing warning shots near the Seine. Soon everyone was at his window, calling for news from houses across the street or from the people below. Between eight and nine, as the news spread, church bells began ringing in every parish in the city. As the ominous drum roll of the call to arms started up, men rushed through the streets, still fastening their uniforms, to join their national guard formations.[20]

Many people hurried to the Tuileries to see for themselves, and by half past eight a huge crowd had burst through the gates and climbed the stairs to the royal chambers, intimidating and shouting insults against guards and servants who had not already slipped away. The soldier assigned to the king's sister was pushed against the wall and threatened, until the crowds were shown a newly discovered secret door built into the bookcase. There were reports of the people destroying portraits of the royal family and a certain amount of furniture in the queen's room. But for the most part, people simply gawked and talked to one another. When municipal officials arrived, urging the need to seal off the premises to preserve evidence, the crowds readily departed.[21] Elsewhere hostile groups of people surrounded Bailly and Lafayette, initially held responsible for the flight, as the two tried to make their way to the city hall. But the imperturbable general stood his ground and led the mayor to safety, accompanied by only a few guards. The duke d'Aumont, commander of the Tuileries guards during the night, was not so fortunate. Cornered by a large crowd, he was beaten and his clothes badly torn before he was rescued by a unit of the militia. In other sections of the city, rumors spread that the prisons housed dangerous counterrevolutionaries who might soon break out and attack the people, and municipal forces had to be rushed in to prevent a potential massacre.[22]

Yet on the whole, after the first shock and excitement, the city remained calm, and almost all observers commented on the relatively mild reaction. "There is complete tranquillity here," wrote the Spanish ambassador, "as well as a kind of stupor, as though everyone has been struck with apoplexy." "Never," observed the

People Rushing to the Tuileries after Learning of the King's Departure. Citizens and national guardsmen cross the Pont-Neuf and head down the quay toward the Louvre on the morning of June 21. The towers of Saint-Germain-l'Auxerois are visible on the right.

roaming reporter of the newspaper *Le babillard* (The Chatterer), "has Paris been both so touched with emotion and so calm. The common people, in particular, have remained orderly." The young German writer Konrad-Engelbert Oelsner wondered at the atmosphere of determined and almost jovial optimism reigning in the streets: "There was much movement and curiosity, but nowhere destruction or disorder. The indignation manifested itself less in bitterness than in amusing pleasantries. People questioned each other, spoke to those they had never seen before, discussed, joked. An extraordinary event, affecting the whole community, had wrenched a million people from their daily affairs; torn them from their petty cares, bringing them closer to one another."[23] In the short term, the open reality of conspiracy turned out to be far less disruptive than the previous rumors and fears of conspiracy.

Clearly, one of the keys to the popular restraint was the immediate and vigorous action taken by the municipal authorities. Hastily convened by Bailly at ten that morning, the city council was to remain in session around the clock for the next six days.[24] The councilors quickly established liaisons with the National Assembly, from which designated officials shuttled back and forth almost hourly. They also attempted to work closely with the neighborhood section committees, each of which was invited to maintain two representatives in the city hall to assure communication with the local bodies. In this way, the new laws decreed by the Assembly to meet the crisis were rapidly proclaimed to the sound of trumpets on street corners throughout the city. In addition, Bailly and the city councilors quickly investigated even the most far-fetched accusations—reports of impending jail breakouts or of "enemies" planning to bombard the city from the surrounding hills. They thus succeeded in disarming fears as soon as they arose.[25]

Even before they had been contacted by the mayor, most of the sections had swung into action. As chance would have it, many were meeting that morning for the election of the new legislature. When word of the emergency reached them, they immediately declared themselves to be in permanent session and mobilized the national guard units in their neighborhoods. For the first time, more humble "passive citizens"—those too poor to qualify for voting rights—were widely welcomed into the units. Some of these inhabitants seized arms for themselves by breaking into government magazines. A few sections went further, claiming complete control over the local militias and denying the authority of Lafayette, whom many suspected of involvement in the king's disappearance. The general and the city leaders had long been suspicious of the radicalism of the sections, and for the time being they were able to reassert their control over all guard units and thwart the creation of independent paramilitary groups. But in the midst of the national crisis, the municipality tolerated the permanent sessions of the sections and acquiesced to their claims as de facto administrative units. These were significant precedents. Within a year after Varennes the sections would evolve into the principal institutional base of the armed "sans-culottes" radicals, a primary force in the overthrow of the king and in the ascendancy of the Terror in Paris.[26]

Equally significant for the future of the Revolution was the dramatic change in attitudes toward the king. Throughout the first two years of the Revolution, Louis had retained a remarkably positive image among the great majority of Parisians of every political persuasion. When the king's elderly aunts emigrated to Rome in February, a female contingent of the Fraternal Society of Les Halles wrote to the monarch: "We love you as our good father, and we want to tell you how sad we are that your family is abandoning you." A month later, when Louis had recovered from a severe cold and sore throat, there was an extraordinary outpouring of affection and goodwill everywhere in Paris, a general rejoicing marked by a thanksgiving service in the cathedral of Notre Dame, a series of cannon salutes, and a special illumination of the city throughout the night. The most serious source of antagonism before June 21 had been the king's refusal to hear mass from the "constitutional" clergy. This was the single most important grievance motivating the events of April 18, and since that time there had been a distinct cooling toward Louis in the radical press. Yet the king seemed rapidly to admit his error and to mend his ways (in fact, as we know, to help screen his plans for escape). Most Parisians were ready to invoke the time-tested formula of the "good king badly advised," and to attribute his "mistakes" to the influence of the aristocrats or the queen.[27]

But everything was transformed by the king's flight. It was not only Louis' departure that stunned the Parisians, but also his letter renouncing much of the Revolution and declaring that his previous acquiescence to the new laws had been coerced. Oelsner was struck by the number of people he saw reading and discussing copies of the king's letter in the street. Here, in his own hand-written note, the monarch made it clear that the flight had been entirely his own idea and not the work of his advisers. It now seemed obvious that Louis had lied to the French. His solemn oath pronounced just one year earlier—an oath sworn before God and the nation to uphold the constitution—had been insincere.[28]

Indeed, after June 21 it was difficult to find a single newspaper—aside from those of the most reactionary royalists—with anything positive to say about the monarch. The *Chronique de Paris* wrote of the king's "perfidious treachery," of his "atrocious and black dissimulation" in plotting his departure. The generally moderate *Journal de Perlet* played on the contrast between the king's previous statements and his new manifesto. "How," the editor asked, "could one ever again have confidence in anything the king might say?"[29] The harshness of the reaction, the veritable flood of scorn, revulsion, and disgust toward the monarch, impressed all contemporary observers. Some reports even commented on the cowardly manner in which the monarch had deserted his ministers and his royalist supporters to the wrath of the crowds. In a deluge of articles and pamphlets—over a hundred published during the next three weeks—he was variously labeled a "traitor," a "liar," a "coward," or simply "Louis the False." "Try to think of the most degrading expressions you could possibly use," wrote the Paris scholar and bookseller Nicolas Ruault, "and you will still underestimate what is actually said." "There are no epithets of shame," concurred Swiss writer Etienne Dumont, "which have not been repeated unsparingly and with cold-blooded scorn."[30]

The Parisian radicals, already obsessively sensitive to plots and conspiracies, felt especially perturbed, even humiliated. How could they have been so blind, lulled to sleep and oblivious to this, the greatest conspiracy of all? "We relied on the king's fine words, his honeyed speeches," protested Jacques-Pierre Brissot, an ambitious journalist and Parisian political figure. "We were lulled to sleep. It seemed a crime even to doubt the king's promises. So now this 'patriot' king has fled . . . and is unmasked." There were endless refer-

The Family of Pigs Brought Back to the Stable. Another version of the return to the Tuileries palace—just visible on the far right. The transmogrified royal family is pulled along in a toy wagon.

ences to the king as a "parjure," one who is faithless to his oaths. William Short found everyone in Paris referring to him as such: "Louis the Traitor, Louis the Faithless." "He has fled," wrote the *Chronique de Paris,* "despite all of his faithless promises. He even chose the moment of his flight to correspond [almost] with the anniversary of the Federation oath taken before heaven and earth and in the presence of the nation, a nation that had forgiven him for his earlier mistakes." The Cordeliers published a paraphrase of a passage from *Brutus,* a popular play by Voltaire:

> Remember the day, at the altar august
> Louis swore he'd forever be faithful and just.
> But such is the bond between people and throne
> That he sundered our oaths, in betraying his own.[31]

There was no clearer evidence of the depths of the popular outrage than the change in the representation of the king. Before

Varennes, simple engraved portraits of Louis had been affixed to walls in almost every home and shop in Paris. But now, almost overnight, they were removed, and large numbers were said to have been thrown ostentatiously into the gutters.[32] Indeed, there was a striking reformulation of the images used to portray the king. Above all, he was pictured as an animal, and especially as a pig. It was an obvious allusion to his reputation for overeating—a trait once viewed as almost endearing but now depicted as disgusting. For weeks thereafter the "pig-king" appeared everywhere in newspapers and brochures, in posters and engravings. Often there were whole families of pigs: a pig-queen and various other pig-members of the royal family in company with the porcine Louis. Someone even attached a sign to the wall of the Tuileries palace shortly after the flight: "A large pig has escaped from the premises," it read. "Anyone finding him is urged to return him to his pen. A minor reward will be offered."[33]

Birth of the Sans-Culottes

It was late on the evening of June 22 when Parisians learned that the missing monarch would indeed be returned to the "premises." At about half past ten the master barber Mangin, dispatched from Varennes almost twenty-four hours earlier, finally arrived in Paris. He shouted as he rode through the streets, "The king is taken! The king has been stopped!" Covered with dust and obviously exhausted after his long ride, he presented the National Assembly with a written report and breathlessly delivered a somewhat garbled and inaccurate version of the events in his hometown. The account was further transformed by those Parisians who had followed him into the Assembly and who then rushed out to relate the story to their friends. But the essence of the capture was soon understood, and the news spread rapidly throughout the city. Most people had already gone to bed, but they were roused by the noise and rushed to their windows or into the streets, anxiously asking for more details, and musing throughout much of the night on the possible ramifications of this unexpected turn of events. They had all assumed that by now the royal family must have escaped to a foreign country and that war might soon be declared. The capture in a small town in Lorraine seemed all but miraculous, bringing a new sense of exhilaration, self-confidence, and power. Once again it seemed that fate, perhaps God himself, was on the side of the Revolution.[34]

As chance would have it, the next day was Corpus Christi, a celebration in honor of the sacrament of the Eucharist and one of the great feast days in the Catholic liturgical year. Plans had been in the works for weeks—as they were each year at this time—to carry the Sacred Host around each of the city's fifty-two parishes, through streets adorned with colorful tapestries, flowers, and other decorations. Religious hymns were to be sung; processions of the national guard would march behind the local clergy, followed in turn by the religious confraternities of various worker groups with their flags and banners. In the evening there would be bonfires and fireworks and a veritable carnival atmosphere.[35]

But now the ceremony was transformed into a citywide celebration of the capture of the king. The most grandiose of all the processions was the one that encircled the parish church of Saint-Germain-l'Auxerrois, the Gothic structure just east of the Louvre and the official parish of the Tuileries palace. The march had originally been conceived to include the king and the royal family, as well as a large contingent from the National Assembly and hundreds of the elite national guard, led by Lafayette himself. But with the king absent, and with the news of his capture, the traditional religious music was replaced in large measure by an array of patriotic songs. Observers were impressed, above all, by the repeated renditions of the vigorous and optimistic popular song that had swept through the city: "Ah, ça ira! Ça ira! Ça ira!" (It'll all work out! It'll all be okay!). The patriot-priest Thomas Lindet, who was present and heard the song for the first time, congratulated the unknown composer "for helping to excite the courage of the French and rekindle their natural cheerfulness." Nor did anyone miss the symbolism in the fact that it was the deputies of the National Assembly who had taken the place in the procession of the missing king—still riding in his carriage somewhere in Champagne on the return route to Paris. One newspaper noted that the Assembly's appearance "had something triumphal about it. Vigorous applause and cries of happiness were mixed with the music of the national guard."[36]

Whether by plan or through improvisation, many of the guardsmen who had marched in the procession followed the deputies back to their meeting hall and asked to be allowed to take the same oath of allegiance to the constitution that the Assembly had administered one day earlier to all deputies who were military men. After a break for dinner, other guards from throughout the city converged on the hall, clamoring to swear an identical oath. The event was perhaps partly staged by Lafayette, who was anxious to reclaim the good opinion of the patriots after his failure to prevent the king's flight.[37] But the general did not plan the remarkable sequel. As though reviving their processions of earlier in the day—and transforming a religious act into a political one—common citizens from all over Paris marched to the Assembly hall through the gathering dusk, arriving by neighborhood or worker confraternity, asking that they, too, be permitted to take the oath. Musicians took up seats in the largely deserted benches on the right side of the hall, where the conservative and aristocratic deputies sat in theory, but were usually absent. Once again the band took up the stanzas of "Ça ira!" and a variety of other patriotic songs. Column after column of citizens passed through the candlelit hall, in one door and out another, joining in the songs and raising their hands to shout "I so swear!" as they passed in front of the Assembly's president. Still in a festive mood, they arrived in an extraordinary mixture of clothing styles and colors. There were guardsmen in bright blue or green and white uniforms, and men in a diversity of more sober middle-class dress with knee breeches, buckled shoes, and three-cornered hats. But there were also large numbers of common people, women with aprons and bonnets, men in the long workingman's trousers—the "sans-culottes" (without knee breeches), as they were now coming to be called. Marching through the hall, six abreast, were butchers and colliers and fishwives, bakers with loaves of bread on the end of pikes, and stocky porters with their large round hats from the central market: men and women of every age and profession, some of the women holding up their babies as they shouted out their oaths, as though the next generation was also to be included in this common allegiance to the nation. They marched by in rapid order for at least two hours. Guittard estimated upward of 15,000; others thought it was more like 50,000. The popular eastern suburbs of Saint-Antoine and Saint-Marcel were particularly well represented. Marie-Jeanne Roland, the thirty-seven-year-old wife of a provincial official and herself a passionate radical Revolutionary, claimed that virtually the entire district of Saint-Antoine had arrived in a column stretching back across town to the neighborhood itself, some two miles away.[38]

After the long hours of uncertainty and fear, this colorful evening festival marked a release of tension and seemed to reinforce a new sense of unity and self-confidence. Mobilized in part, no doubt, by the fraternal societies and the more radical sections, the common people present were also armed with a rough sort of political message. Some carried banners with the words "Live free or die." Others added new verses to "Ça ira," sending both the aristocrats and the king to the devil. Although in general their allegiance was directed toward the National Assembly, they also made it clear that they did not intend to be subservient to the Assembly's decisions if those decisions were not to their liking. "Long live the good deputies!" some of them called out, "but let the others watch out!"[39] And though their mood was generally joyous, the people were also well armed with an incredible assortment of weapons, from sickles to pitchforks, from clubs to pikes. Many of the pikes were covered with bright red "liberty caps"—now the hat of choice among the patriotic workingpeople. But underneath the caps were razor-sharp spikes and hooks, originally conceived for slicing up cavalry horses but more recently used to carry the severed heads of the victims of popular violence. Some of the pikes had almost certainly been seized illegally from the municipal armories during the last two days.[40] It was the first time such weapons had been seen in the Assembly since the harrowing October Days of 1789. In a symbolic sense, then, this extraordinary nighttime procession marked a major moment in the emergence of the sans-culottes as a self-conscious, well-organized political force. It was a force that the National Assembly and the whole of France would soon have to reckon with.

A King Is Not Inevitable

For well over a thousand years the Parisians had always had a king. When one died, so the theory went, another one, his closest male heir, immediately assumed the royal powers—"The king is dead; long live the king!"—even if the monarch in question was only a child and his powers were exercised by a regent. But now, for a great many Parisians, the myth of the kingship had been shattered. Once Louis had been brought back from Varennes, led through the streets of Paris, and reinstalled in the Tuileries, the great question in everyone's mind was what should become of the monarch and the monarchy. The bookseller Nicolas Ruault sized up the situation in a letter to his brother: "We have to decide what we will do with this king, who is now a king in name alone. The question is delicate and awkward in the extreme."[41] Everyone in Paris began mulling over the situation and proposing solutions. Louis should be maintained as king, but only as a figurehead; he should be deprived of all power until the constitution was completed and then offered the throne, to take it or to leave it; he should be exiled from Paris or from the country; he should be imprisoned and tried for treason; he should be deposed, and his power should pass to the little dauphin, who would be carefully educated in the ideals of the Revolution. But from the very first day of the king's flight, and in the midst of the confusion, some Parisians went even further. They asked themselves if the monarchy itself was truly inevitable, if it was not time for the French to live independently in a republic without a king.

To be sure, this was not the first time the word *republic* had been mentioned in Paris. Almost a year earlier Louis Lavicomterie, a future member of the Convention, had published an essay called "Of People and Kings," which openly advocated a government without a monarch. Louise Kéralio, the novelist and historian turned radical publisher, quickly picked up the idea in her newspaper the *Mercure nationale,* an idea that her husband, François Robert, further elaborated in a small booklet at the end of the year. By the spring of 1791 the concept of republicanism had become almost fashionable in certain radical intellectual circles. Yet there was always something speculative and academic about such discussions. The principal preoccupation of the radicals continued to be the expansion of voting rights to all men, regardless of income. And the idea of a French government without a king had virtually no popular support. The young duke de Chartres—the future Louis-Philippe, "king of the French" in 1830—described the reactions of a patriotic audience to a performance of Voltaire's *Brutus.* When an actor pronounced the line "Oh, to be free and without a king," only a few people applauded, while the great majority began shouting, "Long live the king!" followed by the "triple refrain" of "Long live the nation, the law, and the king!"[42]

Yet the flight to Varennes brought a dramatic change in attitude for many Parisians. Within hours after the news had broken a popular onslaught against symbols of royalty began throughout the city. Anything smacking of kings or kingship was removed, pulled down, covered over, or defaced. Establishments with names suggesting royalty in any form—like the Queen's Hotel or the Crowned Ox Restaurant—found their signs removed and destroyed. Coats of arms of the Bourbon family on public buildings or notary offices were blacked out with a mixture of soot and oil. Soldiers and guardsmen were urged to remove the royal fleur-de-lis insignia from their uniforms; busts of kings were pulled over, and larger royal statues, too massive to be moved, were covered in black cloth; even streets like Rue du Roi de Siam (the King of Siam) were renamed with a more patriotic designation.[43] Marie-Jeanne Roland was amazed and delighted by the extraordinary rapidity with which

Parisians Covering Symbols of Royalty. In the days after the king's flight, people cover in black the word *royal* on the lottery office and the crown on the Golden Crown Inn, and remove fleur-de-lis shields from a notary's office.

the new idea seemed to take hold in the popular quarters of the city. "The masses have a healthy and correct understanding," she wrote on June 22. "The word 'republic' is now being uttered almost everywhere."[44]

In addition to the spontaneous attacks by common people on the symbols of monarchy, a significant number of Parisian intellectuals, political figures, and radical newspaper editors openly declared for a republic. Within days, several of the most advanced journalists had come out in support of the idea. Brissot was particularly emphatic as he inveighed against Louis XVI, who "has destroyed his crown with his own hands. One can never convert a despot to the cause of liberty." The writer and founder of the populist Society of the Friends of Truth, Nicolas de Bonneville, began militating for a republic. With his friends, the celebrated mathematician and philosopher the marquis de Condorcet and the Anglo-American liberal Thomas Paine, he launched a newspaper dedicated to the republican ideal. "It is only with the event of June 21," as the abbé Sieyès wrote to Paine, "that we have suddenly seen the emergence of a republican party."[45]

From the beginning, the most effective and dynamic leadership for such a party came from the Cordeliers Club, whose membership included many of the journalists who would most vigorously adopt the new position. On the very day of the king's flight, the club resolved to call into question the whole idea of a constitutional monarchy as it had been elaborated by the National Assembly over the two previous years. The members seem to have adopted a two-pronged strategy. On the one hand, they urged the deputies to redraft the constitution as a republic. But on the other hand, aware that the majority of French citizens might well oppose such a measure until they were properly informed and educated, the members supported a national referendum to elicit a general debate on the issue. "Legislators," they wrote, in a formal petition addressed to the Assembly, "you can no longer hope to inspire the people with the least degree of confidence in a state functionary who is called a 'king.' On the basis of this fact, we beg you, in the name of the fatherland, either immediately to declare that France shall no longer be a monarchy, but a republic; or, at the very least, to wait until all the departments and all the primary assemblies have announced their will on this critical question."[46] Thereafter the club became a whirlwind of activity and energy, promoting and explaining its idea. Members had posters printed and affixed them to walls at street corners throughout the city. They urged all the Parisian fraternal societies with which they were so closely linked to coordinate their efforts and to debate and adopt the same position. In addition, they organized a citywide march of adherents to present their petition to the National Assembly.[47]

The demonstration of June 24 was another signal event in the development of popular radicalism and the politicization of the sans-culottes. In some respects, it might be viewed as the first modern political demonstration in French history—anticipating in its form and its spirit the great Parisian political marches of the nineteenth and twentieth centuries. Coordinated through the network of popular societies and sections, people from all over Paris set off on foot toward the designated rallying point at the Place Vendôme. The organizers built on the success of the previous day's Corpus Christi parade through the Assembly. In this sense, there was another fascinating link between the religious processions of the Old Regime and the new form of mass democratic culture. Men, women, and children—most of them from working-class families, according to witnesses—paraded through the streets, linking arms and walking seven or eight abreast, and occasionally singing or shouting slogans. Many wore armbands or badges on their coats with the eye that symbolized their club and its mission to search for conspirators. Guittard de Floriban, the elderly bourgeois property owner who lived not far from the Cordeliers, looked on as thousands marched by. At first he was frightened, fearing violence and a riot. But then he noted that the participants were calm and well organized. Unlike the previous night at the Assembly, no one carried arms, not even sticks or canes. He followed them as they crossed the river on the Pont-Neuf, heading toward the Place des Victoires, where they converged with thousands arriving from eastern Paris. In the Place Vendôme, just north of the Assembly hall, they were met by Lafayette, who clearly had been tipped off about the demonstration and had gathered a large contingent of national guardsmen with cannons and muskets in readiness. But the crowd remained peaceful, announcing only that they wished to present to the Assembly a petition signed by 30,000 people. After a nervous face-off, seven delegates from the crowd were allowed to deliver their statement.[48]

The demonstrators could only have been disappointed when the Assembly postponed reading the petition until the following day. When it was introduced, according to one member of the Cordeliers, it was read by a mere secretary "in such a manner that it could be heard by no one" and then sent to a committee to be promptly forgotten. Over the next three weeks the Cordeliers and the other fraternal societies in Paris continued their campaign. By one count, seventeen petitions were drawn up between June 21 and July 17, each of them rejected out of hand or ignored by the Assembly. Throughout this period both the Cordeliers and the fraternal societies continued to hold nightly debates on the king and the fate he deserved. Marie-Jeanne Roland, who went out each evening to watch and participate—for many such meetings invited the involvement of women—was stunned by the quasi-millenarian transformation she witnessed. The common people of Paris, who only a few years earlier would "stupidly sing amen" no matter what they were told by the authorities, were now becoming enlightened and were ready to support "our just cause" and demand "the reign of justice." "We are advancing ten years in a single day."[49]

The republican campaign by the popular societies was significantly affected, moreover, by two other developments. In the first place, it coincided with a series of worker demonstrations that contemporaries perceived as better organized and more intense than anything they had previously witnessed. By the first week in July, national guardsmen were being sent out almost daily to suppress labor protests and attempted strikes—by journeymen hatmakers, masons, and street workers, for example—strikes now rendered illegal by the National Assembly's recent Le Chapelier law. At almost the same time the city government, backed by the Assembly, had begun dismantling a system of public works, initiated in 1789 as a dole for the unemployed and now deemed too expensive. These actions generated enormous anxiety and anger, and in late June and early July workers organized several protest marches, many of them again converging on the Place Vendôme. Although these labor movements were not necessarily related to the political events, they helped to intensify the atmosphere of crisis and to energize the sans-culotte movement.[50]

In the second place, the Cordeliers and the fraternal societies, along with several of the more radical sections of Paris, came increasingly to focus their anger on the National Assembly itself. Disenchanted that the Assembly took so little notice of their petitions, they were also increasingly suspicious of the deputies' treatment of the king and queen after their return, allowing them to remain in the palace with their servants and advisers, almost as though nothing had happened. And they were beside themselves with anger and frustration when word began to leak out by the second week in July that the deputies were moving toward exonerating the king.[51] Already prone to paranoid perspectives, the men and women of the Cordeliers and the fraternal societies began to sense a plot being hatched in the Assembly. Rumors spread that the deputies had "sold out to the court," that they had doctored or fabricated the king's private testimony—notably Louis' statement that he had never intended to leave the country. There were even stories that the majority of the deputies were planning the assassination of the small group of Assembly radicals, like Pétion and Robespierre, who were sympathetic to the Cordeliers' position. In the midst of the crisis, the Assembly had postponed the election of a new legislature, and now there were accusations that the representatives were using the situation to perpetuate themselves in power, like the members of the Long Parliament in seventeenth-century England.[52]

On July 12 the Cordeliers and their allies drew up yet another petition. Once again it was rejected by the Assembly, after the president, Charles de Lameth, had read only a few lines and had announced it "contrary to the constitution." Furious at this snub, which resembled only too closely the upper-class condescension they had known under the Old Regime—and Lameth himself was a former count—the Cordeliers resolved to bypass the Assembly and to appeal their case directly to the French people. They drew up an "Address to the Nation" to be published and circulated throughout the country, an address soon supported by most of the neighborhood fraternal societies. Until now the radicals had taken great care to act within the law, carefully obeying the Assembly's decrees on petitions and duly notifying the municipal government before each street demonstration. But the new address could be seen as a veritable call for insurrection, prefiguring the convocation of the National Convention in the summer of 1792. The petitioners summoned each of the eighty-three French departments, the administrative units of the new regime, to send a delegate to Paris, there to constitute a new "executive authority" that would replace the king—and presumably the National Assembly as well—"until the nation can decide the fate of the ex-king and determine the new mode of government." They also denounced the deputies for refusing to allow new elections to take place: "this arbitrary and abusive prolongation of their term in office." The departments should immediately and unilaterally convoke new elections, replacing the current deputies, who had "lost the confidence of the nation." Finally, the local administrators were urged to organize these elections through universal male suffrage, ignoring the National Assembly's laws placing tax qualifications on the right to vote.[53]

During the same period many of the radical newspapers—whose messages were soon being read aloud in cafés and shouted in the streets throughout the city—began pushing even more directly for insurrection. Brissot thundered against the Assembly and its position on the king: "an infamy, an absurdity, an atrocity." Fréron and Bonneville predicted and urged an impending revolt. One article, probably written by the Cordeliers' Pierre-Gaspard Chaumette, was even more blunt. The author reminded the deputies of the fate of the governor of the Bastille in 1789, who had been decapitated by the insurrectionary crowds when he acted against public opinion. "There are moments," he wrote, "when insurrection is the holiest of duties."[54]

Bastille Day 1791

The second anniversary of the storming of the Bastille fell in the very midst of the crisis. Although there had been some talk of canceling the event after June 21, Paris officials decided in the end to follow through with their original scheme. The Cordeliers and the nascent sans-culottes did not speak for all the complex population of the city. Indeed, large numbers of Parisians, including most of the deputies in the Assembly, were appalled by the recurrent street demonstrations of workers and political radicals. Few had been happy with Louis' flight, and most had felt considerable anger toward the king. But the continuing violence or threat of violence from the crowds, and the Cordeliers' scarcely veiled appeals for insurrection against the Assembly, had frightened them and made them all the more wary of radical changes to the constitution. Now the town fathers hoped that a reprise of the Federation Festival of 1790 might somehow resurrect the magic and the unity of the previous year and provide the means for respectable citizens to counter the demonstrations of the republicans. It would be a ringing response to the "fanatics who want to destroy the monarchy, to the treacherous rogues who can only shout for a republic," as one moderate journalist put it. In any case, the great stadium on the Champ de Mars at the western end of the city was refurbished to hold even more people than the year before, and the central "Altar to the Fatherland" was remodeled for the occasion.[55]

The citywide celebration began on the evening of July 13, with a great musical event in the cathedral of Notre Dame, attended by various Revolutionary dignitaries and by the individuals who had led the attack on the great medieval fortress two years earlier. A ritual thanksgiving *Te Deum* was sung by the pro-Revolutionary clergy, and the composer François-Joseph Gossec organized a musical extravaganza titled *The Fall of the Bastille*.[56] The festivities continued the next morning when a long procession set off at ten o'clock from the site of the now-demolished Bastille in the direction of the parade grounds across the city. Led by Bailly and the municipal government, the march included a long line of officials from the government ministries, the judiciary, the military, and the forty-eight sections, all interspersed with bands, batteries of drummers, national guard units, and a model of the Bastille carried like a religious reliquary in an Old Regime procession. For three hours the musical parade wound through the city: past the city hall, down the right bank of the Seine, across the river near the Tuileries, through the Left Bank district of Saint-Germain, and into the stadium. When everyone was in place, around two o'clock, there was a mass and another *Te Deum*, led by the newly elected "constitutional" bishop of Paris. The ceremony ended with a series of military maneuvers by the national guards, directed by General Lafayette astride his white horse.[57]

In certain respects the event appeared to be a success. Most observers thought that the crowds were at least as large as in 1790, and perhaps larger. And no one could deny that the weather was better. The day had dawned warm and beautiful, in sharp contrast to the miserable rain and mud of a year earlier.[58] But there were also ample signs of a sea change in attitudes from the previous year and of the sharp political differences now dividing the Parisians. Claiming that they were too occupied with debates, the National Assembly sent only twenty-four delegates instead of the entire body, which had arrived in procession in 1790. Even more obvious was the absence of the king and the rest of the royal family. No one had even considered asking Louis to renew his oath to the constitution. Some witnesses also noted the apparent last-minute changes executed by unknown artists on the Altar of the Fatherland. There was a bas-relief of the "Triumph of Voltaire," alluding to the anticlerical procession celebrated only a few days earlier in honor of the patriarch of the Enlightenment. There was another scene that witnesses took to be a monument to citizen Drouet, the hero of Varennes. And most conspicuous of all, the word *king* had been effaced from the altar, which now read "the Nation, the Law, the [blank]." References to the monarch had also been removed from virtually all the flags of the national guard units. At several points during the ceremony, people even cried out, "No more Louis XVI, no more king!"[59]

There were also reports of tension and violence of a kind quite unknown twelve months earlier. The visiting Creole noble Henri-Paulin Panon Desbassayns made the mistake of wearing his cross of Saint Louis, an Old Regime marker of aristocratic status, and he was insulted and badly handled by the crowds. Even worse treatment was meted out to two supporters of the refractory clergy, who threw stones at the national altar. Early in the proceedings a rumor spread that the National Assembly was going to profit from the people's presence at the Champ de Mars to vote the exoneration of the king, and some individuals rushed back across town to the Assembly hall. Indeed, members of several of the popular societies, including the Cordeliers, had not even attended the ceremony. They had sent their own procession to the Assembly earlier in the day to demonstrate their continuing opposition to its policies, presenting the deputies with yet another petition. Once again they demanded that the deputies take no decision on the king until all the people of France had been consulted in a referendum. And this time, they went even further. The true sovereign body, they argued, was not the Assembly at all, but "the people." A failure to recognize this reality, they continued, might well lead to civil war.[60]

Clearly, all eyes were now on the deputies of the National Assembly. The men who only a few months earlier had been universally heralded as "the Fathers of the Nation" were being castigated and threatened with insurrection by a vociferous minority of the Parisian population. Now the deputies would have little choice but to act.

The Fathers of the Nation

FOR OVER TWO YEARS the deputies had been at work in the National Assembly, drafting a constitution and reorganizing the country from top to bottom.[1] In many respects, they were an exceptional group of men. The electoral system, patched together by the royal government in 1789, had brought in elites of local, regional, and national stature from every part of the kingdom. There were close to 300 nobles, most of them titled and exceedingly wealthy, representing the greatest families in France. There were several dozen aristocratic bishops and archbishops, and over 200 parish priests from towns and villages across the country. And there were some 600 deputies of the Third Estate, commoners for the most part, from a wide range of professions: lawyers, judges, doctors, merchants, landowners, and a variety of government employees. Most of the Third Estate deputies were men of property, and many had experience in municipal government. But their cultural common denominator was training in the law. Perhaps two-thirds of them had pursued legal studies, and several ranked among the finest legal minds of their age.

For the commoner deputies of the Estates General and for the minority of liberal nobles and clergy who supported them, the early weeks of the Revolution had marked an extraordinary, almost magical moment. Faced with the intransigence of most of the aristocracy and with the near abdication of power by the royal government, encouraged by the support of the Parisian crowds, they had learned from one another, stimulated one another, and pieced together ideas from a whole range of eighteenth-century notions of reform. Soon they found themselves moving further and more rapidly toward a radical transformation of France than any of them would previously have imagined. By the middle of June 1789 they had converted themselves into a sovereign National Assembly, solemnly dedicating themselves—in the dramatic "Tennis Court Oath"—to drawing up the country's first constitution. A few weeks later, on August 4, during a particularly stunning nighttime session, they had swept away large portions of the Old Regime's political and social institutions and the whole system of seigneurial rights and caste privilege. Soon thereafter they had issued their "Declaration of the Rights of Man and the Citizen," anticipating many of the provisions of the Bill of Rights, ratified in the United States just two years later. Following the king from Versailles to Paris after the October Days, and moving their meetings to an adapted indoor riding arena just north of the Tuileries gardens, they had taken up with unflinching energy the task of restructuring the country. Having largely dismantled the previous regime, they had been compelled to rebuild almost everything from scratch: the central government, the regional administration, the courts, the legal code, the tax system, the organization of the armed forces and of the church.

To End a Revolution

But as the deputies moved into the second year of the Revolution, subtle changes in their mood and outlook had begun to appear. In part, it was a question of sheer fatigue. For those who took their mission seriously, for those who attended sessions regularly, participated in committees, read the endless proposals written by other deputies, and maintained correspondence with their constituencies, the relentless responsibilities could easily lead to exhaustion and lassitude. Few had been accustomed to such a pace of life before their arrival in the capital, and few could now afford secretaries. "Our brains can no longer cope with such intense and sustained exertion," wrote one of the deputies. They were "harassed," thought another, "with too much work, with too many sessions, with too many struggles." In their correspondence they described themselves as "exhausted" and "worn out," suffering from headaches, insomnia, and weight loss. By early 1791, absenteeism had risen precipitously. Most of the nobles and a great many of the priests had simply ceased attending, and only about 400 of the nearly 1,200 representatives actually appeared on a regular basis.[2]

The exhaustion and overwork may also have contributed to the terrible factional conflicts that marked the second year of the Revolution. "The Assembly no longer works as efficiently as in the beginning," wrote the deputy Doctor Jean-François Campmas. "It is utterly exhausted and a prey to political passions." Since the end of 1789 the most progressive representatives had begun meeting separately at night in a large abandoned convent a block or two north of the Assembly hall. Here the Friends of the Constitution, or Jacobins—after the convent of Saint-Jacques—debated issues and developed political strategies in advance of Assembly sessions, anticipating in many respects the activities of a modern political party. Soon they had also developed a network of affiliated societies throughout the country—the very network that the patriots of Varennes had joined in early 1791. But only a few months after their creation, the Jacobins found themselves at odds with a breakaway contingent of more moderate deputies, organized as the Society of 1789. And both of these patriot "clubs" were frequently riven by bitter personal and political rivalries. Lafayette, who early left the Jacobins for the "Eighty-Niners," lamented the situation to his friend George Washington in May 1791: "Even among those who call themselves patriots, the passion for factions has gone as far as it can go without leading to bloodshed."[3]

The challenges faced by the deputies were also complicated by a series of unanticipated developments. In the spring of 1790 a diplomatic crisis between England and Spain first raised the threat of international intervention into France's affairs, a threat that continued to preoccupy the Assembly to the eve of the king's flight. The prospect of war seemed particularly unsettling in that rising hostilities between commoner soldiers and aristocratic officers—the same hostilities encountered by General Bouillé in his efforts to organize Louis' escape—had brought the French army to the verge of collapse. Even more disturbing was the opposition aroused in certain areas of the country by the Civil Constitution of the Clergy and the requirement of a clerical oath. Most patriot deputies saw this legislation as a rational and necessary reform of church organization, but some segments of the population became convinced that the Assembly was trying to change the Catholic religion itself. The seriousness of the crisis came home to the deputies when portions of their own constituencies—sometimes including wives and close friends—began attacking the religious policies of the Assembly.

At the same time, the representatives had been forced to confront the problems of ever-increasing popular riots and unrest. The daily threats of "anarchy" in Paris, in the very neighborhoods in which the deputies lived and worked—the bread riots, the labor protests, the insubordination of national guard units—caused many patriots to question the democratic positions they had previously embraced. Once considered the saviors of the Revolution, the common people of Paris were soon viewed by many moderates as ungrateful, unpredictable, and dangerous. They had become all the more dangerous, in this view, through the irresponsible demagoguery of the Cordeliers Club and the radical press. Beginning in the winter of 1790–91 a group of moderate Jacobins began pushing through a series of decrees intended to disarm popular radicalism. These measures included the exclusion of poorer citizens from the national guard; the enforcement of laws against "crimes of the press"; and the Le Chapelier law, banning worker organizations and strikes.[4] At the head of this group were the young lawyer from Grenoble Antoine Barnave and his close friends, the nobles Charles and Alexandre Lameth—both veterans of the American Revolutionary War—and the liberal Paris magistrate Adrien Duport. For Barnave and the group around him, it was now time to end the Revolution, to put the French people back on the normal course of their lives and to reinstill some sense of stability and civic discipline.

Antoine-Pierre-Joseph-Marie Barnave. Leader of the moderate Jacobins, and later of the Feuillants.

Jérôme Pétion. Leader of the radical Jacobins.

Yet ending a revolution was to prove every bit as difficult as beginning one. All of the moderates' measures were opposed tooth and nail by a small group of radical Jacobins in the Assembly, led by Jérôme Pétion and Maximilien Robespierre. An ascetic in his lifestyle, though intensely passionate in his political convictions, Robespierre, like Pétion, refused to abandon his belief in the rights and basic goodness of the common people. Indeed, the two men and the group of deputies who followed them believed that the Revolution was not in fact complete. Democracy should be expanded and suffrage extended to all male citizens, whatever their status or economic condition.

But in the spring of 1791 Robespierre and his allies were rarely able to prevail. As one former radical put it, "a time for moderation has arrived."[5] The desire to curb the popular influence in Paris and to end the Revolution was even pushing many moderates to shore up the power and prestige of the king. The Spanish ambassador had already detected this policy reorientation at the end of 1790. "Through secret intermediaries," he announced in December, "the democratic leaders are now seeking to reach an understanding with the monarchy, and are promising to work toward the prompt restoration of order." By April 1791 Barnave and the moderates had largely ceased attending the Jacobin Club and—as Robespierre suspected but was unable to prove—had even entered into clandestine negotiations with Louis XVI.[6] The majority's desire to strengthen the monarchy helps explain the exceptionally positive attitude toward the king among a great many of the patriot deputies, the wishful thinking with which they evaluated Louis' every action. It was for this same reason that the king's sudden dash for freedom would seem like such a harsh blow.

The Interregnum

When the president of the National Assembly announced the terrible news at nine in the morning on June 21, the deputies sat in stunned silence. One member remembered vividly "the consternation painted on every face" as they all tried to comprehend the implications of the event. Jean-François Gaultier de Biauzat, writing on his lap during the meeting, noted simply: "may God help us now."[7] Over the previous weeks they had all heard predictions that the king might be abducted. But there were always dozens of unproved rumors floating about, and, as jurists trained in sorting evidence analytically, they had learned to dismiss most of the stories out of hand. And if truth be told, these were not rumors the deputies wanted to believe. As they came increasingly to envision the monarch as the linchpin in the constitutional system, they had convinced themselves that the king could be trusted.

A parade of embarrassed officials soon arrived in the Assembly hall, attempting to justify themselves and explain what had happened. Lafayette, who was ultimately responsible for security at the Tuileries palace, entered "with a doleful and downcast appearance." Mayor Bailly and several deputies charged with investigating the earlier rumors also spoke and admitted their failure. Indeed, the rumors in question now appeared far more substantial than most deputies had realized. The queen's servingwoman—the very woman the royal couple had so feared in the weeks before the flight—had informed officials of the coming evasion with great accuracy. Extra guards had supposedly been placed near the door she had indicated, and still the royal family had disappeared as if by magic. Some deputies speculated that Lafayette himself was in on the plot or had knowingly allowed it to succeed.[8] It seems more likely that the general never really believed the rumors. If we can trust his memoirs, he had directly broached the reports with Louis himself, and the king had given "such solemn and forceful denials that [Lafayette] would have wagered his life that the king would not leave." Like nearly everyone else, he had wanted to believe that the king was incapable of lying. Perhaps for this reason he had failed to impress upon the guards the need to be especially vigilant.[9]

In any event, the deputies soon overcame their consternation. They bravely reminded one another of all they had been through, comparing the present situation with the summer of 1789, when obstacles had seemed all but insurmountable. They declared them-selves to be in permanent session, and for the next several days they met around the clock, with a skeleton crew of deputies spending the night at their benches, ready to confront whatever emergencies might arise.[10] And in the face of the unprecedented crisis, they put aside their factional feuds and pulled together. The members were particularly impressed when Barnave, the former Young Turk of the Jacobins, came to the defense of his longtime rival Lafayette. "This act of justice and generosity stunned the Assembly and brought to a halt all accusations against the general. It was a day on which all those previously divided by ideas, passions, rivalries, or personality were brought together." The next morning, June 22, nearly all of the deputies who were members of the military, most of them sitting on the conservative right of the Assembly, came for-ward and, with swords raised and one knee to the ground, swore a solemn oath of allegiance to the constitution. The oath was particu-larly dramatic in that it now lacked all reference to the king. It was the same oath taken the following evening by the colorful proces-sion of Parisians who would march through the Assembly.[11]

Over the next two days there was a flurry of motions and de-crees, most of them passed by unanimous assent. The first order of business was the attempt to halt the royal flight. Lafayette himself had sent out couriers even before the deputies convened on June 21. Now the Assembly did likewise, dispatching messengers along the main roads with orders to stop the king and all members of his fam-ily. In French the same word is used for both "stop" and "arrest," and the sobering ambiguity was clear to all.[12]

Almost as quickly, the representatives took steps to keep the gov-ernment functioning. Never in its history had France been without a king or a king's regent, and now, in these difficult circumstances, the Assembly was forced to improvise. Unanimously and without debate the deputies ended the requirement of a royal "sanction" for the ratification of decrees, adding that all decrees previously voted and still awaiting the king's approval would immediately pass into law. Someone suggested the creation of an executive "committee of public safety" drawn from the Assembly to meet the emergency. But the deputies opted to work through the existing ministers, who were immediately summoned and asked to declare their allegiance to the Assembly. When all had done so, they were set up in an adjoining building in order to maintain close contact with the representatives and to work directly with the appropriate committees in coordinating policy. Other decrees enabled the finance minister to continue paying the nation's bills without the monarch's signature and instructed foreign ambassadors to deal directly with the Assembly through the minister of foreign affairs.[13]

All such decrees, improvised in the space of a few hours, were conceived as temporary, emergency measures. Yet no one really knew if the king would be found or would ever return. Indeed, the rapid reorganization of the government constituted a virtual second revolution, instituting, if only provisionally, a veritable republic. In theory all such changes were perfectly legal, since in 1789 the deputies had declared themselves to be a "constituent assembly," with full powers to make a new government. But in practice they had always sought Louis' approval of their decrees, constitutional or otherwise. In two of his speeches, elaborated on the spot, Charles Lameth proposed another justification for their actions, a justification based on expediency. "At present," he declared, "we are compelled to assume both legislative and executive powers." "In periods of crisis, one cannot subject oneself rigorously to the forms of the law, as one would necessarily do in a period of calm . . . It is better to commit a momentary injustice than to see the loss of the state itself."[14] Such sentiments carried ominous implications. In many respects, decisions taken during the crisis of Varennes would prefigure the policies of another government by expediency, the government of the Terror.

The deputies were also quick to perceive the international consequences of the king's departure. No less than the people of Varennes and Sainte-Menehould, they suspected that the flight had been coordinated with a planned foreign invasion to end the Revolution by force. Thus the Assembly took steps to prepare the nation for war. The principal military commanders then in Paris were ordered to the Assembly and asked to swear their allegiance to the constitution, the laws, and the Assembly; the word *king* was again absent from the oath formula. The deputies were thrilled when General Jean-Baptiste Rochambeau, the friend of Washington and the hero of the Battle of Yorktown, arrived to pronounce his oath. The commanders were asked to work with the ministers and the Assembly's committees to develop contingency plans.[15] Ever conscious of the weakness of French armed forces, the deputies took steps to call up volunteer national guardsmen throughout the country for potential service in the regular army. A first generation *levée en masse*—the general mobilization of the nation for war—established lists of at least 3,000 citizens in each of the eighty-three departments "ready to bear arms for the defense of the state and the preservation of the constitution." The Assembly anticipated yet another institution of 1793–94 by sending four teams of representatives on a mission to the frontier departments to oversee war preparations and to verify the loyalty of the officer corps. Everywhere they traveled, the representatives were authorized to "take all necessary measures to ensure public order and guarantee the security of the state."[16]

Equally worrisome for many deputies was the problem of maintaining the peace in France itself, particularly in the great metropolis surrounding the Assembly. Given the almost continual popular unrest in Paris during the previous six months, most members anticipated outbreaks of panic or violence or worse. Barnave recalled the crisis of July 1789 and the enormous disorders caused by the lower classes in Paris until "property owners and those citizens veritably attached to the nation" had taken charge. The representatives quickly established an armed guard to surround their meeting hall and to prevent anyone but deputies from entering. And they issued an appeal for order directed primarily at the Parisians: "The National Assembly . . . informs all citizens that the protection of the constitution and the defense of the nation have never more urgently required the preservation of law and order." The Parisians were far from unmoved by the disappearance of the king, and several incidents of violence did occur. Yet for the most part, during those first days after the king's flight they remained remarkably calm. The deputies were amazed and extremely grateful. "It would seem to be a miracle," wrote Félix Faulcon, "a great and unexpected good fortune. I am tempted to think that a kind of Providence is watching over the constitution."[17]

At first virtually everyone spoke of the king as having been abducted or kidnapped. The rumors circulating before June 21 had usually involved someone absconding with the king against his will or through trickery. No one wanted even to consider the possibility that the monarch had acquiesced in the venture. But the appearance of Louis' handwritten "declaration" explaining his actions changed everything. Its existence was first mentioned by one of the ministers, and at two o'clock on the afternoon of the June 21 it was formally read to the Assembly. To judge by the deputies' speeches and letters, the declaration caused nearly as much consternation as the initial news of the king's disappearance.[18]

As the implications of the statement sank in, virtually no one outside the extreme right was willing to defend the king. The deputies were horrified by the facility with which Louis had broken his previous oaths. Basquiat, who had been a strong defender of the king, spoke for virtually all his colleagues: "Louis the Sixteenth," he wrote, "this king whose goodness had always seemed to excuse his weakness, has abjured in an instant all of his promises and all of his oaths. With this declaration, written and signed in his own hand, he has revealed to the whole universe that the honor and duty of kings toward their people are utterly worthless." Deputies were enraged by Louis' apparent obliviousness to the consequences of his act, an act that might easily lead to "civil war and the greatest possible disasters." Many were deeply disillusioned that the king who had so often seemed to support the Revolution "in such a candid and faithful manner" could now disavow everything. They had always believed Louis to be "quite incapable of breaking his word or betraying the people's confidence." The king "has deceived us," wrote another deputy, "as he has deceived all of France, who once so adored him." The "good king," the "citizen king" of only a few weeks before, was now described as "an imbecile," "an idiot," "stupid," "pitiful," "cowardly," "a monster," "a pathetic excuse for a king."[19]

Even deputies on the moderate right declared their disgust at the thoughtlessness of the king's actions, "doubly offended," as Lafayette recalled, "that they had not been warned and that they had been left behind, exposed to all kinds of dangers." The conservative marquis de Ferrières wrote to his wife: "[The king] has abandoned to the fury of the mobs not only the nobility, the clergy, and the whole right side of the Assembly, but also his friends, his servants, and his ministers. Such conduct is atrocious." In the heat of the moment certain deputies were initially ready to see the king tried in public, replaced by a regent, or even deposed in favor of a republic. "France is now prepared," wrote the curé Thomas Lindet to his brother, "to give the example of a people who can quite dispense with kings. When one examines the list of the imbeciles and rogues who have defiled their thrones, one is tempted to overthrow the whole lot of them." Antoine Durand felt that the experience "had cured the French of this ridiculous idolatry that makes them treat kings as gods."[20]

Late on the evening of June 22, however, everything was again thrown into question by the amazing news that the royal family had been captured. After two full days of uncertainty, most of the deputies had concluded that the king had crossed into foreign territory. But when the Varennes barber Mangin burst into the hall to recount his story, all the deputies stood on their benches and cheered. In their initial disgust with the king, some had mused that it would be preferable to let Louis go and be rid of him altogether. Yet most greeted his capture with enormous relief. Ferrières wrote immediately to his wife, "You can imagine the joy that this news has caused." Gaultier began his own account to his constituency with a prayer of thanksgiving. "The plot has failed," wrote the Protestant pastor Jean-Paul Rabaut Saint-Etienne, "thanks to our star of destiny, in which I continue to believe."[21]

But the feeling of celebration was to be short-lived. As word arrived of the king's slow progress back to Paris, the mood turned tense and somber. The deputies had initially concentrated all their energies on the immediate crisis, on the tasks of maintaining calm, of holding the government together, of preparing the country for what everyone assumed was an impending war. In their first reactions of shock and betrayal, a surprising number of deputies had been prepared to eject Louis from the government altogether and replace him with a regency or even a republic. But such thoughts were easier to pursue with the king absent and perhaps in a foreign country than with the king returned to the Tuileries palace, only a few hundred yards away. Now they were forced to face the central issue of what the flight meant for the future of the constitution on which they had labored for almost two years and which was now so close to completion, the issue that, as one of them put it, "we have not dared to consider until now."[22]

And the problems seemed endless, ranging from basic matters of procedure—for which neither precedent nor the constitution gave any guidance—to profound questions of political philosophy. How did one investigate a king? Had the king committed a crime? Was it possible for a king to commit a crime? And even if there was no crime before the law, could Louis ever again be trusted and placed in a position of executive authority? A great many deputies agonized over the course of action they should take, feeling themselves in a nearly untenable position. They had staked all their hopes on the new constitutional monarchy. They were increasingly anxious to put that constitution into effect, to end the Revolution, to bring a halt to the agitation and anarchy that seemed to be eating away at the very fiber of their society. But after the recent events, would such a constitution ever again be viable? "We are confronted with pitfalls in every direction," as one of them put it. It was difficult to imagine "by what means we can extricate ourselves from the impossible position in which the king's flight has placed us."[23]

A first round of debates had already begun on the afternoon of June 25. With the king returning from Varennes, only a few hours from Paris, the Assembly was forced to make a preliminary decision on how it would handle the situation. And it was soon clear to everyone that the unity of purpose experienced by the deputies after the first news of the flight had now been shattered. The conservatives and the aristocratic reactionaries held that the king should be immediately reinstated. He had not broken any law in leaving the palace, and in any case he was covered by royal immunity voted by the Assembly itself nearly two years earlier. Anything else, as the conservative speaker Pierre-Victor Malouet said, "would entirely distort the constitution that you have created." Deputies on the extreme left, on the other hand, argued that Louis should be put on trial, perhaps before the newly created national appellate court. "No matter what his rank," pleaded Robespierre, "no matter how lofty his position, no citizen can think himself degraded when he submits to the rule established by law."[24]

After much wrangling, the Assembly opted for a middle position. Responsibility for the flight to Varennes would be determined by the Assembly itself, which would establish itself as a de facto court of inquiry. Investigations into the affair would be supervised by two of the Assembly's regular committees, the Committees on Research and Reports. All those outside the royal family who had taken part in the escape and who had been captured—the three bodyguards, the nurses, Madame de Tourzel, Choiseul, Goguelat, and the other principal commanders—would be imprisoned and carefully examined. The king and queen, however, would be given favored treatment and questioned in their quarters at the palace. A special commission of deputies would then be established to consider all the evidence and make a recommendation to the full Assembly. But at the same time the Assembly made the critical decision to continue the suspension of the king's powers. His right to sanction decrees would remain in abeyance, and all executive activities would be exercised by the ministers and the Assembly's committees.[25]

Three deputies, all eminent men of law, were chosen by the Assembly to question the royal couple. The king's interview took place on the evening of June 26, just twenty-four hours after his return. The queen, however, postponed her meeting with the deputies until the next day, supposedly because she was still in her bath, but in reality so that she could make certain her story matched that of the king. The story agreed upon was the same they had carefully prepared while in Monsieur Sauce's bedroom and had then recounted to Barnave and Pétion during the return from Varennes. The king had never intended to leave the country, but only to travel to Montmédy, where he and his family could be safe from the threats and insults they had encountered in Paris. He had entered into no relations with foreign powers. He had been surprised during his travels to discover that people everywhere in France supported the new constitution. For this reason, as Lindet put it, he was "prepared to put aside his personal unhappiness" with the Revolution and to cooperate. Much of the story was no doubt accurate as far as it went. The denial of links with foreign governments was, however, patently untrue.[26]

Once the results of the interviews had been read to the full Assembly, the whole question was turned over for consideration to a commission that eventually combined the membership of seven standing committees.[27] And then for almost three weeks, from June 27 through July 13, the whole affair was left in limbo. The permanent session, meeting day and night for some 128 hours, was finally brought to an end, and the Assembly returned to its normal order of business. According to the deputy Laurent-François Legendre, the long wait was necessary so that the committees could complete their inquiry into the affair. But for the American statesman Gouverneur Morris, who resided in Paris and knew many deputies, the delay was conceived less for judicial than for political reasons. It seemed clear to him that with the king now safely back in the Tuileries, the moderate deputies in the Assembly had returned to their long-term strategy of preserving the monarchy. "The intention of the Assembly," wrote Morris on July 2, "is I find to cover up if possible the king's flight and cause it to be forgotten." For the American, such a scheme seemed ill conceived and potentially disastrous: "This proves to me great feebleness in every respect and will perhaps destroy the monarchy." In fact the Barnave-Lameth-

Duport faction was secretly negotiating once again with the royal family. The delay in taking a position would, they hoped, permit them to mobilize public opinion in the provinces in support of the king.[28]

But whatever the motives, the Assembly and the nation now found themselves in a veritable interregnum. For all practical purposes, the government had become a "republican monarchy," a kingdom with a powerless king, ruled by deputies who had assumed not only legislative and executive functions but also a critical judicial role. It was the Assembly itself which would judge on the responsibility for the flight to Varennes. In his caustic manner, curé Lindet seized up the situation: "Executive power is now exercised only indirectly. The Senior Government Official [the king] must confine himself to drinking, eating, and sleeping. These are duties which he fulfills perfectly well."[29]

The one major development in the Assembly during this interval was the arrival of a letter from General Bouillé, sent from his exile in Luxembourg. By the general's own account, the statement was conceived as a means of salvaging the king's position after the failure of the escape. Bouillé now assumed entire responsibility for the flight. Mocking and insolent, he expressed nothing but scorn for the Revolution and "your infernal constitution." The king and the queen, he claimed, had not really wanted to leave. It was only after the violence of April 18 and under pressure from the general that the royal couple had been persuaded to flee. "I arranged everything, decided everything, ordered everything. I alone gave the orders, not the king. It is against me alone that you should direct your bloody fury."[30] The letter substantially warped the reality. Even though the deputies could not know all the details of the escape plan, they had ample evidence that the king himself had signed numerous orders for military maneuvers in anticipation of the flight.[31] But Bouillé's statement was quickly seized upon by the moderates in the Assembly who hoped to preserve the monarchy, and in this respect the general's ploy worked better than he might ever have hoped.

While formal debate on the king among the deputies was largely shut down, it raged with enormous passion outside the Assembly. Two groups of deputies, in particular, were anything but passive and patient during the interregnum. On June 28 a large group of conservatives—"the wisest and most enlightened among the minority," according to the noble Irland de Bazôges—met to discuss the situation. They were indignant at the majority's suspension of the king and seizure of executive power. For all practical purposes the king was now a prisoner in his own palace. Yet Louis had, they believed, committed no crimes and should be allowed to travel wherever and whenever he saw fit. His only fault, according to the duke de Lévis, was to have had the weakness to say that he liked the constitution when this was not in fact the case, and "to have wanted to enjoy the very liberty he gave to others and in the name of which he is now enchained." Some of the more staunch reactionaries, like the marquis de Vaudreuil, were even angry that the king had backed away from his declaration of June 21. More royalist than the king and abiding no compromise, the marquis used the occasion to announce his rejection of a whole range of measures passed by the Assembly, including the Civil Constitution of the Clergy and the suppression of the nobility. After a lengthy debate, some 293 conservative deputies formally protested the suspension of the king, and more than 250 of these vowed to boycott all future votes in the Assembly.[32] There can be no doubt that the protest of the royalist deputies inflamed the conspiracy obsessions of a great many Parisians. Some now concluded that the "250" had colluded in the king's escape from the very beginning.

In the meantime, at the other end of the political spectrum, the Jacobin Club was following and commenting on events with particular ardor. All its members, both moderates and radicals, had long seen as one of their principal tasks the discovery and denunciation of conspiracy.[33] But like almost everyone else, they had maintained a generally favorable disposition toward the king, usually portrayed as weak but well-meaning. Now, with the flight to Varennes, a great many club members not only felt betrayed by the king, but were appalled at their own blindness in not anticipating that betrayal, in not rooting out this the most dangerous conspirator of all, dwelling in their midst. Perhaps it was this feeling of guilt, even humiliation, that led many Jacobins to react with exceptional outrage and anger to the king's flight.

Yet the club remained deeply divided, and the evening meeting on June 21 saw a particularly tense confrontation between the two factions. Robespierre, leader of the radicals, arrived first, lashing out in near frenzy against his fellow deputies, accusing "the near totality of my colleagues, members of the Assembly, of being counterrevolutionaries: some through ignorance, some through fear, some through resentment and injured pride, but others because they are corrupt."[34] But the moderate deputies belonging to the club arrived soon afterward, some two hundred strong, determined to regain control. Former bitter rivals like Charles Lameth and the marquis de Lafayette, Barnave and the abbé Sieyès, all appealed for a sacred union in the face of the crisis. When Robespierre's ally Georges Danton, the fiery orator from the Cordeliers Club, accused Lafayette of treason, Alexandre Lameth rushed to his defense. With the feeling of fraternity at its peak, Barnave called for an address to all the Jacobins' affiliated clubs asking full support for the Assembly: "The National Assembly alone, this must be our guide," a proposal that was met with rousing cheers. Moderate deputies were ecstatic at the turn of events: "Now," wrote François-Joseph Bouchette, "there are neither monarchists nor Eighty-Niners, everyone has returned to the Friends of the Constitution."[35]

Yet tensions within the club remained high, and the issue of the king continued to arouse passions. As the Assembly waited, the Jacobins debated the issue almost daily. Although a few of the speakers—like the radical Pierre-Louis Roederer—seemed to advocate a republic, such demands were rare and were quickly denounced by the moderates as going against the constitution, which the society was bound to support. Nevertheless, no one was ready to defend Louis' actions, and a great many nondeputies in the club called for a trial of the king and the creation of a regency government.

As many of the moderate deputy-members tired of attending the rancorous nightly sessions—Barnave and Alexandre Lameth seem never to have returned after June 22—or found themselves preoccupied with committee work in the Assembly, the club as a whole seemed to gravitate toward an unforgiving treatment of the "traitor king" even as it proclaimed grudging support for the monarchy.[36]

The Fate of the Monarchy

The great debate in the Assembly itself was finally launched on July 13 with the formal report of the "Seven Committees," commissioned to draw up a recommendation on the events of Varennes. Over a three-day period some seventeen deputies addressed the issue of the fate of the king and the fate of the monarchy, nine in support of the committees' position of exoneration, eight in opposition.[37] Many were among the finest orators in the National Assembly, and most had carefully prepared their addresses. The leaders of the moderates were masters of parliamentary rhetoric and maneuver, and they brilliantly programmed and paced the debates for maximum advantage. Their opponents, all from the extreme left of the Jacobin group, also developed powerful arguments, but their proposals were more personal and sometimes conflicting.

To present their case the Committees chose a thirty-three-year-old magistrate from eastern France, Hyacinthe Muguet de Nanthou.[38] Muguet made maximum use of General Bouillé's letter to argue that Louis had indeed been "abducted," abducted in mind—through intimidation and pressure—if not in body. To be sure, one could never approve the king's actions from a moral or political standpoint: they had been thoughtless and irresponsible. But it was essential that the deputies follow the law and not the whim of emotion. And legally, the king had committed no crime. His "declaration" of June 21 had been remarkably impolitic, but it was not in itself against the law. His flight would have been grounds for deposing him only if he had left the country and refused to return, and this, by his testimony, he had never intended to do. Yet even if Louis were to have committed a crime, he could not be prosecuted, since the Assembly had voted immunity for the monarch nearly two years before.[39] From their earliest debates on the constitution, Muguet argued, the deputies had decided that France must be a monarchy. A central locus of power was essential "in so vast an empire, whose parts would naturally tend to break apart." In fact, "it is for the nation, and not for the king, that a monarchy has been established." Within this system, it was essential that the king be immune from prosecution. If the king could be indicted, any faction might attack him for its own petty self-interest, and there would be a continual threat of civil war and chaos, just as had occurred in England 150 years earlier. The real villains in the affair, and the only individuals mentioned in the Committees' proposed decree, were Bouillé and his subordinates. France must follow America's treatment of the traitor Benedict Arnold and prosecute these men to the full extent of the law. Curiously, Axel von Fersen was scarcely mentioned. The king and the queen were not mentioned at all.

In reply to the Committees' position, the radicals adopted a number of tactics. Pétion and several of the other orators attacked the very idea of royal immunity. Surely kings must be responsible for their actions, or there would be nothing to prevent a new Nero or new Caligula from committing untold atrocities against the people. The immunity voted by the Assembly in 1789 could apply only to state activities, not to a personal action like Louis' decision to flee the country and abandon his office. For the most part, however, the radicals skirted the Committees' legalistic arguments and appealed to a higher, moral law. How could they accept as their chief executive a man who had flagrantly lied and deceived the Assembly and the whole French nation? "How many times," asked Pétion, "has Louis XVI sworn his loyalty and love for the constitution? Did he not come into this very Assembly, without having been summoned, and affirm his attachment to the constitution. Did he not declare he would be its defender?" "Such actions could only have been designed to lull the French nation to sleep and thus more easily to deceive her." Marc-Alexis Vadier, the grim Jacobin and future Terrorist leader, who rarely spoke in the Assembly, was beside himself with fury. Only a few weeks before he had written self-confidently to his constituency, denying all the rumors of impending flight. Now he felt not only betrayed but humiliated. He bitterly assailed Louis, this "brigand with a crown," this "false, fugitive king, who cowardly deserted his post only to paralyze the government and deliver us up to the horrors of civil war and anarchy; this king who, in a perfidious declaration, dared rip to shreds your constitution."[40]

Several of the speakers raised the fundamental political question of public confidence and legitimacy. Robespierre put it bluntly: how can a government function when it is led by a man whom everyone mistrusts? Without the backing of public opinion, proclaimed François-Nicolas Buzot prophetically, "you can never even hope to have civil peace."[41] All the radicals sensed the deputies' obsessive fear of a republic, and they took pains to assert that they themselves did not wish to abolish the monarchy. But, they concluded, the king must be judged in some way for his actions: either through trial in the regular court system, or through a popular referendum, or through the calling of a national convention.

The moderates took exception, point by point, to nearly all the radicals' arguments. They denied the assertion that public opinion was against the king. One could hardly judge by the passions of the Parisian crowds, riled up by a handful of seditious journalists and club members, "these Machiavellians of consummate perversity who want only to destroy the constitution." Whatever the king's failings, it was argued, the vast majority of the French felt a deep attachment for the monarchy and viewed the person of the king— in Louis-Pierre Prugnon's words—as "necessarily sacred."[42] In any case, society must be based on law, not on the unstable passions of public opinion. Barnave played skillfully on the deputies' fears of the recent popular demonstrations in Paris, many of them directed against the Assembly itself. Whatever their disclaimers, those who called for the king's trial really wanted to create a republic, and a republic could mean only mob rule and anarchy. The Revolution must at last be stopped, or the very basis of a stable society and of individual property would be jeopardized.[43]

The King Speaking to the National Assembly, February 4, 1790. Standing beside
the president of the National Assembly, Louis announces his intention of sup-
porting the constitution. The scene looks toward the conservative "right" side
of the hall, where the nobles are shouting "Long live the king!" and holding
their hands over their hearts. The deputies on the "left," in the foreground,
are much less demonstrative. Women spectators cheer from the balcony.

Yet in the end, the moderates sensed that legalism and fear tactics might not be enough. On July 15 the Committees' original motion was passed into law, but only after additional amendments were promised specifying the grounds on which this king or any future king might be deposed and replaced. The following evening, July 16, final versions of the amendments were introduced and passed. It was now decided that Louis would not be immediately reinstated, but that his powers would remain suspended until the constitution had been completed and he had officially signed his acceptance. If he refused to sign, he would be immediately deposed, and his son would become king under a regency. In addition, the deputies voted two other grounds for dethroning a king in the future: a monarch who either led an army against the French nation or retracted an oath to the constitution that he had previously sworn would be considered, by those very acts, to have abdicated the throne. It was only too obvious that if the law on the retraction of oaths had existed one month earlier, Louis would have lost his crown.[44]

The final vote was never recorded. Antoine Thibaudeau thought that many deputies had originally planned to oppose exonerating the king. But after listening to the debates and after the various amendments had been passed, only eight individuals out of several hundred rejected the Committees' bill.[45] We will never know why the deputies voted as they did. In letters written home they struggled to explain their decision to their friends and family. Many complained how agonizing the choice had been. Most piled reason upon reason, closely recapitulating the arguments of Muguet or Barnave or others, sometimes quoting speeches verbatim, without indicating which arguments had been most decisive. It was essential to follow the law; the king had committed no crime; the king was immune to prosecution; a republic would never work in a large country like France (even though no deputies had ever actually proposed a republic); the trial or deposing of the king would cause internal uprisings and foreign war.[46] Significantly, two of the deputies opposed trying the king because they were convinced that he was guilty and would thus be sent to the scaffold: "The indictment of a king is not a game, for we think that any king who is so indicted will certainly lose his head."[47] One theme that seemed particularly widespread but was never mentioned in the published debates was the deputies' fear of having to scrap a constitution on which they had worked so long and in which they had invested so much energy and emotion. For Félix Faulcon, a victory for the radicals would have meant "that this constitution which had caused so much struggle and sacrifice for more than two years; that this constitution whose completion would end violent upheavals and replace them with public happiness, that this constitution would cease to exist!" The Burgundian wineseller Claude Gantheret wrote much the same in his laconic style: "My work on the constitution has caused me too much pain even to think about changing it."[48]

And yet a great many deputies, in their personal correspondence, expressed deep disillusionment with the whole experience and pessimism about the future. Although he voted with the majority, Gantheret admitted that he was unable to forget curé Henri Grégoire's words: even if the king signed the constitution, how could a man who had already broken three or four oaths ever again be trusted? Durand confessed having a "feeling of terror" when he thought of the decision he had made. Lindet, who seems ultimately to have voted to maintain the king, confided his disgust with the whole affair to his younger brother, a future member of the Committee of Public Safety: "We want a king. But we have to take an imbecile, an automaton, a traitor, a perjurer; a man whom the people will detest, and in whose name scoundrels will reign." And he was convinced that Barnave and the others were wrong and unjust when they attributed popular protest against the king to the sedition of a few journalists. The common people of Paris clearly despised the king. "What can we expect with a leader who is so debased? It is difficult to imagine that the situation will long remain peaceful."[49]

The Massacre at the Champ de Mars

Throughout the previous days the people in question, the citizens of Paris, had closely followed the deputies' debates and had talked of little else. The long interregnum, the National Assembly's delay in taking a position, had encouraged numerous individuals to think through the issue on their own, and many had already committed themselves to one side or the other, for or against retaining the present king, for or against a republic. Word of the Assembly's vote on July 15 raced through the city in the late afternoon like a lightning discharge, sparking an explosion of arguments in cafés and streets and public squares, where large groups of people were already gathered. Substantial numbers of Parisians, especially in the more prosperous parts of the city, vigorously supported the decision, fearing that any other course would be too uncertain and dangerous. At the Saint-Martin's Café in the north of Paris, over a hundred people were said to have cheered their approval. But large numbers also reacted passionately against the decree, accusing the Assembly of "weakness" or of complicity with the "treason" of the king. In the Café Procope on the Left Bank—the celebrated drinking spot where Voltaire and other Enlightenment authors had once gathered—a vigorous shouting match broke out among those taking opposing positions. The Palais Royal and the courtyard outside the Assembly itself filled with "countless groups of turbulent people" crying out their opposition. The visiting Creole Henri-Paulin Panon Desbassayns was stunned and frightened by the clash of opinions and the growing factionalism: "Both sides are becoming so exasperated that they see their opponents as personal enemies." "The common people are furious," wrote the bookseller Nicolas Ruault. "There is a frightful uproar throughout the city, from the square in front of the National Assembly to the smallest café. The indignation and irritation against the king and the Seven Committees seem to be overwhelming."[50]

In the midst of this chaotic spontaneous reaction the Cordeliers Club and the various fraternal societies quickly began mobilizing a more organized response. Several thousand of their supporters—people from the publishing district and sans-culottes from throughout Paris—soon marched to the National Assembly to present yet another petition, drawn up earlier that day, urging the deputies to reconsider their decision. When five of the demonstrators were allowed to enter the hall through the lines of national guardsmen, they were told by Robespierre and Pétion themselves that the Assembly had unfortunately made its decision and that petitions had now become useless. Frustrated and angry, a portion of the crowd then surged into the wealthier Right Bank districts, forcing the closure of theaters and the opera as a sign of "mourning"—much as they had done during the insurrection of July 1789. Others flowed into the nearby Palais Royal, joining a giant outdoor rally launched that evening by the radical club the Friends of Truth. The speakers went further in their opposition than ever before, declaring they would never accept the deputies' decree without a referendum of all French citizens, clearly implying that they no longer accepted the legitimacy of the National Assembly. About nine o'clock several thousand demonstrators then moved on to the Jacobin Club to urge a similar position.[51]

Here the crowds found the Jacobins in the midst of a divisive debate on how best to react to the new decree. When several hundred of the demonstrators managed to push open the locked doors and crowd their way in, disorder broke out in the hall. Shocked by the pressure tactics of the crowds and angered by the radicals' continuing opposition to the Assembly's decision, nearly all the deputies present walked out, vowing to boycott the club altogether. Those remaining initially attempted to negotiate with the Cordeliers and the fraternal societies, promising to draw up and present a petition of their own. But the popular societies were now demanding a republic and a rejection of the National Assembly, and the Jacobins—including Robespierre and Pétion and the few other deputies who had remained in the club—refused to repudiate the Assembly to which they belonged. Negotiations continued that evening, after the crowds had retired, and on into the next day. But in the end the Jacobin leadership renounced the whole idea of a petition, and the Cordeliers and their allies were compelled to push ahead on their own.[52]

The members of the National Assembly followed these events with anger and impatience. For days now the square outside their hall had been a rallying point for all those opposed to reconciliation with the king. Despite the massive national guard contingents positioned in readiness, the representatives were unable to reach their benches without walking a gauntlet between lines of angry men and women, shouting insults, accusing the deputies of treachery, and sometimes brandishing pikes.[53] Infuriated by the unruliness that had been swelling in the city for months, the moderates in control of the Assembly now resolved to force a confrontation and be rid of the popular threats once and for all. On July 16 Mayor Bailly was summoned before the Assembly and publicly rebuked for tolerating the actions of the crowds. Charles Lameth was particularly firm. All the unrest, he argued, had been incited by a small number of troublemakers who were probably paid by outsiders and who were misleading the Parisians into acting against their own best interests. He harshly chastised the mayor and the municipal leaders for "closing their eyes to such disorders," and he demanded that they use "all means allowed by the constitution to discover and punish the instigators and to guarantee peace and tranquillity for all citizens."[54]

Throughout the afternoon and evening of July 16 the Cordeliers and their allies made careful plans for a giant petition-signing ceremony to take place the following day, with or without the support of the Jacobins. Militants from all over the city would assemble at the open square near the demolished Bastille at eleven in the morning and then march across town to the stadium of the Champ de Mars, following the very path taken by municipal and national leaders three days earlier during the July 14 celebration. The symbolism seemed clear: the fraternal societies were now replacing the administrative elites whose authority they no longer recognized. The opposition leaders were also eager to maintain a peaceful demonstration, and instructions went out that no one was to carry a weapon, not even a club or a cane. But some individuals were clearly anticipating trouble, and there was talk of filling one's pockets or apron with rocks in case they were harassed by guardsmen. A few men carried pistols under their coats.[55]

In the end the march across the city never came off. Lafayette and his subordinates had been informed of the militants' plans, and national guardsmen remained busy throughout the night breaking up street meetings wherever they were found. Early the next morning, Sunday, July 17, when popular societies and neighborhood groups tried to converge on the Place de la Bastille, they found hundreds of guardsmen occupying the area and barring their way. After a period of consternation, the demonstrators abandoned the idea of a group march and made their way to the Champ de Mars by whatever route they could.[56]

Despite the efforts of the organizers, there were a number of episodes of violence during the day. On several occasions people threw rocks at guardsmen in the streets, and one man even tried to shoot Lafayette—though the pistol failed to go off. The most serious incident, however, occurred in the stadium itself, and it was to change the whole character of the event. Toward noon, before the fraternal societies and their supporters had begun arriving, a group of people from the neighborhood adjoining the Champ de Mars spotted two individuals hiding under the Altar of the Fatherland at the center of the stadium. A young wigmaker and an older man with a wooden leg were found crouching with a stash of food and wine and a few carpenter's tools. Later commentators were convinced that the two had only planned to drill holes and spy on the women from below as they crossed the altar to sign the petition. The rumor spread rapidly, however, that they had planned to blow up the patriots with a bomb. Some of the crowd tried to escort the culprits to the local authorities for interrogation. But others—led by a group of boatmen, laundrymen, and other workers who lived nearby—seized the two men and dragged them away to be lynched on a light post and then decapitated.[57]

Once the petition ceremony itself got under way everything seemed to proceed smoothly and peacefully. Now that the Jacobins had abandoned the field, François Robert—the journalist and Cordeliers stalwart who had published a republican tract the previous December—sat on the steps of the altar, placed a plank across his knees, and drew up a new petition. The document strongly denounced Louis XVI and declared that the will of the people was to end the kingship. It suggested that the National Assembly was now under the influence of the 250 conservative deputies who had rejected the suspension of the king. Although Robert carefully avoided the word *republic*, the meaning was perfectly obvious: the deputies were urged to "reconsider their decree" and "to convene a new constituent body" that would ensure "a judgment against the guilty party [the king] and his replacement by a new organization of the executive branch." It was a clear call for a new revolution and the election of a National Convention to create a central authority without a king.[58]

Seven or eight copies of the petition were quickly produced and placed at different locations around the stadium; long lines of people soon formed to affix their signatures or their marks. As best we can tell from those who examined the original document—before it was destroyed in the nineteenth century—some 6,000 individuals had already signed it at the time the ceremony was disrupted. They represented all elements of the Parisian population: a few professional men, local officials and national guardsmen, and a great mass of lower-class citizens, both men and women, many of them unable to sign their names. An estimated 50,000 others—men, women, and children—had also come out to watch the proceedings, taking advantage of the hot summer weather for a Sunday outing.[59]

But in the eyes of the National Assembly, the peaceful behavior of the vast majority of the petitioners could not outweigh the earlier murders or the underlying threat to the integrity of the Revolution's leadership. At the beginning of the afternoon the Assembly addressed yet another angry letter to Bailly and the municipal council, demanding "the most vigorous and efficient measures possible to halt the disorder and find the instigators." "It is time," thundered Michel-Louis Regnaud, the eloquent young deputy from southwestern France, "to unleash the full rigor of the law." Indeed, if it were up to him, "I would demand an immediate proclamation of martial law."[60] In a climate of growing uncertainty and under continuing pressure from the Assembly, the city council finally resolved to act. In a speech, the mayor linked the whole affair to a plot of outsiders and foreign agents: "a clearly defined conspiracy against the constitution and the nation, financed by foreigners who are attempting to divide us." It was they who, "hidden behind a variety of disguises, are fomenting the popular movements."[61] We will never know whether the mayor truly believed what he said or was simply seeking to justify himself in an impossible situation. But at half past five in the afternoon, Jean-Sylvain Bailly, Enlightened academician and scientist, the onetime friend of Voltaire and of Benjamin Franklin, ordered the red flag of martial law unfurled above the city hall and issued the general call to arms.

At half past six he set off from the city hall, accompanied by a portion of the city council and by two detachments of armed infantry and cavalry. Witnesses who participated claimed that they were cheered by most of the Parisians as they marched across the city, but that there were also scatterings of angry jeers, especially after they had crossed the Seine to the Left Bank. Near the stadium they were joined by General Lafayette and additional contingents of guardsmen, who were already on the scene.[62] By this time the demonstrators and bystanders in the stadium were well aware of the arriving forces. But the official decree of martial law specified that no force could be used until the mayor had pronounced three successive summons for the crowds to disperse. The leaders of the demonstration urged everyone to remain calm and not to leave until the first of the three commands had been given.

As the first armed guardsmen entered the passage into the stadium through the earthen embankment that served as a grandstand, many of the demonstrators began shouting their disapproval: "No bayonets, no red flags!" Soon some pelted the guardsmen with rocks from the surrounding stands. What happened thereafter is somewhat confused, and interpretations depended in part on the political positions of the witnesses. Apparently, after a few moments a lone gunshot rang out, the ball passing precariously close to Bailly himself and hitting a cavalryman in the hip, knocking him off his horse. Alarmed by the violence against them, the guardsmen then entered

Declaration of Martial Law at the Champ de Mars, July 17, 1791. Troops and guardsmen attack republican petitioners on the national altar, atop which a lone man holds copies of the petition toward heaven. Bailly, wearing his mayor's sash, is visible in the left foreground, near the red flag of martial law.

rapidly with their drums beating a double-time cadence and took up position inside the stadium, facing the central altar from the north. No formal summons to disperse, as specified by the law, was ever pronounced. The soldiers claimed that they had first fired several warning shots in the air. But with stones raining down on them and with other demonstrators trying to cut the skins of their drums, the guardsmen opened fire on the crowds, aiming primarily at those in the stands, but also at others on the floor of the stadium. Soon a second column of guardsmen entered from the opposite side of the altar and charged to the north, catching many demonstrators in a pincers movement. Apparently some soldiers on horseback even pursued people outside the stadium into the surrounding fields and gardens, trampling some, cutting down others with their sabers. According to the elderly Nicolas-Célestin Guittard de Floriban, who was present and who was far from sympathetic with the aims of the protesters, the firing continued for at least three minutes. General panic broke out, and "in trying to save themselves, people knocked over and trampled on women and children." Many of the casualties, he reported, were among the bystanders, "people of every condition, attracted to the site by curiosity and by the beautiful Sunday weather."[63]

When the troops finally ceased their attack, many dozens of men and women, wounded or dying, lay inside the stadium or in the surrounding fields. No careful count was ever made. Bailly himself, in a report the next day, claimed that only twelve demonstrators and two soldiers had been killed. But the usually cautious Guittard was angered when he heard Bailly's statement: "His account is not right! It's outrageous! Everyone knows there were a great many deaths." A nearby resident who visited the hospital outside the stadium testified that he saw "the dead and the dying on every side." Various contemporary estimates ranged from a few dozen to over two thousand. But François Robert, who successfully fled and hid out for a time with Marie-Jeanne Roland and her husband, claimed that about fifty had been killed and far more had been wounded. This was the figure used at the time of Bailly's trial during the Terror, and it probably represents the historian's best estimate.[64]

THE KING'S ATTEMPTED FLIGHT and the National Assembly's efforts to deal with its effects had led to a bloodbath on the outskirts of Paris. Even those Parisians—undoubtedly a large number—who sympathized with the Assembly's decision on the king were shocked by the shootings at the Champ de Mars. No one, wrote Guittard, would ever forget "this terrible atrocity."[65]

CHAPTER 6

Fear and Repression
in the Provinces

FOR MANY PARISIANS at the time of the Revolution and for most historians since, the massacre at the Champ de Mars was the single most dramatic event in the wake of the king's flight. Yet the city of Paris represented only one small portion of the total French nation in 1791—perhaps 700,000 people out of the 28 or 29 million inhabiting the tens of thousands of villages and towns across the kingdom. It is impossible to understand the full impact of Varennes without leaving the banks of the Seine and following reactions across the great expanse of French territory, from the North Sea to the Mediterranean, from the Rhine River to the Pyrenees, from the Breton peninsula to the Alps.

In the provinces as in Paris, news of the departure and then capture of the king caused an extraordinary sensation. "France," wrote curé Lindet, "has been struck by an electric shock. It traveled from one end of the kingdom to the other with unbelievable rapidity."[1] Initially word went out from the capital by official messengers. As soon as General Lafayette learned that the monarch had disappeared, early on the morning of June 21, he commissioned several trusted subordinates to ride at full speed along different roads in an effort to find and halt the royal family. A few hours later the National Assembly followed much the same procedure, dispatching its own couriers carrying handwritten summaries of the deputies' first decrees toward the Austrian and German frontiers, the most likely directions of the flight.[2] But soon a whole array of unofficial messengers had also set out from the capital. Several deputies in the Assembly hired private horsemen to inform their constituencies as rapidly as possible, horsemen who spread the story haphazardly wherever they rode. A number of Parisian clubs and even neighborhood sections appear to have done the same. Thus, Saint-Quentin in northern France first learned of events from the Quatre-Nations Section, perhaps at the instigation of the Cordeliers Club. Parisian newspapers were also quick to capitalize on the breaking story with editions dispatched rapidly into the provinces.[3]

Once the news had breached the walls of the capital, it rapidly resonated through local communications networks in much the same manner as the Great Fear two years earlier, with a variety of individuals on horseback, in carriages, and on foot fanning out across the nation. Incidental travelers and impromptu local messengers teamed up with official couriers. Townspeople and villagers who heard the story through unofficial sources, sometimes in garbled and fantastic versions, grew even more tense: "our anxiety increased," remembered the citizens of Bar-le-Duc, "as time dragged on and we waited for more news." In their apprehension, officials sent their own messengers back along the chain, seeking confirmation and further details. Soon there was a press of riders charging about in every direction, all exchanging information and misinformation as they passed one another on the roads.[4]

By midnight on Tuesday, June 21, knowledge of the king's disappearance had spread about a hundred miles from Paris in an amoeba-shaped area extending along the principal roads.[5] After a delay in passing the city gates—where overzealous guardsmen initially halted all movement—the messengers had ridden scarcely beyond Châlons-sur-Marne to the east and Cambrai to the north. But by the end of Wednesday, moving day and night at about five or six miles per hour, "like fire along a powder trail," knowledge of the royal flight had reached most of the northern frontier, as far as Metz and Nancy in the east, Rouen in the west, and Moulins in the south.[6]

One messenger—perhaps commissioned by the Breton deputies—had even reached Nantes, at the mouth of the Loire River. By Thursday the event horizon had attained the northeastern frontier along the German and Swiss borders and most of the Atlantic coast from Dunkerque to La Rochelle—with the exception of the Breton peninsula. Riders pulled into Strasbourg, on the Rhine, at five in the morning, and into Lyon, the nation's second-largest city, by half past ten that night. By Friday at dawn, the great seaport of Bordeaux received reports, forwarding the startling news up the Garonne River to Toulouse, where a messenger arrived about eight that evening. On Saturday, at the end of the fifth day, couriers had reached Marseilles and the Mediterranean, racing along the coast as far as the port of Toulon to the east and Perpignan to the south, within twenty miles of the Spanish border. At about the same time, word finally arrived in Brest, at the tip of Brittany. But it would take another day or two to reach the most isolated mountain villages in the Pyrenees, the Alps, and the Massif Central. The village of Aumont, accessible only by mountain track through the southeastern mountains of Gévaudan, still appeared uninformed at the beginning of the following week.[7]

Once Louis and his party had been identified and halted, another wave of news spread out from Varennes in much the same manner. The master barber Mangin, riding around the clock, had brought his account to the National Assembly in less than twenty-four hours. But elsewhere the second surge of news often moved slightly more slowly, perhaps because it first traveled primarily by the chain of local messengers, until official notification could be relayed from the capital on June 23. It reached Bordeaux only on the fifth day, Toulouse on the sixth, and Perpignan on the morning of the seventh day after the king's arrest. In the confusion of currents and crosscurrents, radiating from multiple sources, many towns learned of Varennes only a few hours after—and in some cases before—hearing of the king's disappearance from the Tuileries.[8]

It was one of those events with such a powerful emotional impact that people would remember all their lives where they had been

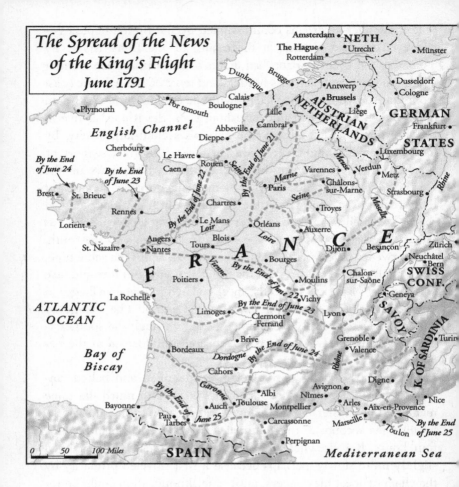

The Spread of the News
of the King's Flight
June 1791

Amsterdam • NETH.
The Hague • Utrecht • Münster
Rotterdam •

Dunkerque
Brugge • Antwerp • Dusseldorf
AUSTRIAN
Calais NETHERLANDS Brussels • Liège • Cologne
Boulogne • Lille •
GERMAN
Plymouth • Portsmouth Abbeville • Cambrai • Frankfurt •
Dieppe • STATES
English Channel
Cherbourg • Luxembourg •
Le Havre • Rouen • Varennes • Verdun
By the End Caen • Meuse Metz •
of June 24 By the End Marne Châlons-
of June 23 • Paris sur-Marne Strasbourg •
Brest • St. Brieuc • Seine
Rennes • Chartres • Troyes •
Lorient • Le Mans Orléans • Auxerre •
Loir
Angers • Blois Loire Dijon • Besançon • Zürich
F St. Nazaire • Tours • Bourges N Neuchâtel •
Nantes Vienne By the End • Moulins Chalon- SWISS Bern
Poitiers • of June 22 C sur-Saône CONF.
La Rochelle • Vichy • Geneva
ATLANTIC By the End Clermont- Lyon • SAVOY
OCEAN Limoges • of June 23 Ferrand
Brive • Grenoble • K Turin
Bay of Bordeaux • Valence • OF
Biscay Dordogne By the End of June 24 Rhône SARDINIA
Cahors • Digne •
Garonne Avignon • • Nice
Bayonne • Albi Nîmes • Arles • Aix-en-Provence
Auch • Toulouse Montpellier •
Pau By the End Carcassonne • Marseille • By the End
Tarbes • June 25 Toulon • of June 25
• Perpignan
0 50 100 Miles
SPAIN Mediterranean Sea

and what they had been doing when they were first informed. Depending on the day and the time when the various messengers arrived, the news caught people in their fields, or at work in their shops, or marching in Corpus Christi processions, or asleep at home, awakened by church bells in the middle of the night. In a number of towns, citizens were in the midst of primary assemblies, convoked to elect a new legislature, when "the deplorable event of the king's disappearance threw everyone into turmoil."[9] Almost everywhere, as citizens recounted in moving letters to the National

Assembly, the unexpected news provoked intense grief, consternation, and stunned incredulity. In the southern town of Auch, "emotions have reached their peak"; in Beauvais, north of Paris, "everyone is filled with intense sorrow over this frightful event which has afflicted the nation"; in Châteauroux, in central France, "people sense an abyss of evil and suffer the torments of an agonizing situation." The Jacobins of Montmorillon must have described the feelings of a great many others when they recalled their hopes, on the eve of Varennes, that the Revolution had at last come to an end, that threats of counterrevolution had disappeared, that they might now return to normal lives: "But the disappearance of the king has crushed all our hopes, and has warned us not to count on such a return."[10]

The Meaning of Fraternity

Confronting this unprecedented emergency throughout the country were the officials of the newly transformed regional government. The Revolution had brought a dramatic reorganization and democratization of the administrative system, with the thirty-odd intendants, the king's appointed governors under the Old Regime, replaced by thousands of elected officials. It was they who staffed the new bureaucratic system into which France was now divided: the 83 departments, the 500 districts, and the 40,000 municipalities large and small. With little or no experience in such positions, the officials had been undergoing massive on-the-job training over the previous year. At times they had struggled with the sheer number of new laws and directives passed down to them by the National Assembly on almost every aspect of economic, fiscal, religious, and agrarian life. Yet for the most part—especially at the department and district levels and in the larger towns—the new administrators were drawn from the educated professional and merchant elites. They had closely followed and embraced the Revolution from its beginning, and they were ready, confident, and resolutely determined to perform their duties as best they could.

Jolted into action by the crisis, the officials quickly organized emergency committees, bringing together representatives from the various power centers in their areas. In a typical regional capital—in Lyon or Beauvais or Auch—the departmental authorities summoned deputies from the district directory and the local municipal council, as well as from the principal law courts, the patriotic clubs, the national guard, and the regular army. If a town was divided into neighborhood sections—as was the case in the largest municipalities—or if the electoral assemblies happened to be meeting, these bodies, too, were invited to send representatives. Thus, in the northeastern town of Thionville over a hundred people had crowded within minutes into the mayor's office, the largest assembly space available, where many of them remained around the clock for the next three days.[11]

Whether or not this collective approach to crisis management was the most efficient means available, it did provide a much-needed sense of unity and solidarity. Especially in the larger communities, where multiple levels of authority existed side by side, fierce rivalries had often arisen during the previous year—between department and district, or district and town, or department and town.[12] But now, confronted with this stunningly unexpected emergency, officials everywhere made unity and cooperation their highest priorities. Numerous patriots attested their newfound sense of harmony in letters to the National Assembly. "There exists in this town," wrote the leaders of Dieppe, on the English Channel, "the greatest possible unity between the different bodies holding power." In Lyon patriots were convinced that their security depended on "the rapid unification of all authority, and on the general confidence which such power will inspire."[13] To reinforce the sense of common purpose, the town of Saint-Quentin required all men and women to wear specially manufactured ribbons with the words "Union! Live free or die!" Indeed, in a number of towns local authorities ordered all citizens to affirm their solidarity by displaying Revolutionary cockades, the tricolor bull's-eye badge that had become one of the symbols of the patriots in Paris.[14]

Even more dramatic emblems of unity were the emotion-filled

oaths organized by people almost everywhere as soon as they learned of the king's disappearance. Residents of the small town of Juillac, in central France, meeting in their electoral assembly, vividly recalled the moment the news arrived. At first they all sat stunned in "mournful silence." Suddenly the president of the assembly rose to his feet, raised his hand to heaven, and pronounced an impassioned oath: "I swear to defend to my last drop of blood the nation, the law, and the National Assembly. I swear to live free or die!" Immediately all the others present stood, raised their hands, and shouted in unison: "I, too, so swear." Everyone then filed out of the room, sustained with a new sense of purpose, and walked to the city hall, where members of the local Jacobin Club and the national guard took a similar oath.[15]

In town after town, civic leaders and common citizens, men and women, old and young, national guardsmen, soldiers, and even a scattering of patriot nobles and clergy—all clamored to enunciate oaths of their own. They did so spontaneously, for the most part, even before learning of the similar declarations sworn with such fervor in Paris on June 23. And in most cases they replaced "king" with "National Assembly" in the oath formula that had previously been used. In Valenciennes, near the Austrian border, "we all swore to shed our blood for the defense of freedom and the happiness of the nation." In Tours the ceremony took place out of doors near the Loire River, with "a thousand voices" uniting in a vow to sacrifice their lives for the preservation of the constitution. Beneath the walls of Saint-Malo, on the Breton peninsula, 4,000 armed guards, along with 2,000 women and children, swore their allegiance to the nation and the constitution. In Cahors, in south-central France, oaths were also pronounced by women as well as men, each occupying a separate space: "the women, standing nearby in the garden imitated the men, repeating in a touching manner their affirmations of fraternal and patriotic love."[16]

In their near obsession with oathtaking in a moment of crisis, the French were using a symbolic language with which almost everyone was familiar. They lived in a world in which solemn vows of this sort retained a religious character and remained requisite acts for entry into the army, the clergy, or the law courts. Those with any education were also familiar with the oathtaking tradition of classical Greece and Rome—a tradition given new immediacy by the stirring oaths of the National Assembly at the beginning of the Revolution. The oath of June 17, 1789—when the Assembly was created—and the Tennis Court Oath three days later had been widely publicized, inspiring the whole nation to excited emulation. Even more pervasive had been the waves of oathtaking in February and July 1790—the latter as part of the federation ceremonies celebrated throughout the country. But the earlier oaths had always been somewhat abstract, pronounced in moments of general calm. Now the French found themselves facing the very real danger of invasion and war. It was in this context, in a moment of great tension, that they frequently attached the coda "to live free or die." For people who were now confronted with the prospect of living in a nation without a king, the one individual who had always represented the unity of that nation, oathtaking held an additional relevance. It was the visible symbol of patriotic union and a willingness to work together and die together for the greater good of the national community. In this way, the great surge of oathtaking in June 1791 played a major role in easing anxiety and instilling a sense of common purpose.[17] It was a signal moment in the emergence of French nationalism.

The Enemy Without

But oaths of allegiance and a determination to die for the country were hardly sufficient in themselves to confront the crisis. Emergency committees throughout France were faced with the need to organize an immediate response to the various dangers their communities might encounter. The National Assembly's initial decrees provided only the roughest outline for action. The printed proclamation sent out on June 22 ordered administrators to halt all movement across frontiers of people, arms, munitions, precious metals, and horses, and "to take all necessary steps for the maintenance of law and order and the defense of the nation."[18] But there would be enormous variation from region to region in the ways in which local people interpreted and implemented those decrees.

For towns adjoining coastlines or foreign frontiers, the most immediate concern was the threat from abroad. For a great many people, both in Paris and in the provinces, the implications of the king's flight seemed obvious. Whether Louis had left of his own will or had been abducted, everyone expected him to leave the country. And once the royal family had crossed out of France, war seemed an inevitable consequence. For the town of Mézières, only a few miles from the frontier, the flight could only have been "assured through the authority of the house of Austria, which now reveals its clear intention of waging war on France." The town leaders of Dole, close to the Swiss and German borders, generally agreed: "At present, we should consider ourselves to be in a time of war and of imminent peril." And they issued detailed instructions for the mobilization of the whole society, establishing procedures by which all citizens were to contribute both time and money for the defense of the nation.[19]

Almost as soon as they learned of the crisis, leaders in frontier or coastal areas sent out units of the national guard and the regular army to establish lines of defense and brace for invasion. The city of Strasbourg took the initiative in stationing guardsmen up and down the Rhine. Longwy, on the northern frontier near Luxembourg, urged all border communities to arm themselves and prepare for war. In Provence a protective cordon was set up along the neighboring Italian states, and in Perpignan detachments were directed to guard both the passes of the Pyrenees and the Mediterranean coast near Spain. Similar steps were taken along the Atlantic coast. Bordeaux and Dieppe temporarily closed their ports, going well beyond the instructions from Paris. Rouen established observation posts on the English Channel from Le Havre to the department border at Le Tréport. A semaphore chain was prepared along the south Breton coast to relay word quickly of suspicious sightings.[20]

But even in locations a considerable distance from coasts or frontiers, citizen militias were called up for service to patrol the streets and guard city gates and bridges. Rusty cannons were dragged into position to defend local stores of ammunition and strongboxes containing public funds. Barricades were established at central positions—the city hall, the courthouse, the offices of the department and the district—to protect against the uncertain threats that everyone feared but no one could quite name.[21]

The situation was particularly tense in the northeastern sector of France. This was the zone traversed by the king in his attempted escape, and it took no feat of genius to conclude that he had been heading for the border of the Austrian Netherlands. Since General Bouillé and his entire general staff had deserted to the enemy, the armed forces in the region had been left leaderless, and civilian authorities had to step in and improvise as best they could.[22] All along the frontier, from Metz to Givet and Rocroi, volunteer citizens' brigades and patriot soldiers rushed to shore up the frontier fortresses, left in disrepair since the previous war thirty years earlier. In Sedan city administrators even organized a special festival dedicated to the defense of the fatherland, a festival that conveniently coincided with the Corpus Christi ceremony. After the celebration some three thousand citizens, joined by infantrymen garrisoned nearby, set to work repairing the walls and moats protecting the town.[23]

But although teams of citizens could help shore up the defenses, they could do nothing about the problem of arms. And almost everywhere municipalities found that their stores of muskets and powder were distressingly meager. General Bouillé had surreptitiously removed armaments from most of the strongholds in Lorraine in order to concentrate them in Montmédy for the protection of the king. When local administrators discovered what had happened, many assumed that it was part of a general conspiracy to weaken defenses in anticipation of invasion. Everywhere in the northeast, in the hours and days after Varennes, people began looking out for the arrival of enemy armies. Not surprisingly, perhaps, some began to see them.[24]

The origins of the invasion panic that swept across northeastern France can be precisely identified. Early on the morning of June 22 General Bouillé, still hoping to rescue the king, ordered a regiment of Swiss infantry in the pay of France to march westward from the town of Metz to the Meuse River, only ten miles from Varennes. In fact, when the regiment arrived near its destination late that night, most of the soldiers mutinied and refused to advance, announcing that they were not paid to fight against the French people. The officers then fled, and the remainder of the Swiss retreated in good order to Verdun. But coming as it did in a moment of supreme tension, this strange cross-country movement away from the frontier of several hundred heavily armed, German-speaking soldiers provoked pandemonium among the local population.[25]

Late in the afternoon of June 22, authorities in Verdun sent word to the surrounding villages that an army was moving toward Varennes, and that all available guardsmen must march to the Meuse and burn all the bridges, if necessary, in order to halt the attack. Soon thereafter the panic-stricken leaders of Varennes issued their own urgent call for help.[26] Within hours, the messenger chain that had spread the word of the king's arrest was set in motion once again to announce the approaching "enemy" troops. For the second night in a row, guardsmen were mobilized all across the region to come to the aid of Varennes.

Invariably some towns and villages, in relaying the appeals for reinforcements, exaggerated or expanded on the original message. In the atmosphere of fear and tension, there were inevitable misunderstandings and miscommunications. But it was also natural for terrified officials to exaggerate a bit, to make certain that the situation seemed sufficiently critical to rouse others to their aid—and to justify their own panic. Thus, when citizens in Clermont relayed Varennes' plea to "fly to the assistance of your brothers in arms," they inflated the story somewhat, announcing that fighting had already broken out between patriots and "the enemy." The next village to the south embellished the message further, asserting that a battle was now raging and that many French citizens had been killed. By the next morning, as the news reached the southern edge of the department of Meuse, the word *enemy* had subtly changed meaning: the threat was no longer from a regiment of Swiss mercenaries in the pay of France, but from the "Imperials" themselves, an invading Austrian army, which was now said to be advancing rapidly beyond the Meuse.[27]

In the meantime, the news had traveled westward across the Argonne Forest and arrived in Sainte-Menehould. The small town was just recovering from an exhausting and harrowing night. The confrontation with Damas' German dragoons, the sudden appearance of the king and queen, and the havoc wrought by the duke de Choiseul's cross-country cavalry ride just north of the town had thrown the citizens into near panic. Now they heard, or imagined they heard, that Austrian soldiers had taken and destroyed Varennes, were heading directly west, and would soon fall on the people of Sainte-Menehould themselves—perhaps planning to punish them, as they had punished Varennes, for their part in the capture of the king. "Imperial troops have sacked Varennes," they wrote in a desperate call for help: "In the name of the Fatherland, we implore you to come to our aid. Quick! We are short of arms and munitions, and especially of men."[28]

By the morning of June 23, the rumored invasion had produced a wave of terror not unlike the Great Fear of 1789. Toward nine the story arrived in Châlons-sur-Marne, where the royal family had just spent the night on their return trip to Paris. Rumors spread rapidly through the town that the Austrians had arrived and were just outside the gates. Soon a riot broke out as people desperately sought arms for their protection. The doors of the city hall were beaten down, and the mayor was surrounded by an angry crowd and forced to throw open the municipal arsenal—before leaping from a second-story window and making his escape. Terrified both by the imagined Austrians and by fellow townspeople clamoring for action, officials mobilized the national guards throughout the department, urging all citizens to come to their aid: "Take courage! Let us show ourselves worthy of our freedom by daring to defend it!"[29]

To many people it now seemed obvious that the Austrians had invaded France in an attempt to recapture the king. And from this point on, the panic closely followed the monarch's procession back toward Paris. Guardsmen, sometimes accompanied by women and children, were on the road everywhere, advancing to the aid of Varennes or Clermont or Châlons, or returning home when they discovered that the enemy had "retreated." Thousands of others were hurrying to join the escort of the monarch—now, in part, to protect him from the Austrians. The weather was hot and dry. The myriad of marching men and women raised great clouds of dust in the light chalky soil of northern Champagne. The dust, the confusion, the noise of drums and plodding feet at night or in half light, could easily confirm one's worst fears that the invading army was just over the hill or in the woods beyond the river.

Within two days the terrifying news had spread throughout much of Champagne and parts of the provinces of Lorraine, Picardy, and Ile-de-France. In Lorraine, the fortress city of Metz mobilized its guardsmen and sent them off toward Verdun for the second time in two days. Thionville, north of Metz, also heard of the invasion, but now there was confusion as to the direction of the attack, and citizens set to destroying all bridges across the Moselle River, in anticipation of an invasion from the German states farther east. In the meantime, moving from village to village, intensified everywhere by the warning sounds of church bells, the panic had surged to the northwest as far as Charleville and the northern frontier. When citizens in the cathedral city of Reims heard the rumor, they relayed it westward toward Soissons and Laon, and by the morning of June 24 the fear had swept into the province of Picardy beyond the river Oise. Now the threat had taken on epic proportions. The king, it was said, had already been stopped by an army of 40,000 to 50,000 Austrians—some said 60,000. They had destroyed Varennes and Sainte-Menehould, had moved beyond Châlons, and were ravaging everything in their path, "burning and killing everywhere."[30] That afternoon, a day ahead of the king, rumors of an "invasion" from the east incited "a movement of unrest among the common people" in Paris itself.[31]

In the following days four other regions in the kingdom were touched by similar invasion panics. A shootout between soldiers and smugglers in the western Pyrenees ignited rumors that the Spanish army had crossed the frontier and was marching down three mountain valleys into southwestern France. Soon dozens of communities from Pau to Bayonne and as far north as Bordeaux rushed off guardsmen to confront the enemy.[32] Along the central Atlantic coast, "the appearance of several unknown sails off Saint-Hilaire-de-Riez" prompted a report of an English invasion that spread throughout much of the province of Poitou.[33] In Brittany a small fight near Saint-Malo between guardsmen and emigrant nobles sailing to Jersey sparked yet another rumor. The story spread that six thousand troops had disembarked from forty British ships and were now moving west along the coast. Guardsmen, mobilized from as far away as Rennes and Brest, rapidly converged on the "invaders" to save the fatherland.[34]

Then, abruptly, almost as rapidly as they had begun, the various panics evaporated. Urgent messages from the "invasion sites" themselves soon made it clear that no foreign troops had appeared —or that if they had appeared, they had now "retreated." The National Assembly took steps to denounce the stories as unfounded. Yet the rumors also encountered skepticism from some local administrators. Significantly, all the invasion fears had begun in areas little touched or untouched by the Great Fear of 1789. But once the rumors arrived in regions that had experienced the violence and anarchy of the previous panic, they were frequently greeted with disbelief. In Château-Thierry, for example, a town that had been profoundly shaken by the Great Fear, district leaders concluded that the announced invasion was so inherently incredible that the story must have been an enemy fabrication, a plot to disrupt the nation. Not only did they refuse to pass on the rumor, but they set out to investigate the source of the falsehood.[35] Particularly among the elites, the memory of the widespread violence and anarchy of that earlier encounter with imaginary enemies seems to have acted like an inoculation against ensuing panics.

The Enemy Within

Everywhere in France, even in regions where no panics had occurred, the king's sudden disappearance provoked fears of possible invasion. But the crisis also aroused fears of internal enemies, secretly plotting against the Revolution. A conspiratorial view of the world was hardly unique to the Revolutionary period. For centuries people had attributed grain shortages to the concealed maneuvers of various groups of scoundrels out to make a profit or to take their revenge for wrongs previously suffered. Despite the appearance of new modes of analysis, based on rational "scientific" explanation—linking famine, for example, to meteorological conditions or to poor transportation—a great many people continued to relate all that went wrong in the world to the willful actions of individuals operating through plots and conspiracies.[36] Even to the more enlightened members of provincial society, such a hypothesis seemed by no means impossible in the context of the Revolution. Patriots knew only too well that the transformations wrought since 1789 had excited the bitter opposition of two groups, in particular: the nobility and the clergy.

Although a small group of liberal nobles had early thrown in their lot with the Revolution, the great majority were anything but pleased by the course of events. Unhappy with the National Assembly's attack on their feudal rights and privileges, they were even more angered by the suppression of the very status of "noble" in June 1790. In their racial view of society, the idea that one could legislate the nobility out of existence seemed absurd, as though—in the words of a baron—one could change an oak tree into a pine by a simple decree.[37] To be sure, after the summer of 1789 most provincial nobles remained cautious, watching their language and retiring to their chateaus or townhouses, where they hoped to ride out the storm. But a few were unable to hold their tongues, taunting the local patriots, rejecting the very existence of a National Assembly or of the "rights of man," and predicting that the recent changes would never last. When they gathered among themselves for social occasions and commiseration, they were even less restrained in their condescending remarks about the Revolution and the Revolutionaries and in their angry prophecies of catastrophe for both. Such predictions, born of impotent rage and frustration, were invariably overheard by servants and neighbors. Duly embroidered and passed on to the community, such talk could be transformed into proof of conspiracy.

The conspiracy interpretation was all the more credible in that everyone knew of the armies of émigrés gathering across the Rhine, counterrevolutionaries who had fled France and were dedicated to ending the Revolution. With the advantages of hindsight, it seems clear that such armies, manned with large numbers of noble officers but very few common soldiers, posed little real danger to the nation. But for patriots in the spring of 1791, the reality of the threat was much more difficult to assess. It was hard to believe that men who had always wielded so much power in society would now suddenly cease influencing events. Many were convinced that the émigré leaders, the count d'Artois and the prince de Condé, were secretly lining up support among provincial nobles.[38] In the months before Varennes, a citizen in Picardy told the National Assembly of groups of nobles gathering at a nearby chateau, and of his conviction that "plots were being hatched" among "men with the evil intention of starting a counterrevolution." In southern Lorraine, there were reports of another "known counterrevolutionary schemer who was moving from chateau to chateau" to organize the local nobility and "overthrow the constitution." A letter from Provence claimed proof of a vast network organized in every region of the country by émigré nobles, an "aristocratic, chivalrous, Jesuitical association" sworn to obey the count d'Artois.[39] Whether real conspiracies existed in any of these cases is difficult to know. But such letters revealed the widespread conviction in the spring of 1791 that whole segments of the provincial nobility were engaged in counterrevolutionary activities.

And such fears were intensified by the religious crisis brewing in France since the beginning of 1791. By the spring of that year almost half of the parish clergymen in the country had refused to swear the loyalty oath in the words specified by the National Assembly, and orders were issued for the replacement of the "refractory" priests. In strongly refractory areas like western France or the peripheral zones of the east and south, many leaders felt themselves threatened and under siege. Wherever there were significant clusters of oath refusals, administrators were tempted to see collusion and hidden conspiracies, perhaps initiated by the refractory bishops, now living abroad and closely tied to the émigrés. Already in May department directors in Laon, northeast of Paris, had become obsessed with the "critical situation" created in their region by the oath crisis. There was no doubt in their minds that the clerical refusals were linked to "centers of sedition and plotting, both inside and outside the kingdom."[40]

Thus, when news of the king's flight broke, patriots throughout much of the country already assumed the existence of internal conspiracies dedicated to the destruction of the Revolution and undoubtedly linked to foreign enemies. "The disappearance of the royal family," wrote the leaders of one town, "excited a general movement of indignation against the enemies of the public good. The audacious statements of some, the emigration of others, the refusal of the oath by clergymen, all are indicative of a criminal conspiracy."[41] The real problem for administrators—the problem that would beset the Revolutionaries for years to come—was how they should respond to such threats. And here they were deeply torn. On the one hand, most officials were committed to the concept of equal justice and the rule of law, for nobles and clergymen as for everyone else. Such ideals were, after all, part and parcel of the Declaration of the Rights of Man and the Citizen. As men of substance themselves, the officials remembered only too clearly the chaos and disorder of the first summer of the Revolution, and they were anxious that accused "suspects" should be dealt with by the courts and not by mobs. Their directives in June and July 1791 were filled with admonishments on the need to preserve law and order. Officials in Auch, for example, urged everyone to show "a perfect submission to the laws. Citizens! now we must decide whether we can truly be free or whether we will be fettered with the new chains of anarchy."[42]

On the other hand, the very values of equal justice and the rule of law were dependent on the continued existence of the new constitution, and the administrators were aware of the threat posed by the king's departure and the perceived conspiracies to the survival of the Revolution. Were there not emergency situations in which the defense of the nation justified repressive actions that would normally be illegal; when, as Charles Lameth had put it, "It was better to commit a momentary injustice than to see the loss of the state"? In this context, the Assembly's instructions on taking all necessary steps for "the maintenance of law and order and the defense of the nation" were particularly ambiguous and elastic. They could easily be interpreted as a veritable blank check for repressive action.[43]

Local officials, moreover, were not acting in a vacuum. They had always to take into account the opinions of the people they were supposed to administer and whose suspicions and penchant for violence were only too well known. Two groups, in particular, pushed local leaders toward more repressive measures in the days after June 21: the urban masses and the national guards. In numerous communities, news of the king's flight and his arrest in Varennes set off spontaneous outbreaks of popular violence against local nobles and clergyman.[44] Sometimes the authorities acted immediately to redirect such emotions. The notables of Cahors were unusually creative in this respect, organizing a special "federation" ceremony—perhaps advancing plans already afoot for the July 14 celebration. There were marching guardsmen, bands, patriotic speeches by the constitutional clergy, rousing renditions of "Ça ira!" and a solemn oath pronounced by all men and women to be faithful to the nation and the laws. In Strasbourg a veritable public charivari was organized with straw effigies of Bouillé and his subordinates, Klinglin and Heyman, carried through the streets in a cart and subsequently burned in the central square before the cheering population.[45]

But for many officials, acquiescence to popular pressure seemed

Conspirators in the King's Flight Burned in Effigy in Strasbourg, June 25, 1791.

the better part of valor. Administrators in Brittany were particularly articulate in their description of the dilemma. "The unrest and resentment of the people has reached an extreme degree," they wrote in late June. "In the midst of this agitation, it is impossible for reason alone to be heard. We must soothe and accommodate such passions if we are to prevent them from falling out of control . . . and maintain our favor in public opinion, without which it would be impossible to govern."[46]

Perhaps no single issue aroused greater apprehension among the common people than the control of the town fortress. The keys to such strongholds were held by local military commanders who were themselves invariably nobles. The treason of General Bouillé and his entire staff had intensified suspicion against all such officers. In Strasbourg, in Verdun, in Dunkerque, in La Rochelle—in virtually every fortress city up and down the coast and along the frontiers—civilian administrators were compelled by popular demand to take control of the local citadels. As the town fathers in Cambrai explained, "the people consider priests and nobles to have been the authors of the king's abduction." Officials thus felt compelled to seize control of city defenses, "since, in the present state of things, it would be dangerous to oppose public opinion, which is an essential element of patriotism."[47]

Pressure for various forms of extralegal action also came from the national guards. Throughout the country, as we have seen, the mobilization of the local militia was among the first measures taken when administrators received word of the king's flight. The National Assembly had decreed that lists be drawn up of guardsmen prepared to go to war if the country should be invaded, and almost everywhere men rushed to enroll with extraordinary enthusiasm. In Lyon more than eight hundred new recruits were welcomed from the city alone; in La Rochelle "spontaneous meetings of citizens by street or by neighborhood determined the formation of six new companies." Even in the small southern village of Cuxac, peasant guardsmen were said to be "burning with the desire to save the nation."[48]

Most of the guards were strongly committed to the goals of the Revolution. They had vowed to preserve the constitution against all its enemies, and the experience of Varennes strengthened their suspicions of aristocrats and refractory clergymen. Several units quickly expelled all nobles from participation, since "prudence and the safety of the state prevent us from confiding troops to individuals whose interests are opposed to those of the Revolution."[49] Moreover, if they were to perform their functions properly and obtain the status they felt they deserved, these newly minted militiamen would obviously require arms and ammunition. The guardsmen's vigorous search for muskets and powder would have the advantage not only of disarming counterrevolutionaries, but also of placing more weapons in patriot hands.[50] Almost everywhere in the days after June 21, the guardsmen formed the shock troops of repression in the provinces.[51]

Responding to popular pressures and adapting the National Assembly's blank check to do everything necessary for the defense of the nation, administrators throughout the country took a range of measures against the "enemies within." Many of these measures were both illegal and in violation of the Declaration of the Rights of Man. But the crisis appeared so unprecedented and the danger of conspiracy so real that officials resolved to take "all necessary and appropriate measures to thwart the treacherous plots of the enemies of society."[52]

Thus, almost everywhere local officials began opening and reading letters sent through the post office—despite repeated decrees on the "inviolability" of the mail.[53] The council of one small town in Lorraine carefully explained its reasoning: "Our internal and external enemies will not fail to do everything possible to achieve their infernal designs against the nation. Thus, it will perhaps be prudent, without revealing any family secrets, to scrupulously examine in the post office any correspondence that might seem suspicious."[54] In practice, the definition of suspicious correspondence varied greatly from one town to another. Some officials examined all letters addressed to or from foreign countries. Elsewhere they focused on mail sent from refractory bishops or received by any "suspect" noble or clergyman. Most of the letters so examined were unrevealing, despite the patriots' best efforts to read conspiracy into inane family chatter. Large quantities piled up in the archives of the Assembly's Committee on Research, never delivered, and as little enlightening to the deputies in 1791 as to historians today. But occasionally the opened letters had major consequences for individuals. A seemingly innocent note from an émigré noble to his business agent near Orléans—a certain Monsieur Petit—intercepted and revealed to the public, led to the near lynching of the agent and his lengthy incarceration in the town jail. "At every minute," wrote the terrified Petit, "I seem to hear the mobs crying out for a victim."[55]

Many officials also sanctioned the illegal arrest of travelers. Broadly interpreting the Assembly's interdiction on individuals crossing frontiers, administrators began stopping unknown travelers wherever they were found, especially those who appeared to be nobles or who had unlikely dress or strange speech or who seemed a bit nervous. It was clearly not the moment to leave on a trip, and the National Assembly was flooded with appeals from unfortunate people who found themselves imprisoned in the midst of the crisis, sometimes for weeks on end, denied the right of habeas corpus guaranteed by the constitution. In Cahors guardsmen fell upon two Belgian businessmen with obvious foreign accents on their way to Italy. The townsmen justified the arrest in terms of their fear of "an impending invasion of foreign troops. To save the constitution from destruction . . . we felt the need for extraordinary precautions." In any case, the two were still in jail in the middle of August, bitterly lamenting their fate. Elsewhere authorities summarily arrested a down-and-out clarinet player, a physician from the royal stables on his way to Brussels, and a suspicious count "prowling" through town and "suspected by everyone."[56]

Usually, however, provincial patriots were less worried about outsiders passing through than about local inhabitants who had already aroused mistrust for their opposition to the Revolution. All over France, teams of officials and national guardsmen rushed to scrutinize nearby chateaus and religious houses staffed by clergymen who had refused the oath. They searched for evidence of secret meetings of counterrevolutionaries. They looked also for arms and munitions, arms that might be used against the Revolution and that, in any case, were badly needed by the patriots themselves.

For the first time in many provincial towns the term *suspect* entered widely into the administrative vocabulary. But what it was that aroused distrust, what it was that indicated "suspect intentions"—as officials in Montpellier put it—was often far from clear. In many cases, suspicion seems to have arisen from specific statements made by individuals, either sometime in the past or immediately after Varennes, words that classified them in the minds of their neighbors as "citizens notorious for their antirevolutionary principles." A woman in Meaux was incarcerated for an "aristocratic outburst" during a dinner with friends several months earlier. A priest near Verdun was arrested for publicly musing that "it would not have been a disaster if the king had escaped"—words taken entirely out of context, according to the "suspect" in question. Two refractory priests were nearly hanged by an angry crowd in Vendôme for insulting a prorevolutionary clergyman. Unfortunately, officials were unable to save a noble in Brest from popular revenge for his mocking depiction of a Revolutionary ceremony with "obscene graffiti" on the walls of a cabaret. Soon after news of the king's disappearance arrived, the noble was murdered and his head paraded through the streets on a pike.[57]

Elsewhere, individuals had attracted mistrust because of known links to emigrants or because they themselves had expressed a desire to leave France. We have seen the sad predicament of Monsieur Petit when his correspondence with an émigré was intercepted. A young man named Boubert was tracked down and arrested after asking a relative for money to finance his emigration.[58] More common, no doubt, were the fears aroused by the reputed secret gatherings of nobles and clergymen in local chateaus. Reports of "hidden conclaves of aristocrats and refractories" in Saint-Denis, just north of Paris, prompted district authorities to search a nobleman's home at two in the morning. The nobleman claimed that the visitors had come only to celebrate Pentecost, and in fact the inspection turned up neither arms nor mysterious strangers. A similar search of a chateau near Chaumont-en-Vexin—where a noble family was surprised in the midst of a game of whist—turned up nine antiquated hunting guns and a souvenir pike from the battle of Fontenoy, all duly confiscated for the arsenals of the nation.[59]

In some cases, attacks on individual nobles seem to have arisen from antagonisms long predating the Revolution. In the wake of Varennes, guardsmen from several villages near Reims converged on the chateau of the marquis d'Ambly, deputy to the National Assembly. Finding few arms, they compelled the marquis' wife to give them money to purchase guns and then marched off with the nobleman's terrified young grandson, whom they claimed to have adopted as their "mascot." In this case the guardsmen seem to have picked on d'Ambly in part because of his reputation as a reactionary in the Assembly, but also because of a grudge over feudal rights that had pitted villagers against their lord for some twenty-five years.[60] Far more violent was the attack on Guillin du Montet, the lord of Poleymieux, in the countryside near Lyon. Guillin was already hated before 1791 for his brutal treatment of the peasants and his general refusal to accept the Revolution. Soon after the Varennes crisis broke, inhabitants arrived a hundred strong to seize the large store of weapons that Guillin kept in his chateau. When he resisted, a gun battle broke out, ending only after the chateau had been stormed and Guillin had been killed, his body torn to pieces and thrown into the burning castle.[61] The events in Poleymieux were soon widely publicized, to the horror of people throughout France. Yet extreme violence of this kind was rare during the crisis. Only four individuals, all nobles, are known to have been killed in the wake of the king's flight, and at least three of these were already detested for a variety of long-standing grievances.[62]

In most instances, the repression practiced by local leaders and guardsmen was pursued on a case-by-case basis, targeting specific "suspect" individuals. But in certain instances the authorities, fearful of real plots or succumbing to popular pressures, gave orders to search or arrest without trial whole categories of persons. Here the status of suspect arose not from any act that a particular man or woman was thought to have committed, but from the fact of belonging to a specific social or political group. Such reasoning was probably widespread among elements of the common people. In Varennes, at the height of the invasion panic, a crowd of peasants and guardsmen fell upon one of the cavalry commanders who had been attempting to cooperate with the patriots. "He's an officer! He's a noble! He must be a traitor!" they shouted, with a lapidary logic, reducing guilt to the fact of wearing an officer's uniform.[63]

More significant were the actions of public officials who classified suspects in this manner. The most obvious targets for such collective indictments were the clergymen who had refused the oath of allegiance. In those regions struggling with large numbers of refractories, local patriots were immensely impatient with the National Assembly's decrees on "freedom of religion" and toleration for refractories who stayed out of trouble. Was not the very refusal to take an oath an affront to the constitution and a threat to the nation? Liberals might push "freedom of opinion"—as citizens of one small town argued—but "dear God, what kind of opinion is fanaticism, which can only offer a vision of carnage, scorched villages, and a devastated kingdom!" In some areas the repression of refractories was sweeping indeed, unlike anything previously pursued in the Revolution. As soon as they heard news of the king's flight, officials in the city of Nantes ordered the immediate deportation of all refractories in the region and the arrest of any priest suspected of counterrevolutionary activities. Some district leaders in Normandy and Brittany did much the same, arguing that such clergymen were threatening a return to the Wars of Religion and that all refractories, "without exception, are enemies of the state."[64] Within a short time similar measures were taken, illegally arresting or deporting hundreds of nonjuring priests, in a total of at least nine departments throughout the country.[65]

A second target of blanket repression was the nobility. In the departments of Cher and Indre, in the center of the kingdom, refractories were relatively rare and not generally perceived as a danger, but the news of Varennes raised fears that aristocrats in the region were organizing counterrevolutionary aggression. Several districts sent out guardsmen systematically to disarm every chateau. The town of Bourges went even further, ordering all resident nobles to remain in town and guarding the city gates to ensure that none slipped out, so as "to prevent joint action by all those who openly profess principles contrary to the general will." For the most part such policies were pursued peacefully, with guardsmen specifically instructed to act "in a reasonable and polite manner, without violence."[66]

Nowhere, however, was the collective repression of nobles more violent than in the province of Brittany. Here officials found themselves plagued not only with one of the highest proportions of refractory clergymen in the country, but with long-standing tensions between nobles and commoners that had been exacerbated by provincial politics on the eve of the Revolution. Following the king's flight, and encouraged by local administrators, Breton national guardsmen from many towns launched a veritable terror in the countryside, harassing suspect nobles and clergy, searching for arms, and occasionally destroying chateaus. In one department authorities gave free rein to pursue all members of the two suspect groups: "Our enemies," they wrote, "are making a final push. Hatred and fanaticism will be stirring up trouble as never before, and there is no limit to the measures we should take in order to thwart their efforts." Following these orders, guardsmen began breaking into every manor house to "remove from the enemies of the constitution the means they might use to overthrow the state." Leaders in a neighboring department went even further and ordered the seizure of the property of all nobles who had already emigrated. Since the National Assembly's June 21 decree had forbidden the carrying of money or precious metals across frontiers, it seemed justifiable to impound the profits of absentee nobles, profits that might otherwise be sent abroad in support of counterrevolutionary schemes against the nation.[67]

With administrators encouraging repression and tensions raised to explosive levels by the invasion panic, Brittany would be the scene of several especially violent incidents. In the region east of Rennes, the news of Varennes sent some three to four thousand citizen militiamen into the villages looking for refractories. Frustrated at not finding a particular nobleman who had supported the dissident clergy, the guardsmen burned down his castle, and soon several other chateaus in the area went up in flames. With word of the king's flight, another detachment of a hundred guardsmen was dispatched to the chateau of Le Préclos near Vannes, where a group of suspicious nobles were said to have gathered. Arriving at four in the morning and awakening the residents with drums and musket fire, the patriot militia carried away eighteen men in carts, their hands tied behind their backs, to be interred in a local citadel as "prisoners of war." Leaders in La Roche-Derrien, near Brittany's northern coast, had also set out to disarm all the "former privileged" in their region. Apparently no one resisted until guardsmen arrived at the chateau of Tralong, where the irascible count du Roumain greeted them with shots from a seventeenth-century blunderbuss and a "Breton Billy," an antiquated device that fired stones. After several citizens had been wounded and another unit of guardsmen had been called in, the patriots stormed the castle, killing du Roumain in the process.[68]

As the crisis of June and July abated and as the central government received more reports from the provinces, the National Assembly began criticizing the more flagrant examples of collective repression. Department officials in Quimper, perhaps under pressure from Paris, took the district of Landerneau to task for its massive arrests of nobles and refractories, people "whose only crime was to have been suspected of anticonstitutional opinions, but who had never done anything to disrupt public order." Not only were such activities against the law and the rights of man; they could further inflame the situation: "To incite trouble in this way, to frighten individuals and to threaten their property, is all the more reprehensible in that it compromises liberty and the principles of the constitution." But the district of Landerneau forcefully defended its actions. The circumstances of the crisis and the fundamental goal of saving the Revolution justified all the measures they had taken. "Blood would soon have been spilled," they declared. "We had only one choice: to seize our enemies before they could commit crime and murder." Refractories and nobles were simply too dangerous to be trusted, even those—perhaps especially those—who hid behind "the hypocritical mask of patriotism." In the end, Landerneau officials remained unrepentant: "We have served both humanity and the constitution, in separating out those who would cause trouble and disorder. . . . We strongly denounce them and we will not cease pursuing them until the sacred fire, which we hold in our breast, has purified every corner of the French nation."[69]

The debate between Landerneau and Quimper was emblematic of the quandaries encountered by French people everywhere in the face of the crisis of the king's flight. Even in the twentieth century, in societies where liberal democratic culture is deeply rooted, periods of war and the threat of terrorism have created legal dilemmas over demands for "preventive repression." For men and women who had lived most of their lives under authoritarian rule and who were only just learning the meaning of equal justice and civil rights, the events of June 1791 posed problems that were particularly perplexing. Revolutionaries found themselves forced to negotiate a delicate balance between principle and expediency, between the rule of law and the needs of "public safety," between individual liberty and community defense, between preserving the rights of man and preserving the state. In their groping efforts to confront these dilemmas, many citizens in the provinces had wandered into the byways of repressive actions—guilt by association, guilt by unproved suspicion, lengthy imprisonment without due process—that were clear harbingers of the tactics of the Terror.

CHAPTER 7

To Judge a King

THROUGHOUT THE THREE WEEKS following the king's flight and return, the citizens of Paris had continually referred to opinion in the provinces. For the Cordeliers Club, a nationwide referendum was essential before any decision could be made on the fate of the king, and the members were hopeful that the majority of the country would opt for a republic. Moderates, on the other hand, were convinced that the French, both inside and outside the capital, overwhelmingly backed the monarchy. In the meantime, the National Assembly had put off its decision on the question, in part to wait for reactions from the hinterlands, reactions that were aggressively solicited by the deputies in letters addressed to their constituencies.[1] In short, everyone realized that Paris was not France and that the views on the king of the great majority of citizens were still unknown. Everyone, in a sense, was waiting for the French to speak.

And eventually the French would speak. Beneath all the sound and fury of the nationwide mobilization—the marshaling of the national guard, the shoring up of border defenses, the preventive repression—people everywhere had begun to ponder the fate of the one individual whose actions had launched the whole episode. How were they to explain Louis' sudden disappearance? What were the implications for the new constitution that the National Assembly was struggling to complete? What was the place, *was* there a place for a monarch—this or any monarch—in the brave new world that the Revolutionaries hoped to construct?

A Citizen King

Such questions were particularly wrenching and unsettling in that people throughout the country, no less than in Paris, had long linked themselves to their king through exceptionally strong bonds of emotion and tradition. Of course, individual kings had never been free of reproach, and the present monarch's two predecessors, Louis XIV and Louis XV, had often been the subject of caustic criticisms from both intellectuals and the popular classes. Yet the myth of the monarchy—as opposed to the reputation of individual monarchs—persisted with extraordinary vigor. It was built on a whole array of classical and historical traditions and of secular legends, as well as on the images of grandeur cultivated by seventeenth- and eighteenth-century monarchs through their military prowess and the splendor of their palaces and court life. French children and adults alike were continually exposed to a folklore of popular stories in which the existence of a monarchy and the ideal of the good king—as opposed to the bad king or the weak king poorly advised—remained as undoubted assumptions. Many among the lower classes maintained to the end of the Old Regime their belief in the "king's touch," his magical powers to cure the common skin disease scrofula. And the virtues of the first Bourbon monarch, Henry IV—his strength, his good sense, his love for his people— were still mentioned at the beginning of the Revolution when people described the ideal sovereign. Indeed, from 1788 to 1791 Louis XVI was himself commonly compared to "good king Henry."[2]

To be sure, the royal image had evolved somewhat in the decades before 1789. Over the centuries all kinds of descriptive phrases had been used to extol the king's grandeur: the king as great warrior, as chief magistrate, as highest feudal lord. But by the eve of the Revolution the portrayal of the monarch as "father of the people"—a designation mentioned at least since the sixteenth century—had increasingly come to predominate. There can be no doubt that the image was consciously encouraged by Louis XVI himself. He had been enormously proud of his own paternal success, a success achieved only after a long period of sexual failure and psychological turmoil, and he took great personal interest in the upbringing of his children. He had continually drawn on the paternal metaphor in his statements to the National Assembly. He had done much the same in Varennes, when he revealed his identity to his "faithful children" in Monsieur Sauce's apartment. Of course, the figure of the father, like the image of the king, had complex and sometimes ambiguous meanings. It could imply the *paterfamilias*, with his near-absolute authority in law and custom over wife and children, a figure patterned to some extent on the religious conception of an all-powerful God the Father. But as the image came to be embraced in the late eighteenth century by large elements of the educated population, the paternal king was perhaps linked above all to the literary fashion of the family melodrama. In plays and novels of the period there was endless praise for the "good father," a father who was not authoritarian but conciliatory, even egalitarian with his wife and children, treating all members of his family almost as friends and companions.[3]

There can be no mistaking the feelings of respect shown for Louis XVI in the grievance lists of 1789, the thousands of formal statements drawn up by the French during the elections to the Estates General. Almost everywhere people continued to address the king with the traditional epithets of honor and consideration— "Sire" or "His Majesty"—coupled with formal phrases of supplication. "His Majesty is most humbly beseeched" to grant such-and-such a request, as the expression commonly went. More than half of the grievance lists opened with statements of enthusiastic praise for the reigning monarch, and well over a third made references to his paternal virtues. Nearly as many stressed his goodness, and a fourth commented on his justice—though none made mention of his military prowess. Almost one in five specifically used the word *sacred* in reference to the king. Although this word was also occa-

"How Precious Is This Image to All Good Frenchmen!" Rural people of all ages kneel before the portrait of Louis XVI in 1789.

sionally used in speaking of abstract concepts, such as the "sacred right of property" or the "sacred constitution," in no other instance was it utilized to describe a specific individual.[4] It was the cultural strength of the royal mystique—coupled with gratitude for Louis' actions in summoning the Estates General—that rendered most patriots so tolerant of and forgiving toward the king during the first two years of the Revolution.

We have seen that from October 1789—if not earlier—Louis had self-consciously followed a policy of deceit. Even while he publicly accepted the laws sent to him by the National Assembly, he secretly announced to the king of Spain that he was signing them under duress. But the French in general knew nothing of this. The moderate patriots, determined to strengthen the constitutional monarchy, had done all in their power to promote Louis' image through carefully orchestrated speeches and appearances that they persuaded the king to make.[5] And if we are to judge by the letters flooding into the National Assembly, Louis' popularity may even have increased during the first two years of the Revolution. Soon after the king's speech to the deputies in February 1790, the small western town of Ernée wrote of "this happy and blessed day, forever memorable, when the best of kings, the restorer of French liberty, the gentle father of the nation, honored our Assembly with his presence and gave his approval to all its labors." The leaders of Troyes were scarcely less enthusiastic in describing their filial links to the king: "Children of a common father, listen to the king's words and unite behind him as he desires. The paternal heart of His Majesty asks for this proof of our love."[6]

There could be no doubt that the Revolution had substantially diminished the authority of the king. The constitution had transformed his status from that of absolute monarch to that of chief executive, with institutional powers not unlike those of the American presidency only just created across the Atlantic. Yet for most citizens the special, semireligious aura of the monarch persisted. They remained convinced that the king supported the Revolution and that ultimately the will of the monarch and the will of the nation would always correspond. The smattering of critical remarks from Jacobin clubs in the first half of 1791—some urging the king to ban refractory clergymen from his court—were overwhelmed by a chorus of affection and respect. The small town of Coudray, not far from Paris, expressed its indignation over the violent acts committed in the royal palace on February 28 and the supposed insults to "the sacred person of our good king."[7] When Louis came down with his sore throat in March of that year, hundreds of municipal councils and Jacobin clubs held solemn masses for his recovery, and virtually every town in France organized thanksgiving celebrations upon learning of his return to good health. "The God who oversees the destinies of empires did not wish to deprive us of our strongest supporter, the anchor of our happiness. Our churches ring out with prayers of thanksgiving" (Laval, in western France); "as the adoptive children of the Great Henry, we will forever maintain our attachment to this Bourbon prince, so worthy of his name and so precious to France" (Belley, in eastern France); "may God save the idol of the nation" (Bourges, in central France). A few weeks later, the small town of Châteaurenard in Provence unveiled a portrait of the king on the wall of the city hall, and the recently elected mayor gave a dedication speech. The French monarch, he argued, had created an entirely new relationship to his people, so that Louis seemed hardly even to belong in the same category as other monarchs: "Kings seek to be powerful through the use of terror, but Louis XVI wants only that confidence which his virtues inspire; kings command respect and obedience, Louis XVI asks only for the love of the French; kings wish to be the masters of their people, Louis XVI wants only to be his nation's father; kings work to enchain their subject's freedom, Louis XVI is the restorer of ours. O friend of mankind! O citizen king!"[8]

Everywhere in the provinces, on the eve of Varennes, the overwhelming majority of French citizens continued to feel affection, even reverence, for the person of the king. They continued to think of the monarchy as central and integral to the unity and coherence of the nation.

Tears of Blood

Perhaps it was the very intensity of their attachment to the monarch that prompted so many French to recount their experiences during the traumatic days following the king's flight. Between June 21 and the end of July more than 650 letters were received by the secretaries of the National Assembly from a variety of collective bodies all over the country: from every department, from virtually every town of any size, and even from a surprising number of villages.

The ostensible purpose of this mass of correspondence was the reaffirmation of allegiance to the Assembly in what was undoubtedly the greatest political crisis since the beginning of the Revolution. But a great many of the letters contained heartfelt testimonies of changing attitudes toward the monarch in the face of the crisis. Municipal and administrative councils, patriotic clubs, national guard units, women's societies, regional tribunals, and unspecified collections of "citizens" all sent in statements, statements undoubtedly drafted by local elites, but frequently signed by dozens or hundreds of others. Taken as a whole this correspondence constitutes a poll of provincial opinion over time, as people throughout the country attempted to come to terms with the king and the king's place in the nation in the weeks after Varennes.⁹

In the first days of the crisis—after citizens had learned of the king's disappearance, but before they had heard of his arrest—reactions depended in large measure on how and from whom the news was received. The petitions of the Parisian clubs and the reports of the radical newspapers were anything but gentle with the missing monarch. But the early announcements of the Assembly itself were much more ambiguous, never mentioning the king's antirevolutionary declaration, and leaving ample room for the belief that the royal family had somehow been kidnapped. Many provincial groups were eager to accept such a scenario and to give Louis the benefit of a doubt. Overall, close to a third of those sending in views during this early period persisted in their positive and sympathetic views of the monarch.¹⁰ They spoke bitterly of "the frightful crime of the abduction of the king and the royal family"; of "these monsters of humanity who have carried away the best of kings"; of "France now having been left an orphan." The Jacobins of Arras, usually linked closely to their compatriot Robespierre, were particularly poignant in their initial reaction to the event. "They have taken him away from us," they lamented, "this king who seemed to live only for his people, this king who so frequently offered his homage to the National Assembly, and whose patriotic actions were imbued with such candor and truth." When they learned that the king had been found and was being returned to Paris, many provincial towns launched spontaneous celebrations. Within minutes the courtyard of the Rouen city hall "was filled with a prodigious number of citizens, both men and women, attracted by the news of the event. They expressed their happiness with a spontaneous dance that lasted until three in the morning." Everywhere church bells, fireworks, thanksgiving prayers, and public celebrations marked the moment when their "bitter sorrow," as Limoges described it, was transformed into "the exhilaration of joy."[11]

In general, it was only at the end of June that people in the provinces began to appreciate the full significance of the events which had just transpired and that a veritable crisis of conscience began to sweep across France. As the National Assembly entered into its three-week interregnum, placing a moratorium on considerations of the king, its official pronouncements were no longer the preeminent source of information in the provinces. Towns were inundated with circular letters and petitions from the various clubs and sections in the capital and with Parisian newspapers of every political stripe. The great mass of newspapers, in particular, enormously broadened the range of information and interpretations available. "The public papers," as the patriotic club of Vendôme explained, "have continually helped us develop our opinions. Like all French people, we have closely followed the regular rhythms of their publications."[12] Many of the circumstances surrounding the flight had been neglected or censored in the Assembly's initial accounts. It was from newspapers and brochures that people in the provinces first heard of the Parisians' disapproving reception of the returning royal family on June 25, and of the early efforts of the Cordeliers Club to have the king deposed. Only now did they read of the king's personal declaration in which he implicitly repudiated his earlier oath and denounced many of the Revolutionary decrees that he had previously signed into law. Local leaders in Toulon first learned of the king's letter on July 1. When citizens in Bergerac first saw it, four days later, they publicly burned a copy in the town square.[13]

In the evaluation of this mass of information, local patriotic clubs played a particularly important role. By the middle of 1791 several hundred such clubs had already been created, including some four hundred directly affiliated with the Jacobins of Paris.[14] But although the provincial clubs closely followed the debates of the Jacobins in the capital, they were never blindly subservient to the mother society. The British agent William Miles was struck by the continual interchange of ideas among the various societies throughout the country, a process that reminded him of "the whispering gallery of Saint Paul's Cathedral"—the circular walkway inside the great dome in London from which visitors could hear one another speaking, no matter where they were standing. With the Parisian Jacobins unable to reach a consensus, provincial clubs became even more independent in the range and subjects of their debates. Dozens of societies began circulating copies of local deliberations throughout the correspondence network of provincial clubs, resulting in a rapid dissemination of ideas and proposals. In Bordeaux, in Bergerac, in Bar-le-Duc new tracts and petitions arrived daily from sister societies around the kingdom without even passing through Paris, tracts that seemed to grow more radical from one day to the next.[15]

In this liminal period of flux and uncertainty, in which the king seemed to have disowned the Revolution and the National Assembly had not yet taken a position, people everywhere began a sweeping reevaluation of the foundational assumptions of the new constitution. Not only in the local political clubs, but in the diverse administrative councils and the various ad hoc meetings set up to meet the crisis, citizens pondered and debated and passed in review the options available. In Toulouse "everyone made an effort to publicly pronounce his opinion, no matter how bold, on the question of the king." In Tours, as one townsman described it, debates soon focused on "the most interesting and probing questions ever discussed since the beginning of the monarchy. Ah! How can we describe it, the joy we felt in the midst of all our tensions and fears. We saw shy adolescents stammer out their thoughts, bold young men express the ardor and impetuosity of their feelings, mature men offer advice dictated more by reflection and prudence. What a touching spectacle it was!"[16]

And opinion now swung decisively against the monarch. During the pivotal period between late June, when news arrived of the capture in Varennes, and mid-July, when the Assembly issued its decrees, only about one in six of the testimonies from the provinces revealed any sympathy for the runaway king.[17] Even those who did show compassion frequently joined their remarks with harsh commentaries, linking the king's actions to his weakness of character in accepting bad advice. "The monarch is unfortunate, weak, deceived, and taken advantage of," wrote one town council. "We would like to believe," wrote another, "that it was through weakness and a blind submission to odious courtiers that Louis XVI was led to desert his post and abandon a people who had overwhelmed him with their love; that it was not through his own initiative, but in order to yield to the desires and unrestrained ambition of those who surrounded him. Because of this possibility we will remain silent and not judge him."[18]

By contrast, close to three-fifths of the correspondents were distinctly negative in their assessment of the monarch.[19] In statements that were striking for the anger and bitterness of their rhetoric, administrators, club members, and national guard units in every corner of the nation castigated the king for a whole range of sins. Louis was indicted for having deserted the palace without any consideration for the consequences of his actions for the French people. The man they had once considered their strongest supporter had "abandoned his post in a cowardly manner and betrayed all his oaths." His "desertion of the most admirable throne in the universe could have turned France into a vast tomb." Despite Louis' disclaimers, most correspondents had little doubt that the king's real intention had been to flee France and seek the aid of foreign powers against his own country. "The supreme commander of the nation planned to leave and take refuge in a foreign state that promised him money, assistance, and troops in order to reconquer the imaginary rights he claimed to be his." "He sought in vain to bring down foreign swords upon us." Such actions could only have led to war and could only be characterized as "treasonous." The king had abandoned his throne "to travel to foreign soil and transform our fertile plains into an ocean of blood. He would have delivered France over to desolation and to foreign and civil war." Even if he had been following the advice of others, he was "no less guilty of utter treason against the nation." It was only too clear that his ultimate aim had been to return "at the head of an army" and to re-impose "the former system" of the Old Regime. "Imbued with the principles of despotism, Louis will forever be the enemy of our liberty."[20]

Nothing more angered the provincial patriots than the king's famous "declaration," announcing to all the world that his previous oaths to the constitution had been insincere. In the Revolutionary ethos, imbued with the ideals of transparency and authenticity, there was perhaps no greater sin than to swear false oaths, and this is precisely what Louis admitted he had done. Again and again, they described him as a "parjure," one who is disloyal and a traitor to his promises. "We are horrified by any Frenchman who is so deceitful as to betray his sworn oath, thus violating the most sacred of principles." He was "cowardly and faithless," "perfidious and disloyal," "a traitor to his oaths"; "his supposed goodness was only the most base hypocrisy."[21] Several groups directly compared the king's false oath to their own recent vows, assuring the Assembly that they, unlike the king, would forever maintain "the religion of their oaths." For the Jacobins of Nantes, Louis had covered himself with "eternal infamy." No longer would they link him to good king Henry, but to Charles IX, the treacherous French king who had invited Protestant leaders to a wedding on Saint Bartholomew's Day 1572, only to have them massacred.[22]

In addition to the small group of patriots showing a modicum of sympathy for Louis and the large mass harshly condemning him, another fourth made no mention of the king at all in their correspondence: a disregard of the monarch's very existence that was, in itself, unprecedented and implicitly damning.[23] Most such respondents made it clear that they had now transferred all their allegiance to the Assembly. The Jacobins of Saint-Lô, in Normandy, described the psychological process through which they had passed in late June, after they learned of the recent events. "At first we were at a loss for words to describe our feelings, for one phrase had destroyed all our hopes: 'The King has abandoned us!' We hesitated. We tried to discern what it meant. Were his promises then totally frivolous? Were his oaths merely vain words? But then we realized, gentlemen, that you were taking charge. The voice of the nation can still be heard. And we all repeated a solemn oath to accept the new decrees. The destinies of free nations are no longer affected by the actions of kings." It was the deputies themselves who were now described as "the fathers of the nation," "the fathers of the people," "the restorers of liberty," paternal attributions once largely reserved for the king. The letters abounded with comparisons of the deputies to the heroic figures of Greece and Rome: they were the new Lycurgus, giving laws to the people; they were Roman senators battling "against Nero and Catiline." Other writers used religious references in praise of the Assembly: "your work has been touched by the finger of Divine Providence"; even on their deathbeds they would turn their heads toward Paris "and pronounce these words: for God and the National Assembly." In the present circumstances, they announced, they would follow the fathers of the nation no matter what their decision—even, they implied, if the king were to be tried or deposed. They would remain "faithful to the nation, to the law, and to executive authority, however you should choose to organize that authority." "We leave to your discretion and firm judgment the punishment or the pardon of the crimes of Louis XVI."[24]

Many of the statements were intensely moving, expressive of a deep disillusionment with the king. Until June 21, wrote the Jacobins of the village of La Bassée, in northern France, they had all considered Louis XVI the greatest man and the greatest monarch who had ever reigned. How different he had seemed from the sixty-five kings who had preceded him. But in one day, through a single act, "this prince has entirely lost his reputation." Louis' famous silence, once construed as the silence of wisdom and caution, was now attributed "either to stupidity or to treachery." Even the names used in designating the monarch, the dramatic slippage from "His Majesty" or "Sire" or "the king" to the pervasive use of his first name alone—"Louis" or "Louis de Bourbon"—underscored the fact that the king was no longer viewed as the embodiment of an eternal throne, but as a deeply flawed, if not depraved and perverse individual. In forsaking his vows, in violating "his solemn oaths," Louis "had deserted the just cause of a magnanimous and sensitive people who had always worshipped their kings as idols, loving them in spite of their vices." Indeed, the image of the idol, "a king previously the idol of the French," an idol now smashed and destroyed forever, appeared again and again in the rhetoric of the provincial correspondence.[25]

A few of the letter writers even began recasting the history of the Revolution and of the king's place in that history. The municipal leaders of one small town in central France wondered if Louis had not, after all, "always been moved by the principles of despotism." And they wrote a lengthy reinterpretation of the two years since 1789 in which the king was portrayed as attempting to "create a bastion of despotism in the midst of the National Assembly itself. It was he whose use of force compelled the deputies to take refuge in the Tennis Court. Paris would today be a vast graveyard, if it had not been for the courageous action of its inhabitants [who stormed the Bastille]." For the Jacobins of Versailles it now seemed that this "deceitful king" must have been responsible for "all the difficulties that have afflicted France over the last two years," just as he recently "prepared the cold-blooded massacre of the nation, a nation that had always covered him with kindness." Only recently, recalled the citizens of Alès, in southern France, "we formed a religious chorus to sing his praises. Too trusting, we thought of him as

The Overturned Idol. The female figure of France, having donned the royal robes, is about to crush the overturned bust of Louis XVI. Behind her, guardsmen, citizens, and sans-culottes indicate that they will maintain the monarchy to the last drop of their blood, even if they no longer trust the present king.

the restorer of our rights." But "rather than being our father, he preferred to be our tyrant, we might even say our executioner. Ah, gentlemen! Our hearts are broken and our eyes are filled with tears of blood."[26]

Monarchy or Republic?

Most of the groups sending testimonies in late June and early July took no direct stance on what should be done with the king, promising to abide by the Assembly's decision, whatever that decision might be. But about a fourth of the correspondents went a step further.[27] They felt themselves so deeply betrayed, they deemed Louis' behavior so reprehensible that they could never again trust him with responsibilities in the government, and they urged the National Assembly to take action against him. About half of this group seemed prepared to maintain the present constitution, although they encouraged the Assembly to remove Louis from the throne or to place him on trial before the nation.[28] The town leaders of Montauban agonized at length over the steps that should be taken. They still loved the institution of the monarchy, they said, but what could France do when faced with "a man who grudgingly refuses to carry out the law? A fugitive king who abandons the honorable post in which the constitution placed him, who violates the decrees which he himself had accepted, who tramples under foot his most sacred oath, who gives citizens the example of base deception: such is the sad spectacle before us." In the end they resorted to a contract theory of royal authority to justify the suspension of his immunity from prosecution: "a monarch who violates the constitution has destroyed the social contract in which his right to rule is inscribed." The Jacobins of Limoges fell back on a more direct logic of emotion: "Louis XVI should no longer sit on the throne of the French," they advised, "because he no longer reigns in the hearts of the people who now despise him." In Nantes the assembled body of citizens proposed a French version of the Glorious Revolution of 1688, when the English Parliament deposed James II and replaced him with William and Mary. The English taught us, they wrote, "that to dethrone a king who is faithless to the laws of his country is not to overthrow the monarchy itself."[29]

Yet all such proposals immediately posed an array of difficulties. Could the Assembly itself simply declare Louis deposed, as the citizens of Nantes seemed to advocate, or would he first have to be formally tried, presumably before the new supreme court established in Orléans? What would happen if such a tribunal found the king not guilty? And if the king were removed, who would take his place? The king's legal successor, the young dauphin Louis-Charles, was only five years old, and the problem of choosing a trustworthy regent seemed altogether daunting. The most likely such regent would have been the duke d'Orléans, the king's prorevolutionary cousin. But many patriots distrusted the duke almost as much as they distrusted Louis. Perhaps, in the face of such difficulties, it would be preferable to modify the constitution itself. And a small group of correspondents proposed various schemes for severely limiting the authority of the king, leaving him only "the ghost of his authority," as the officials of Brest proposed. "Never," wrote the town leaders in Lyon, "will you see Louis XVI regain the confidence that he has lost. If we must have a hereditary king sleeping on the throne, he must never have so much power that he could abuse it." Some suggested ending the king's right to veto legislation, a power unthinkable in the hands of "a cowardly and deceitful king." Others recommended giving all real authority to a cabinet of ministers, ministers to be chosen by the legislature or even by the people, moving France ever closer to the English parliamentary system. "If the monarchy is to be preserved," wrote the Jacobins of Dijon, "the French nation must so restrain its authority that the people will always be protected from the threat of despotism."[30]

But should France, in fact, conserve the monarchy? Clearly, a number of groups throughout the nation, like the club of Dole, were seriously considering the next step in the train of logic: to "cut the Gordian knot" and eliminate the monarchy altogether.[31] In the context of eighteenth-century Europe, it was a stunning proposi-

Henry IV Shocked by the Present State of Louis XVI. Good King Henry is appalled to find his descendant transformed into a pig. The caricaturist plays on the king's reputation for overdrinking, portraying him "drowning his shame" in a wine barrel. Empty bottles of the "wine of June 21," the "wine of the aristocracy," litter the ground.

tion, flying in the face of almost all contemporary thought, all common wisdom as to the danger and impracticality of a republic for so large and populous a territory as France. Only a handful of groups were prepared to take such a collective position. Those who did justified themselves with extraordinary rhetorical periods and angry denunciations against Louis XVI and the whole regime, often seeking inspiration from the classical heroes of republican Rome. None seems to have mentioned the nascent American republic, considered far too rural and sparsely populated to be comparable with France.

National guardsmen in the small town of Saint-Claud, in southwestern France, thundered against their "barbarous king" who had "sold his trust, his glory, and his country to a race of foreigners," while "harboring in his breast the horrible plan of overseeing the massacre of the French people." They then enumerated the twelve centuries of "scourges with which the scepters of kings have devastated the earth," before urging the National Assembly to overthrow the modern-day Tarquins—the last kings of Rome—and to establish a republic. Club members in the nearby town of Niort appealed to a contract theory. Louis XVI "has violated the treaty he had contracted with the nation; he betrayed his oath, thus the pact is broken and henceforth the nation has the incontestable right to end his political existence." "If we must do battle with the Tarquins," they concluded, "never forget that all true Frenchmen have already pronounced the oath of Brutus"—the Roman leader who had led their overthrow. "Citizens and compatriots," intoned the national guard of Arras, "the book of destiny is now open! Great events have brought forth great treason; but an atrocious crime, secretly plotted, can yield unexpected good fortune. Let us now forget that we have a king and he will be a thing of the past."[32]

How patriots in a small number of French provincial towns arrived at such positions is by no means clear. In the case of Clermont-Ferrand, Marie-Jeanne Roland, the Parisian patriot with ties to the Cordeliers Club, is known to have sent regular advice on fostering support for a republic to one of the local patriot leaders.[33] It is not impossible that partisans of republicanism in Arras and Chartres had been influenced by the rhetoric of their own radical deputies, Robespierre and Pétion respectively. But other townspeople seem to have adopted such positions independently, before letters and petitions could have arrived from Paris. And indeed, the single most important inspiration in the provinces for the destruction of the monarchy came not from Paris at all, but from Montpellier.

The origins of republicanism in this small provincial capital and university town near the Mediterranean remain rather mysterious. In their 1789 statement of grievances, signed by several of the future radicals, townsmen had revealed themselves unusually fervent in their support of the king.[34] The first motion to abolish the monarchy came on June 27, only one day after the town had learned of Louis' arrest in Varennes and almost certainly before the arrival of republican petitions from Paris. The proposal was presented to the local patriotic society by Jacques Goguet, a twenty-four-year-old physician, only recently graduated from Montpellier's medical school. But it was enthusiastically adopted by much of the local leadership, not only by the club, but by the town, district, and departmental administrators as well.[35] In its final version, approved on June 29, the petition to the National Assembly was tightly argued and succinct. The present monarch, the members of the club argued, "is debased, and we despise him too much to hate him or fear him. We leave to the law courts the sword of vengeance. We ask only that henceforth the French might have no other king but themselves." And once again, the demand was buttressed with a reference to antiquity: "All that remains, for us to become true Romans, is the hatred and the expulsion of kings. The first of these is already a fact. We await your actions to ensure the second." "Today," they concluded, "all prejudices have been destroyed and the people are enlightened. Popular opinion allows you, requires you to deliver us up from the evil of kings."[36]

Not only was the petition sent to Paris, where it was read before the Jacobins on July 6, but dozens of copies were circulated directly through the national network of patriotic clubs. Wherever it was received, it seems to have been the subject of serious and spirited debate. Bordeaux took it up as early as July 2; Toulouse and Aix-en-Provence read it on July 4 and 5. By July 10 it had reached Strasbourg, in the far northeastern corner of the country. Poitiers, in western France, began debating it two days later; while Bar-le-Duc, near Varennes, read it on July 13, and Limoges on July 15. In the end, only five clubs are known to have fully endorsed the petition.[37] Several adhered initially, but then reconsidered and decided to await the National Assembly's decision or opted to reject the present king but not the monarchy itself. But even when the majority rejected the Montpellier petition, a strong minority frequently emerged in favor of a republic. In both Poitiers and Bordeaux republican contingents argued their case vigorously, and these contingents might well have prevailed if debate had not been cut short by the arrival of the Assembly's decrees exonerating the king.[38]

Our Duty to Obey

News of the Assembly's decision and the Champ de Mars shootings put an abrupt end to the period of intense political reevaluation. Faced with this new crisis, local elites affirmed their adherence to the July decrees almost without exception. Nowhere outside Paris did the decrees become the target of mass demonstrations or violence. The deputies who had launched the Revolution and who had led the nation successfully through so many previous difficulties continued to command enormous respect and prestige among the provincial patriots—much to the frustration of the Parisian radicals and the Cordeliers Club.

Yet a great many citizens had clearly agonized over the issues at stake. In their letters to the Assembly, townsmen and local administrators often referred to the speeches of individual deputies, speeches that had been read, compared, and carefully weighed. "Robespierre, Vadier, Salle, Duport, and Barnave" was one town's list—indicating by the choice of speakers that both sides of the debate had been duly considered. Some groups recounted step by step their entire reasoning process, examining all the possible solutions to the crisis, eliminating those that seemed unworkable, and then offering their own reflections on the Assembly's final decision. "There were so many complications!" wrote the electors of one small town, as they pondered the unprecedented predicament. "The king seemed guilty, and nevertheless he had legal immunity. How could he then be accused? How could he be judged?"[39]

And acceptance of the Assembly's decision was by no means synonymous with support for the king. Indications of sympathy for Louis continued to decline precipitously, dropping from 31 percent of those writing at the beginning of the crisis, to 17 percent during the interregnum, to a mere 7 percent in the second half of July. By the final period scarcely anyone mentioned the old excuse of "a good king badly advised." Only a single letter—from a small town in central France—made reference to the "sacred" character of the king. To be sure, only one letter in five written after mid-July explicitly condemned Louis. But nearly three-fourths made no mention of him whatsoever.[40] Many provincial leaders clearly preferred to "cover with a veil of silence the sad episode of his flight." The principal objective of the vast majority of letter writers was to reaffirm their allegiance to the Assembly as the sovereign authority in the land, the supreme representative of the general will. The deputies were once again praised to the heavens as "fathers of the country" or as heroes modeling themselves on the Romans. Whatever the previous views of the local patriots—as they announced again and again—they now felt duty bound to follow the National Assembly: "Obedience is the duty of any good citizen," wrote the Jacobins from a town in northern Brittany, "and we will all now give the example." Almost everywhere their compatriots agreed: "You have spoken, and a single cry is heard throughout the land: 'It is the law!' And for this, we are all prepared to die." Even if they had earlier argued for stronger action against the king, "the general will" had now been determined by the Assembly, and "what had previously been an error, would now become a crime."[41]

When they did offer commentaries on the political situation and the Assembly's decision, most correspondents spoke far less of their love for the monarch or the monarchy than of their fear of a republic and of their anger over the "seditious" actions of the republicans in Paris. They returned repeatedly to the arguments of the National Assembly itself—many of them attributed to various philosophers from Montesquieu to Rousseau—that a republic would be impractical and unworkable in France. Such a government was perhaps feasible in small city-states, like those in Switzerland or ancient Greece; but in a large nation it might easily lead to disorganization and chaos. "This country is too vast ever to be turned into a republic. Sooner or later the neighboring powers would attempt to pick away at its pieces." Those proposing a republic had considered "neither the lessons of experience, nor the moral of history, nor the possible results, nor the facts of French customs, population, geography, and attitudes." "We believe that in a nation weighed down with an immense population, there must be a center of unity, a single site of supreme executive authority, from which, with the lever of the kingship—like a new Archimedes—all the vast estates of the nation can be moved."[42]

Many French citizens seemed fearful of the internal chaos that might arise in France if the Assembly were to tamper with the monarchy. For the most part, the Parisian protest movements received a decidedly negative reception in the provinces. There were numerous references to the sedition of the Parisian crowds, events that seemed to demonstrate only too clearly the dangers of placing power in the hands of the people in the absence of a single central authority. "The petition of the citizens of Paris made us tremble with indignation"; "Our hearts were filled with anxiety. We feared that under the pressure of this tumultuous crowd, incorrectly called 'the voice of the nation,' you might have been forced to sacrifice your principles." There were endless condemnations of "the abyss of anarchy," of "the frightful scourge of anarchy," of "the fury of the common people who have gone astray."[43] Many provincials shared the deputies' suspicions that protest in the capital was being incited by counterrevolutionaries or foreign powers, conspiring to bring down the constitution. "Hidden behind the mask of patriotism, such conspirators seek only to infect us with the disease of discord." "The license of anarchy" had been promoted by "monsters," by "traitors and refractory priests," by enemies of the state who were "clothing themselves in the mantle of patriotism in order to overthrow the constitution and push the nation into chaos."[44]

A small minority of the provincial groups sending in letters— perhaps one in eight—suggested that they were not entirely happy with the Assembly's decision, even though they were ultimately persuaded to adhere to that decision.[45] In some cases local citizens had initially opposed the decrees and had been won over only after carefully reading the debates. "If we had followed our hearts," wrote one corps of officials with disarming frankness, "a decision to act against the king would have been clear. But Legislators are compelled to resist the emotions to which ordinary men so easily succumb." In the end, the Assembly had convinced them that a constitutional monarchy was the only system capable of "maintaining the energy and unity necessary for the stability of a large nation and providing an insurmountable wall against the influence of factions." Another group of citizens agreed: "After the king had responded to our love and confidence with the violation of his most sacred commitments, we all hoped the tribunal of the nation would rule against the crime." But the Assembly "has risen above the considerations and the passions of the moment and has delivered, through its decree of July 15, a new pronouncement on the fundamental laws of the nation." The leaders of a small village near Bordeaux were more blunt: "At first we disapproved of your decree, considering it to be at odds with your principles." But after long reflection, they concluded that "we would rather be burdened with a king who is worthless and deceitful, than be forced to face the horrors of civil and foreign war."[46]

Others declared their adherence to the laws even while emphasizing their profound skepticism with regard to the Assembly's decision. In the view of officials in the Breton seaport of Brest, the country would now be placed in the hands of "someone who, through his flight and his declaration, has revealed himself to be our greatest enemy." Another town in Brittany agreed to accept Louis as their king "only because we are ordered to do so by the law." And leaders in Montpellier, who had so vigorously pushed a republic, accepted the decrees with a touch of cynicism: "In society," they reflected, "man can choose only between different sets of chains." In the present situation, they had no option but to place themselves "beneath the honorable and salutary yoke of the law." A few groups made it clear that their adherence to the Assembly's decrees was conditional and contingent on the good behavior of the king. They would accept Louis "only as long as he continues to use his powers to maintain the constitution," only as long as he recognizes that a king "is intended to serve the people and not the people him." And a handful sharply criticized the Assembly. The Jacobins of Périgueux were far from certain that the recent decrees "conform to the cry of conscience and to the general will of the nation." They warned the deputies never to forget that "you are only the organ of the people's will." If they wished to be obeyed in the future, they must not lose sight of the importance of "maintaining the universal confidence" of the people. Indeed, close to a dozen groups of respondents agreed to accept the decrees only if the Assembly would immediately see to its own replacement. It was high time that the deputies returned home and let others take their place. Otherwise, as one town warned bluntly, "your persistence might be mistaken for obstination."[47]

LOUIS XVI'S FLIGHT to Varennes had shaken French provincial society to its very roots. By the end of the interregnum period, and after intense debates, opinion had turned decisively against the reigning monarch. Rhetoric at least as virulent as that emanating from Paris had spread across the land. Although only a small minority of towns had taken a collective stance in favor of deposing the king or creating a republic, individual converts to such positions had emerged and had pushed their views in almost every region of the kingdom. Everywhere people had debated the idea and considered the possibility of a fundamental change in the basis of government—even when such a change was ultimately rejected by the majority. A large proportion of all groups sending in statements of adherence indicated, implicitly or explicitly, that they were prepared to abide by the deputies' decision, even if that decision involved the permanent assumption of power by the Assembly itself. Indeed, not a single letter condemned the Assembly's suspension of the king on June 21. When, fourteen months later, a new National Convention would create a republic, a great many French people, in the provinces as in Paris, would already have reflected on the possibility of living in a France without the present king, and perhaps without any king at all.

CHAPTER 8

The Months and Years After

As FRENCH MEN AND WOMEN in the provinces ended their debates on the fate of the king, a wave of repression was engulfing the city of Paris. For more than a week after the shootings at the Champ de Mars, the red flag of martial law continued to fly above the city hall. The moderate patriots dominating the National Assembly pursued their attack against all those perceived as republican "troublemakers." To strengthen the repression, the deputies rushed through a new antiriot decree. Harsh penalties were imposed on anyone thought to have incited violence through their words or their writings. The law was even drafted to take effect retroactively, targeting actions committed during and before the July 17 demonstration.[1] Only three days earlier, many of the same legislators had argued the illegality of retroactive penalties proposed against the king.

Although the investigations were officially directed by the municipal courts and the Parisian police, they were supervised by the Assembly's Committees on Research and Reports. Within days after the Champ de Mars, more than two hundred people had been jailed for throwing stones or shouting nasty comments against the national guards or for various other "crimes." The government also went after the republican leadership, the principal speakers of the fraternal societies, and the editors of several radical newspapers—people such as Marat, Danton, Desmoulins, Kéralio, and Robert.[2]

And like many provincial officials faced with the crisis of the king's flight, the National Assembly and the Parisian leaders had no qualms about running roughshod over laws only recently enacted. They ordered guardsmen and police to close publishing houses and political clubs, imposing limited press censorship for the first time since the fall of the absolute monarchy. They also reactivated a system of secret police informants, largely abandoned since the Old Regime. Men were sent to eavesdrop on private conversations in taverns or on street corners, listening for possible attacks against the government. Using the pretense of a citywide census, they dispatched municipal agents to apartments throughout Paris, looking for suspicious individuals or documents. The jailings and indictments continued well into August. Many complained of being held for weeks in solitary confinement without seeing a judge, without even being told the reason for their arrest. Cochon de l'Apparent, one of the directors of the investigating committees, was frank about the logic of such actions. "In extraordinary moments of crisis," he argued—echoing the language of Charles Lameth—"when the survival of the state is at stake, illegal arrests are justifiable."[3]

Repression seemed all the more warranted in that widespread secret conspiracies were now thought to have been organized against the Revolution. It was simply impossible, or so the moderates tried to convince themselves, that the petitioners of the Champ de Mars had acted on their own against the decrees of the sovereign National Assembly. They must have been corrupted or misled by outsiders. Although deputies had made similar accusations since the beginning of the Revolution, most had long resisted a conspiratorial explanation of events. In late 1790 the deputy Gaultier had reflected on recent predictions of insurrections that had never in fact materialized: "I have never really placed any credence in them," he wrote, "and you have seen that such beliefs were totally unfounded. Nothing can more surely arouse fears among the common people than false announcements [of conspiracies]." But now almost everyone seemed to slip into a paranoid mode. Not only in their speeches but in letters home to friends and constituents, they spoke of insidious counterrevolutionary plots and money distributed by foreign powers: "Paris has been influenced by a horde of paid foreign agents"; "Prussian and English gold has been widely circulated in the capital to corrupt the less Enlightened segment of the common people." Some moderates even convinced themselves that their more radical opponents in the Assembly—Robespierre, Pétion, and others—were in the pay of such agents.[4]

Although spies were undoubtedly present in Paris, no reliable evidence has been found for the summer of 1791 linking foreign emissaries to Republican agitation. Inevitably, a whole segment of the Parisian population fiercely opposed both the actions and the interpretations of the National Assembly. Marie-Jeanne Roland and her husband, who secretly sheltered Kéralio and Robert from the police, were incensed and frustrated by the turn of events. Every technique possible, she wrote, had been mobilized in a general "system of persecution against good patriots" to blacken their reputations, including "fallacious tracts, *agents provocateurs,* every kind of prejudice, and fabricated testimony." The American William Short was also profoundly shocked: "the true principles of liberty," he wrote to Jefferson, "are avowedly violated every day under the long known pretext of public good." "No true act of habeas corpus existing . . . there is difficulty in extracting an innocent person from prison."[5] Many of the republicans became convinced, in turn, that their opponents in the Assembly were controlled by aristocrats or foreign governments.

Entire neighborhoods in Paris were now polarized by the affair, divided between those who sympathized with the Champ de Mars demonstrators and those who supported the repression. In Saint-Marcel, for example, individuals who served in national guard units known to have fired on the July 17 petitioners were spat upon or attacked, and threats were made against their houses. The two principal leaders of Paris, Mayor Bailly and General Lafayette, were praised by large segments of the citizenry. But for others "they have become the object of an extremely violent hatred."[6] The confrontation was dramatically illustrated by the terrible rift dividing the

Paris Jacobin Club. In the midst of the crisis nearly all the deputies sitting in the club had walked out of the meeting, claiming that the society was now under the thumb of unruly outsiders who wanted to depose the king. Only a handful of representatives, including Pétion and Robespierre, initially remained with the faithful. Little by little, in the course of the summer about sixty radicals from the Assembly returned to the society. But a larger group of dissidents, led primarily by Barnave and the Lameth brothers, created a rival club in the abandoned Feuillant convent just across the street from the Jacobins. They rejected all efforts to arrange a reconciliation. For the next several months the two clubs, Jacobins and Feuillants, faced off in increasingly bitter competition, vying for power and influence, not only in Paris but across the nation. Many of the electoral assemblies for the new legislature, unfolding during the summer in towns throughout the realm, were marked by rivalries between local supporters of the Jacobins or Feuillants.[7]

The bright days of the early Revolution, when patriots felt confident that a new age of happiness and national unity was within their grasp, now seemed only a distant memory. In the wake of the king's flight and the ensuing republican movement, Paris was swept by a climate of suspicion and hatred. Men and women who had once thought they shared common goals now accused each other of treacherous links with counterrevolutionaries or foreign powers. Members of the two rival clubs were afraid to be seen in public with those of the opposing faction, even with individuals who had once been close friends. Rabaut Saint-Etienne, a Protestant pastor from southern France and a key member of the Constitutional Committee, was overwhelmed with frustration to see himself accused of complicity with the king—or with the English or with the Austrians. Like many of his colleagues, he felt besieged and attacked by both the right and the left: by "factional" radicals on the one side and "hypocritical friends of Louis XVI and false zealots of religion" on the other—as Gaultier put it. Theodore Vernier felt as though "a sword is now suspended over our heads." Under such conditions, the deputies' exhaustion and lassitude grew worse than ever. "No one could even describe our impatience to be finished." "The great majority of the deputies," lamented Bouchette to a friend in Flanders, "think only of the moment they can leave. Our life here is wretched. If it doesn't finish soon, we will no longer be able to hold up."[8]

King Again

Sensing a growing public impatience with the length of time they had spent drafting a constitution—now well over two years—the deputies pressed forward to finish their work as soon as possible. The powerful Constitutional Committee and an associated Committee on Revisions had been at work for months, sorting through the great mass of decrees passed haphazardly since the beginning of the Revolution, attempting to decide which measures were truly "constitutional" and which were merely "legislation." Yet the whole process was prolonged for several weeks by the terrible factional feuds within the Assembly. The Feuillant group, which dominated the two committees, had come to believe that the danger from the republicans was far greater than any potential threat from the monarchy. Since late June, Barnave, Duport, and the Lameth brothers had reinitiated secret negotiations with the king. During a moment alone with the queen, while he accompanied the royal family on their return from Varennes, Barnave had proposed a deal. He and his friends promised to do everything in their power to preserve the monarchy and to strengthen the king's authority. In return, they asked only that Louis accept the constitution and obtain recognition of the new French government from the Austrian empire.[9]

But as the Feuillants tried to push through changes in the constitution, reinforcing the power of the king and limiting democracy, they were strongly opposed at every step by Pétion and Robespierre and the Jacobin group. And the Jacobins now found unexpected allies. A whole segment of the unaligned center of the Assembly began to suspect the motives of Barnave and his friends. Thibaudeau, the moderate judge from Poitou, was convinced that the Feuillant leaders wanted only to make themselves ministers under the new government: "We have grown suspicious of these men who once passed as such firm patriots but whom we now know to be ambitious intriguers." Others were stunned that individuals who had previously seemed so strongly democratic had abruptly reversed their position.[10] In the end, the two factions and their allies battled to a draw, and only a small number of changes were made to the constitution as originally voted.

At last, on September 3, utterly exhausted by their struggles, the representatives reached a final agreement, and the constitution was declared complete. About nine that evening a delegation of more than two hundred deputies, marching by torchlight and accompanied by national guardsmen on foot and on horseback, delivered the document to the king at the Tuileries palace. Louis met them in his great council hall with his ministers beside him and announced that he was ready to examine the constitution. Everyone realized that if Louis rejected it, the Assembly would have to remove him from the throne and deal with all the problems of a regency in the name of the young dauphin, the designated successor. "Now we will learn," wrote Bouchette, "if the king will be the friend or the enemy of the nation. Everything hangs on his decision."[11]

As the deputies waited and as tensions continued to build, Louis carefully read the text and considered his options. He was well aware that more than two hundred noble and clerical deputies, deputies who had boycotted all debates in the Assembly since late June, had already rejected the document. But finally, on September 13, he announced that he would indeed accept the constitution. The next day he appeared before the Assembly to affix his signature and pronounce his oath of adherence. He also issued a statement explaining his position, a statement actually written by one of his ministers but signed by Louis as though it represented his own words. In it he attempted once again to explain the flight to Varennes. Entirely ignoring his declaration of June 21—which he *had* written himself—he claimed that he had only wanted to escape from the factions and violence of Paris: "I desired to isolate myself," he said, "from all the conflicting parties and determine which position truly represented the will of the nation." He admitted that he was still not convinced that the new government would have "all the energy necessary to control and unify the diverse parts of so vast a nation as France." Nevertheless, he announced his willingness to give it a try: "I consider that experience alone will judge whether it can work." And he took an oath to do everything in his power to enforce the constitution: "I will accept it," he promised, "and I will ensure that it is executed."[12]

At the same time—whether through his own initiative or through the urgings of his ministers—the king proposed a general amnesty for all those convicted or indicted for actions related to the Revolution. "To extinguish the hatreds, to ease all the troubles invariably created by a revolution of this kind, let us agree to forget the past." By acclamation, the Assembly immediately approved the king's proposal. And throughout the country, jail doors were opened to political prisoners of every stripe, both those awaiting trial and those already convicted. Republican radicals, counterrevolutionary nobles, refractory priests, as well as those implicated in the king's flight—all were immediately granted their freedom. For the first time in almost three months, the duke de Choiseul, Goguelat, and Damas, key players in the "sublime conspiracy" to rescue the king, were allowed to leave their prison cells.[13] Soon thereafter all three departed to join the emigrant armies across the Rhine.

Louis, too, was granted freedom of action, to take up again his functions as "chief executive" of the constitutional monarchy. For many weeks the royal couple had been prisoners in their palace. Guarded day and night, strictly limited in the number of people they were permitted to meet, they were forbidden even to close the doors of their chambers except to dress. Foreign ambassadors had been allowed no contact with the king, but only with the minister of foreign affairs. Yet now the monarch was given leave to resume a "normal" life and to move freely within the capital. He was present at several of the festivities in the weeklong celebration of the completion of the constitution—band concerts, dances, fireworks and nighttime illuminations. As he traveled about the city, according to some reports, he was met with cheers and the cry he so loved of "Long live the king." About the same time, the Assembly voted to reinsert the word *king* into the formal oath of allegiance that all officials and military officers were required to pronounce.[14] At the end of September, with the "executive" in place again, the National Constituent Assembly formally retired. After two years and three months of existence, it handed over its power to an entirely new group of deputies, the recently elected members of the Legislative Assembly. In theory at least, the Revolution was over. In theory at least, the king's flight had been forgiven and forgotten.

But could it really be forgotten? Louis had now solemnly sworn to protect the constitution, yet only a few weeks earlier he had unilaterally annulled a previous oath to the same constitution. What reason was there to think that he would not repeat the maneuver? Like French men and women everywhere, the representatives agonized over this question. Many now believed, hoped to believe, that the king had at last changed his ways and had sincerely accepted to abide by the rules of the game. According to the Breton deputy Legendre, the Assembly "is now persuaded that the king, enlightened by the school of hard experience, will freely accept and cherish the constitution." His colleague Vernier agreed: "After much reflection, we continue to think that the king is quite sincere." But not all deputies shared this optimistic view. Thibaudeau was haunted by the evil influence of the aristocrats who again seemed to surround the monarch: "'Go ahead and accept the constitution,' they have told him. 'And then, when times have changed, you can say that you were forced to do so and had no choice.'" Faulcon, too, brooded that the monarch "may have taken yet another false oath, in swearing a commitment he has no intention of keeping." The sardonic abbé Lindet arrived at much the same conclusion: "The king has sworn to uphold the constitution. He will keep his oath only insofar as it is convenient."[15] The deputies could easily have appreciated a caricature of the king widely circulating in the weeks that followed. Louis was represented Janus-like, with two heads. One head,

The Janus King. At one and the same time the king promises to uphold the constitution and—with his crown slipping off—to destroy the constitution.

looking approvingly toward a deputy, proclaimed: "I will uphold the constitution." The other, contemplating an émigré priest, announced: "I will destroy the constitution."

Such suspicions were only too well founded. Despite all their assurances to the contrary, both the king and the queen were as duplicitous after their attempted flight as they had been before. They rapidly resumed a secret correspondence with the crowned heads of Europe, disavowing in private all their public statements of support for the constitution. Marie-Antoinette's actions in this regard were particularly noteworthy. Whether the queen ever took seriously her discussions with Barnave during the return from Varennes is difficult to say. Over the following weeks, she continued her clandestine meetings with the young deputy from Grenoble. Using all the wiles of the practiced courtier, she led him along with fine affirmations of her frankness and honesty and her deep appreciation of his sympathy for her cause. But again and again she smuggled out letters written in code—to Fersen or the Austrian ambassador or her older brother the emperor—letters in which she repudiated everything she had said to Barnave. She raged against the "insults" committed toward the royal family after the attempted flight, denouncing the deputies as "brutes," "rogues," and "madmen." She condemned the whole constitution as "totally impractical and absurd."[16]

And no less than the queen, the king continued to pursue a double game. Only a few weeks after his abortive flight, Louis managed to slip out a note written in his own hand to the Austrian emperor. He regretted, he said, that he had been unable to "recover his liberty" on June 21 and to "join with those French who truly desire the best interests of their country." He continued to feel himself a prisoner with no control over his fate, and he wanted his brother-in-law to know this fact. And for the first time, he urged the emperor to "come to the aid of the king and the kingdom of France."[17] The strong implication was that he hoped for military intervention. By September, plagued perhaps with the old vacillation in decision-making, he may have modified his position somewhat. In a secret letter to his two brothers in exile, he argued that the best policy was to wait and allow the Revolutionary government to collapse from its own absurdities. He exhorted the two princes not to foment a war, fearing the consequences for the country that such an act might involve. But he also announced his conviction that the very idea of the "Rights of Man" was "utterly insane." Even though some commoners now "hope to rise above the station where nature has placed them," he still believed that the link between himself and the nobility was "the oldest and most beautiful jewel in my crown."[18]

In any case, by December 1791 the king appears to have again reversed course. In a letter to his "foreign minister" in exile, the baron de Breteuil, he recommended the creation of "a Congress of the principal powers of Europe, supported by armed forces." This would be the best means, he believed, of "reestablishing a more desirable situation and ensuring that the evils which beset us do not spread to the other states of Europe." Now, apparently, he had quite set aside his moral scruples against war. He seemed to be pushing for direct intervention by the great powers to alter the constitution he had sworn to defend.[19]

SUCH WAS THE SITUATION at the beginning of 1792. In another time and another place, Louis XVI might have finished out his reign in peace. He might even have been judged by posterity as a better-than-average monarch. He undoubtedly desired the best for his people. Prodded by a fiscal crisis of unprecedented proportions, and in his own uncertain and inconsistent manner, he had attempted sweeping reforms in his government. "Never has a king done so much for a nation," he had proclaimed in all sincerity before the National Assembly on June 23, 1789. But by the time he gave this speech his vision of reforms and that of the patriots to whom he spoke had already sharply diverged. Indeed, it was only through wishful thinking on the part of the patriots and deception on the part of the monarch that the myth of the "citizen king" had survived so long. Now, with the pressure of events and under the influence of his queen, Louis had fallen back on the values he had been taught since childhood, values that included his own God-given right to rule and the hierarchical and fundamentally unequal nature of society. It was a vision that set him on a collision course with the men and women of the Revolution.

The Terror and Beyond

The months and years that followed in the French Revolution would not be kind to France or to many of the individuals encountered in this story. The constitution, which the men of 1789 had struggled more than two years to perfect, and which they hoped would "serve as a model for all nations of the world," would survive only eleven months.[20] The new Legislative Assembly, created by that constitution, was deeply torn from the beginning by bitter struggles between Jacobins and Feuillants. Even more than the first group of deputies, the "Legislators" were haunted by suspicions of betrayal on the part of the king, especially after Louis used his veto powers to block decrees against émigré nobles and refractory clergymen. Rumors continued to circulate that a secret "Austrian Committee," organized around the queen, was undermining the new regime from within—rumors that were in fact not far from wrong.[21] Such fears were reinforced by the joint agreement signed in August 1791 in the German castle of Pillnitz. Here the queen's brother Leopold—reacting perhaps in part to Louis' urgent plea—had urged all European powers to use armed force to "restore" the French monarchy. Fearful of conspiracies hatched by foreign powers in secret alliance with the French court, and spurred by the rhetoric of Jacques Brissot and others, who pushed for a great crusade to spread the ideals of the Revolution throughout Europe, the deputies declared war on Austria in April 1792. Soon they found themselves involved in a conflict with Prussia as well. The Legislative Assembly thus launched the nation into the very war that their predecessors had so hoped to avoid.

Initially the war went badly for the French. By the summer of 1792, the invasion everyone feared at the time of Varennes had become a reality. The Prussian and Austrian armies broke through France's barrier fortresses, capturing Verdun and Varennes itself and beginning a slow, methodical march toward Paris. Faced with the approach of the German armies and convinced more than ever of the king's treachery, the Parisians rose up in August of that year in a veritable second revolution. Following ideas first promoted by republicans in July 1791 and urged on by many of the same men and women who had participated in that movement, Parisians and national guardsmen from the provinces led a general insurrection against the monarchy. On August 10 Louis and his family were forced to evacuate the Tuileries palace, which was stormed by the insurgents in a bloody confrontation that left close to a thousand people dead in the heart of the city. This second revolution brought a new surge of democracy, with virtually all French men, regardless of wealth, now granted the right to vote and hold office. Six weeks later a hastily assembled National Convention officially deposed the king, and on September 21, 1792, it created the first French Republic.

Fortunately for the new republic, the French armies managed to pull themselves together. Building on the nationalist fervor and self-confidence revealed at the time of the king's flight, they halted the Prussians at the battle of Valmy, only a few miles from Sainte-Menehould, where Drouet had first recognized the king. Eventually those same armies would advance beyond the French frontiers to invade and "liberate" whole areas of western Europe. But during the following years, the nation would be gripped by periods of obsessive suspicion, fratricidal infighting, and near anarchy. With civil wars and peasant uprisings breaking out over large areas of the country, with most of Europe arrayed in battle against the French, with sans-culottes radicals pushing for better economic conditions and revenge against their enemies, the republican government instituted a repression vastly greater than that of 1791. Before the storm had ended some eighteen thousand men and women of every social group would be judicially executed, and many tens of thousands more would be killed in civil wars and unofficial reprisals.

Of all the executions, none would be more dramatic and consequential than that of Louis XVI himself. In the last weeks of 1792, after several months of imprisonment, the king was placed on trial before the Convention. Throughout the proceedings he and his lawyers insisted that the constitution of 1791 guaranteed him immunity from prosecution and that before the constitution was signed there had been no formal laws regulating his actions. He continued to dismiss the flight to Varennes as a mere "trip." And he eloquently rejected any suggestion that he was responsible for the shedding of French blood. "The multiple proofs that I have given at all times of my love for the people" should be clear to all. "My conscience reproaches me for nothing." But shortly before the trial began, the revolutionaries had uncovered a secret safe, hidden behind the woodwork of the Tuileries palace, containing a cache of the king's private papers. Many of the documents were written in Louis' own hand, and they provided massive evidence of the king's past deception and deceit, his efforts to oppose and obstruct the Revolution, and his collusion with certain counterrevolutionaries.[22] Most of the formal accusations against the king were directly based on these documents. The single longest article of the indictment concerned Louis' attempted flight, his expenditure of public funds to carry out this plan, and his denunciation of the constitution in the statement he left behind on his desk.[23] After prolonged debate, the Convention voted almost unanimously that the king was guilty of "conspiracy against liberty and the security of the state." Soon thereafter, and by a far closer margin, he was sentenced to death. On January 21, 1793, before tens of thousands of Parisians solemnly attending in the Place de la Révolution—the future Place de la Concorde— Louis XVI went bravely to the guillotine. He protested his innocence to the last.

By 1795 only two of the six passengers in the berline who had fled from Paris on that midsummer's night in 1791 would still be alive. Marie-Antoinette, whose treasonous activities had been even more flagrant than those of her husband (she had even smuggled out the French war plans to the Austrians), followed Louis to the scaffold in October of the same year. The king's sister, Elizabeth, guilty of little beyond her Bourbon name and her loyalty to her brother, was decapitated in May 1794. A little over a year later, the young dauphin, whom the royalists insisted on calling Louis XVII, succumbed to sickness in prison. His older sister might have fallen to a similar fate, but in one of the great ironies of the whole episode, she was liberated in 1796 in a prisoner exchange for Jean-Baptiste Drouet. The man who had played a central role in halting the king's flight—and who, as a member of the Convention, had voted for Louis' death—had been captured by the Austrians two years earlier while on mission with the French army. After his return to Paris and an amazing series of adventures, in and out of France, in and out of prison and politics, Drouet married and assumed a new identity in another provincial town. He died there peacefully in 1824.[24]

But in general, the principal patriot figures in our story did not fare well. Neither of the two deputies who accompanied the royal family back to Paris survived the Revolution. After the failure of the Feuillant party and his retirement to his home province, Barnave was arrested and executed for "royalism" in late 1793. Pétion, who had served for a time as mayor of Paris, eventually broke with his friend Robespierre, fled the Convention, and committed suicide while in hiding in southern France. The philosopher and academician Jean-Sylvain Bailly withdrew from politics in late 1791. But he, too, was arrested and sentenced to death for his part in the shootings of July 17, executed at the very Champ de Mars where the event had taken place. Rabaut Saint-Etienne and Condorcet, Brissot and Marie-Jeanne Roland, Danton and Robespierre were also led to the guillotine, along with many of the leaders of the major Revolutionary factions. General Lafayette survived, but only after languishing for five years in an Austrian prison, where he shared captivity with his friend Latour-Maubourg and his onetime political rival Alexandre Lameth. Monsieur Sauce, the Varennes grocer who had arrested the king and welcomed him to his upstairs apartment, also lived on through the Revolution. But his life was marred by unhappiness. Execrated by the royalists as an archvillain, he was also suspected by the Revolutionaries for monarchist sympathies. After fleeing for his life and losing his first wife during the Prussian invasion, he moved away from his hometown, dying in obscurity in 1825.[25]

For the most part, the royalist conspirators of 1791 did far better than their patriot opponents. After their release from prison through the general amnesty of September, Choiseul, Goguelat, Damas, and the three bodyguards soon joined General Bouillé and his sons in exile. All but the elder Bouillé survived both the Revolution and the Napoleonic period, to reenter France after 1814, honored as heroes by the conservative Restoration government. Axel von Fersen also survived the Revolution. With singular audacity, he had slipped into Paris in February 1792 from his exile in Brussels, visiting the queen one last time at the Tuileries palace. Eighteen months later, crushed by the news of Marie's execution, he returned to Sweden. "If only I had been able to die at her side!" he wrote to his sister in despair. He never married and continued to refer to the queen with great feeling even as he rose to a position of eminence in the Swedish court.[26] He was massacred during a popular uprising in Stockholm on June 20, 1810. It was nineteen years to the day since he had launched the great escape that came so close to changing the destiny of France.

Conclusion:
The Power of an Event

DID THEY DESERVE THEIR FATE, these men and women, celebrated or humble, commoner or king, almost all of whom had begun the year 1789 with such firm hopes for a better future? For more than two hundred years historians have struggled with the problem of violence and terror in the French Revolution. Was there something in the nature of the social situation in France or even in the ideas and political culture on the eve of the Revolution that made the slide into violence inevitable? Was there a necessary link between the inception of the Revolution and the Reign of Terror, between the National Assembly and the Committee of Public Safety, between the Bastille and the guillotine?

The story of the king's flight cautions us against making such simple linear connections. It serves to remind us of the contingent, unpredictable character of the Revolution—and perhaps of every major historical movement. What might have happened in the history of France, in the history of Europe, if events had taken only a slightly different course, and Louis and his family had reached Montmédy and subsequently taken refuge across the border with the Austrian army? In fact, during those two days in June when everyone believed that Louis was gone for good and that war was imminent, there had been an extraordinary surge of unity in the Assembly, in Paris, and throughout the nation. Might that harmony have been sustained if the king had not returned and war had broken out? Might the French have moved immediately toward a republic—as even moderates like Lafayette and Dupont de Nemours were suggesting on June 21? Might the Terror have been avoided or at least greatly attenuated? And what of that other parallel universe—less likely, to be sure—in which Louis resisted the influence of the queen and never fled Paris at all; in which he adapted himself to the role of citizen king that most of the French so ardently desired? Might France have then evolved peacefully toward genuine democracy—following more closely the path of events in the United States? The solution to this string of "what-ifs" is, of course, imponderable and impossible to resolve. Yet such reflections underscore the potential impact on the Revolution and on history of certain critical events.

The liberal regime initiated by the French in 1789, so close in many respects to the American system just under construction across the Atlantic, was not necessarily doomed to failure. There can be no doubt that on the eve of the king's flight the leaders of the National Assembly confronted an array of extremely difficult problems and sources of instability. Some of these problems were clearly of their own making. The deputies' decision to reform the Catholic church and to compel much of the clergy to swear a loyalty oath had brought deep unhappiness to whole segments of the French clerical and lay population. Other difficulties seemed to arise out of the nature of the Revolutionary process itself. No development was more typical in France after 1789 than a progressive questioning of authority, a questioning that quickly penetrated many levels of society. In the army, in the national guard, in the guilds, in the presence of the tax collector, within the civic culture of the cities, almost everywhere men and women began refusing to follow the rules established by either old regime or new, often with extremely disruptive results. At the same time, the very act of transforming society had aroused opposition among those whose vested interests and social positions had come under attack. By the spring of 1791, intransigent nobles and aristocratic bishops living in self-imposed exile across the Rhine were already threatening to reimpose the Old Regime through violence and the force of arms.

Yet the leaders of the Assembly were well aware of these problems. Although they would never have considered reestablishing the rights of nobles or rescinding the church reforms, they had made a great effort to promote toleration, establishing provisions for those who chose not to accept the religious reforms, and attempting to handle disputes with nobles and refractories in an orderly fashion through the regular court system. The Assembly also set out as rapidly as possible to establish a whole new set of administrative and judicial structures. By June of 1791 most of these structures were already in place and functioning, and it could be argued that they substantially reduced—though by no means eliminated—political and social unrest in the provinces and restrained the decline in civil obedience. Moreover, the Assembly could continue to draw on deep reserves of support for the new regime from common men and women, not only in Paris but in communities large and small throughout the nation. The reaction of the citizens of Varennes to the crisis of June was a case in point.

In the spring of 1791 the deputies had been hopeful that with the completion of the constitution and the installation of a permanent new regime, the Revolutionary period would come to an end. And it is not impossible that the constitutional monarchy might have worked and eventually returned some measure of stability to the nation; it is not impossible that the period of state-sponsored violence and terror might have been avoided, if only the monarch himself, the central personage in the new system, had given his wholehearted support. At the beginning of June the majority of the French did think this was possible. The majority—especially outside Paris—continued to believe that their "citizen king" endorsed the Revolution. They continued to imagine Louis as a central father figure around whom the sovereign nation might rally.

But in opting to flee from Paris at a critical moment, when the constitution was almost complete, and in repudiating his solemn oath to uphold the Revolution, the king greatly contributed to the destabilization of the state and the society. In the short term, his action exerted a deeply traumatic effect on the whole population. A great wave of emotion swept across the country, emotions that ranged from crippling anxiety to outbursts of violence to chain-reaction panics over imagined invasions. Rapidly thereafter patriots took hold of themselves and organized as best they could for the war that they all assumed to be inevitable. But the king's flight also initiated a sweeping reconceptualization of the political nation. Within days after the news had been received, everyone realized that the king had not been kidnapped, that he had fled of his own volition. For a great many people the shock was brutal. They had imagined the monarch as a good father, and now they experienced a profound sense of desertion and betrayal. In language that was often exceptionally harsh and angry, Louis was denounced as a liar, a coward, a traitor, a despot. The reaction was particularly strong in Paris, where the Cordeliers Club and the network of fraternal societies quickly launched a popular movement to depose the king and abolish the monarchy. The succession of petitions, marches, and street demonstrations constituted a signal moment in the history of popular Parisian radicalism and the emergence of the sans-culottes as a political force. But in many other areas of the country as well, during that three-week period of uncertainty when the National Assembly chose not to make a public judgment, a minority of people—far more than historians have realized—reflected seriously on the possibility of ousting the present king, even on the possibility of creating a republic.

The king's flight also enormously reinforced the arguments of all those who held to a conspiratorial view of the world. As the National Assembly delved into the affair, it became patently clear that a comprehensive plot had been afoot for months, involving numerous participants in Paris, in the army, and among the émigrés in Germany; entailing, as well, a pattern of boldfaced deceit on the part of Louis himself. Never, since the Revolution began, had there been more extensive proof of the reality of grand conspiracy at the highest levels. Almost everywhere nobles and refractory priests, already suspected before the crisis, now became the objects of extreme mistrust. The popular suspicions were intensified by the new waves of emigration as noblemen in large numbers, inspired by the king's attempted flight, crossed the frontiers and joined counterrevolutionary armies.

Far more than ever before, the Revolutionary leaders internalized this "paranoid" perspective. In Paris members of the Feuillant faction came to suspect not only the refractory priests and the émigré nobles, but also those intellectuals and popular groups who were pushing for greater democracy. Wielding the logic of expediency, the need to save the Revolution at all cost from the enemies—real or imagined—who now seemed to threaten it, patriot leaders readily violated the very laws and the "rights of man" that they themselves had only just proclaimed. For the first time, they crossed the threshold of state-sponsored violence, vigorously promoting the armed repression of the demonstration at the Champ de Mars. Thereafter, in both Paris and the provinces, whole categories of citizens were rounded up, without any attempt to determine individual guilt or responsibility. Freedom of the press, freedom of assembly, habeas corpus, judicial due process—rights guaranteed in the constitution—were all set aside in the name of the greater end of preserving the Revolutionary state. In this sense, the weeks following the flight to Varennes marked an anticipation, a prefiguration of both the psychology and the procedures of the Terror.

Louis' attempt to escape the Revolution did not in itself "cause" the great expansion of state-sponsored violence in 1793–94. In the summer of 1791 there were as yet no Committee of Public Safety, no Revolutionary tribunal, no guillotine. Only a small number of people lost their lives during the entire crisis. And the war that everyone had feared did not in fact begin so soon. By the end of August, the Assembly was self-consciously attempting to end the state of emergency and return to a rule of law. Yet this single event, the flight to Varennes, with all its ramifications and reverberations, profoundly influenced the social and political climate of France. For better or for worse, it helped set the nation on a new and perilous trajectory toward the future.

Abbreviations

Notes

Index

Abbreviations

AC	Archives communales of
AD	Archives départementales of
AHRF	*Annales historiques de la Révolution française*
AM	Archives municipales of
AN	Archives Nationales, Paris
AP	*Archives parlementaires de 1787 à 1860, recueil complet des débats législatifs et politiques des chambres françaises. Première série (1787–1799),* ed. Jérôme Mavidal et al., 82 vols. (Paris, 1867–1913)
BM	Bibliothèque municipale of
BN	Bibliothèque Nationale de France, Paris
RF	*Révolution française*

Notes

Full documentation of sources cited in the Notes is provided in the Bibliography.

Prologue

1. Antoine-François Delandine, *Mémorial historique des Etats généraux*, 5 vols. (n.p., 1789), 3: 4.

1. Sire, You May Not Pass

1. Aimond, *Histoire de Varennes;* and Beauvalet-Boutouyrie.
2. Unless otherwise noted, the account that follows is taken from the minutes of the municipality of Varennes on June 23 and June 27, 1791, as reprinted in Fournel, 310–329; from the account of Jean-Baptiste Drouet in *AP* 27: 508–509; and from Aimond, *Enigme* and *Histoire de Varennes*. The last two works, by an outstanding local historian, relied on documents in the archives of Varennes destroyed in 1914, and on local oral and written testimonies now apparently lost.
3. Fournel, 311.
4. Fournel, 322; Fischbach, 91.
5. For this and the following paragraphs, see especially Aimond, *Histoire de Varennes*, 288–313.
6. AD Meuse, L 2144.
7. Aimond, *Histoire de Varennes*, 292–293.
8. Ibid.
9. Ibid., 293; AD Meuse, L 1266.
10. Aimond, *Histoire de Varennes*, 298–299.
11. Aimond, *Enigme*, 38–39; Aimond, *Histoire de Varennes*, 308–310; Aimond, *Histoire religieuse*, 112, 192; Boutier and Boutry.

12. Aimond, *Histoire de Varennes,* 304–308; Tackett, *Religion, Revolution, and Regional Culture,* 343.

13. Aimond, *Enigme,* 42–43; Aimond, *Histoire de Varennes,* 301–302.

14. For this and the following paragraph: Aimond, *Enigme,* 31, 44–45, 111; Aimond, *Histoire de Varennes,* 299–300, 315–316.

15. *AP* 27: 544.

16. Aimond, *Enigme,* 39–41, 111; letter from Sauce, July 21, 1791, AD Ardennes, L 78.

17. Raigecourt, 187–195; Aimond, *Enigme,* 126.

18. Choiseul-Stainville, 90–92; Damas, 230–232.

19. Fournel, 321.

20. Fournel, 323; *AP* 27: 508.

21. Letter from Sauce, July 21, 1791, AD Ardennes, L 78.

22. Lesort, 10–11; Pionnier, 108.

23. AN D XXIX bis 36 (1), dos. 370.

24. Lesort, 10–12, 14–15; Bimbenet, 187–193, 235–238; Fournel, 335; Pionnier, 108; AD Marne, 1 L 329; AD Aisne, L 605; AD Haute-Marne, L 274.

25. Aimond, *Histoire de Varennes,* 326; Aimond, *Enigme,* 149–152; Fournel, 324.

26. Fournel, 311–312, 325.

27. Aimond, *Histoire de Varennes,* 325; Aimond, *Enigme,* 143.

28. Damas, 237.

29. *AP* 27: 358.

30. Choiseul-Stainville, 101; Tourzel, 201; Aimond, *Enigme,* 154–156.

31. AN D XXIX bis 38, dos. 388.

32. *AP* 29: 532–534; Lenôtre, passim.

2. The King of the French

1. Campan, 113.

2. Bachaumont, 104.

3. Hardman and Price, 243–244, 297.

4. Nicolardot, 112–113.

5. Hardman and Price, 294; Nicolardot, 207; Campan, 113; Padover, 16–17; Saint-Priest, 2: 49–50, 62–63.

6. Nicolardot, 117, 120, 151–160, 189–214, 233.

7. Falloux, passim; Padover, 15–16; Hardman, 20.

8. Falloux, 1, 7, 27, 35; Nicolardot, 49–50; Hardman and Price, 167.

9. Bachaumont, 57–59; Padover, 128–129; Lever, 184–195.

10. Falloux, 98.

11. Tourzel, 103; Campan, 114.

12. Zweig, 4–6, 82–83; Girault de Coursac and Girault de Coursac, 21–22; Saint-Priest, 2: 62; Hardman, 24.

13. Bachaumont, 79; Zweig, 21–24; Padover, 33–36, 96–104.

14. Nicolardot, 62; Arneth, 4–18; Padover, 96–104.

15. Bachaumont, 155; Arneth, 20–21; Zweig, 136–137.

16. Bachaumont, 126.

17. Bachaumont, 67, 143, 165, 226; Saint-Priest, 2: 65–66; Zweig, 34–38, 187, and chap. 10; Hunt, *Family Romance,* chap. 4.

18. Wick, passim.

19. Saint-Priest, 2: 67, 72, 80, 84, 90, 92; Zweig, 226–247.

20. Hardman and Price, 263, 288.

21. Nicolardot, 107, 112–13; Padover, 135.

22. Saint-Priest, 2: 48–50; Fersen, 82–83. See also Bachaumont, 36; Padover, 89.

23. Arneth, 2, 38–39, 110; Bachaumont, 226; Padover, 92–95.

24. Campan, 224; Lescure, 270; Saint-Priest, 2: 77, 82–83.

25. Saint-Priest, 2: 88–90.

26. Saint-Priest, 2: 90–91.

27. Mousset, 228.

28. Saint-Priest, 2: 24–25; also Arneth, 126–127; Feuillet de Conches, 2: 46–48; Tourzel, 105, 142.

29. Tourzel, 78, 80, 102; Tackett, *Becoming a Revolutionary,* 297–298.

30. Arneth, 129, 132; Campan, 279.

31. Arneth, 134, 139; Tourzel, 158.

32. Tourzel, 81; Arneth, 126–127, 129; Feuillet de Conches, 2: 41–42; Mousset, 241.

33. *AP* 27: 378–383.

34. For these and other such plans, see Tourzel, 20–21; Saint-Priest, 2: 14, 83, 93; Campan, 267–268, 273–274; Bouillé, 228.

35. *AP* 27: 383; also Feuillet de Conches, 2: 10–11; Tourzel, 160–161; Mousset, 264; Legendre, letter of March 2, 1791.

36. Tourzel, 173–176, 185; Feuillet de Conches, 2: 46–48; Arneth, 155; Campan, 286; *AP* 27: 552–553.

37. *AP* 27: 383; Tourzel, 160–161, 163, 174; Irland de Bazôges, letter of March 4, 1791; Mousset, 249.

38. Fersen, 97, 103–105.

39. Bouillé, 215–216; Bouillé fils, 17–19, 21–22.

40. Fersen, 113.

41. Feuillet de Conches, 2: 38–40; Fersen, 82.

42. E.g., Arneth, 165, 169, 151, 162, 177–179; Tourzel, 176.

43. Louis XVIII, 45–77.

44. Bouillé, 240; Fersen, 128; Bouillé fils, 39; Damas, 207.
45. Bouillé fils, 43; Tourzel, 193; Bimbenet, 36, 51; Choiseul-Stainville, 44.
46. E.g., Bimbenet, 44, 57–62; 65–82; Choiseul-Stainville, 75–77; Weber, 324–325.
47. Choiseul-Stainville, 50, 52; Tourzel, 190–92; Campan, 286–90; Feuillet de Conches, 2: 14, 127–128; Bimbenet, 26, 40–44.
48. *AP* 25: 201, 312–13; Fersen, 87; also Fersen, 108; Tourzel, 179; Arneth, 155; Feuillet de Conches, 2: 48–49.
49. Bouillé, 202, 226–233, 247–249, 215–216; Bouillé fils, 17–19, 21–22, 24–25, 56–59; Heidenstam, 44–45.
50. Bouillé, 219–220, 240, 255; Bouillé fils, 37–39, 44, 87; Fersen, 121.
51. Bouillé fils, 37–39; Fersen, 118, 121; Tourzel, 196.
52. Campan, 282; Fersen, 121; Bouillé, 251; Choiseul-Stainville, 55–56, 58; Bouillé fils, 70–71; Damas, 207.
53. Bouillé, 253; Damas, 205–206 and 208; Choiseul-Stainville, 63; Fersen, 130.
54. Bouillé fils, 72–73; Choiseul-Stainville, 49.
55. Fersen, 136; Bouillé fils, 70–71.
56. Bouillé, 243–246; Bouillé fils, 33–41, 62–63, 80.
57. Fersen, 130; Bouillé, 220–222, 242; Bouillé fils, 64–65; Damas, 203–205; Choiseul-Stainville, 37; Aimond, *Enigme*, 131.
58. Bouillé, 254–255, 252; Fischbach, 205–206.
59. Choiseul-Stainville, 38, 55; Bouillé, 222; Fersen, 101, 109, 128, 132, 136.
60. Fersen, 137; Bouillé fils, 77–79; Bouillé, 254–255; Choiseul-Stainville, 42–43; Damas, 208.
61. Bouillé, 223; Fersen, 110; Choiseul-Stainville, 34, 53, 55–56.
62. Feuillet de Conches, 2: 101–125; Lefebvre, *Recueil de documents*, 274–284; Fersen, 128; Choiseul-Stainville, 34; Bouillé, 223.
63. Bouillé, 200–201; Arneth, 152–154, 171; Feuillet de Conches, 2: 129–130; Campan, 290; Choiseul-Stainville, 53. Bouillé seems to have made preparations for the king's arrival in the Abbey of Orval, just across the frontier; *AP* 27: 558.
64. Arneth, 152–154; Feuillet de Conches, 2: 55–59, 127–128, 63.

3. The King Takes Flight

1. Madame Royale, in Weber, 313–314; AN D XXIX bis 38, dos. 389; Bimbenet, 44.
2. Valory, 257–259; Moustier, 4; Bimbenet, 92–128; Louis XVIII, 40–41.
3. Bimbenet, 28–29, 51, 57–62; Moustier, 6–7.
4. Choiseul-Stainville, 69–74; Aimond, *Enigme*, 56; Lenôtre, 270–276.
5. Bimbenet, 8–11, 65–82.

6. Aimond, *Enigme*, 57; Lafayette, 3: 77; Weber, 325; *Almanach de la ville de Lyon*, xix.

7. Tourzel, 191–192; Weber, 314–316. By some accounts Tourzel was accompanied out of the palace by Malden, or Fersen, or even the queen herself; Lenôtre, 41–42.

8. Choiseul-Stainville, 75–77; Bimbenet, 35–36, 92–103; Tourzel, 192; *AP* 27: 553; Aimond, *Enigme*, 56–57.

9. Tourzel, 193–194; Choiseul-Stainville, 78–79; Aimond, *Enigme*, 58; Bimbenet, 57–62.

10. Bimbenet, 61–62; Choiseul-Stainville, 78–79.

11. Bimbenet, 8–12, 36, 51.

12. Aimond, *Enigme*, 8–9.

13. Valory, 270; Bimbenet, 82–92; *AP* 27: 552–553; Vast, 15; Arbellot and Lepetit, 18.

14. Aimond, *Enigme*, 13. They traveled the 146 miles from Paris to Varennes in about 20.5 hours, or 7.1 miles per hour. With the nineteen relay stops subtracted, the road time was more like 9.2 miles per hour.

15. Fournel, 356; Lacroix, 128; Weber, 316. Others report that the accident was near Chaintrix: Vast, 24–25; Aimond, *Enigme*, 65–66, 74.

16. Tourzel, 193–195; Weber, 315; Moustier, 9–11; Vast, 1; Pétion, 194.

17. Bimbenet, 65–82, 92–103, 115–128; Moustier, 11; Aimond, *Enigme*, 64–65.

18. Aimond, *Enigme*, 64–65, 68–69; Vast, 16–19, 27, 39–41.

19. Weber, 316; Aimond, *Enigme*, 74–76; Vast, 41–43.

20. Vast, 62, 67–69, 72; Aimond, *Enigme*, 76–78; AN D XXIX bis 36 (1), dos. 370.

21. Tourzel, 195–197; Valory, 270; Vast, 97–99; Aimond, *Enigme*, 79.

22. Bouillé, 256–257; Damas, 209, 212–213; Bouillé fils, 79, 86, 122–129; Raigecourt, 187–195; Bimbenet, 238–239; Aimond, *Enigme*, 106–110.

23. Bimbenet, 177–178.

24. Damas, 107, 210, 214, 218; Vast, 175; Aimond, *Enigme*, 96.

25. Bimbenet, 183–185; Lagache, 449–453; Buirette, 546–550; Vast, 101–107; Aimond, *Enigme*, 33, 84–86.

26. Choiseul-Stainville, 80–84; Damas, 233–234; Aimond, *Enigme*, 80–81.

27. Fersen, 138; Choiseul-Stainville, 80–84, 109–110; Damas, 233–234; Bouillé fils, 95–98; Aimond, *Enigme*, 80–81.

28. Damas, 218–221; Bimbenet, 183–185; Raigecourt, 187–195; Aimond, *Enigme*, 108–110.

29. Tourzel, 197; Valory, 270–274; Moustier, 13; Lagache, 451; Fournel, 340–341; Buirette, 547–548; Vast, 107, 111–118; Aimond, *Enigme*, 84–87.

30. Laurent, 248–249.

31. *AP* 27: 508; Buirette, 547–548; Vast, 111–119; Aimond, *Enigme*, 87–91.

32. Bimbenet, 183–185; Lagache, 452–453; AN D XXIX bis 37, dos. 386: report of municipality of Sainte-Menehould, July 28, 1791; Buirette, 547–553.

33. Damas, 221–229; Valory, 276–277; Tourzel, 196; Weber, 316; Bimbenet, 187–193; Lagache, 453–454; Aimond, *Enigme*, 103.

34. Weber, 316.

35. Valory, 258, 279–285; Moustier, 15–18; Weber, 316; *AP* 27: 508–509; Aimond, *Histoire de Varennes*, 317–318.

36. Tourzel, 198.

37. Choiseul-Stainville, 105–108; Damas, 239; Tourzel, 202; Campan, 298–299; AD Ardennes, L 12 and 78; AN D XXIX bis, dos. 385; Fournel, 326; Aimond, *Histoire de Varennes*, 328; Aimond, *Enigme*, 156–159.

38. Bouillé, 241–246; Bouillé fils, 122–135; Bimbenet, 238–239; Planta de Wildenberg, 444–446; Aimond, *Histoire de Varennes*, 328–329; Aimond, *Enigme*, 161–166.

39. Fischbach, 209.

40. Valory, 312; Pétion, 197; Tourzel, 209–210. On the weather: Guittard de Floriban, 64–66.

41. Moustier, 26; Pétion, 191–192; Buirette, 555–556.

42. Tourzel, 203; Aimond, *Enigme*, 167–168; Buirette, 555–556.

43. Buirette, 561–562; Nicolas, 60–61. See also Chapter 6 of this volume.

44. Valory, 295–296; Pétion, 194; Dumas, 1: 497–499; Nicolas, 61–62.

45. Fischbach, 87; Valory, 298–299; Buirette, 556–559; Lefebvre, "Le meurtre du comte de Dampierre," 393–405.

46. AD Marne, 1 L 329: letter of municipality of Neuf-Bellay.

47. Tourzel, 204–205; Valory, 300–306; Nicolas, 60–62; Aimond, *Enigme*, 171–173.

48. Tourzel, 205–206; Gillet, 37–42; Aimond, *Enigme*, 173–175.

49. Dumas, 1: 489–490; Pétion, 192; *AP* 27: 428; Aimond, *Enigme*, 175–176.

50. Dumas, 1: 490–493; Pétion, 193, 201; Tourzel, 206–211; Aimond, *Enigme*, 177–179.

51. Dumas, 1: 500–502; Tourzel, 211; Pétion, 202.

52. Pétion, 202–203; Tourzel, 211; Valory, 312; Roger, 71; Rabaut Saint-Etienne, *Précis*, 248.

53. Valory, 315–323; Moustier, 52; Pétion, 203–204; Dumas, 1: 503; Tourzel, 212–215; *AP* 27: 527–528; Aimond, *Enigme*, 179–180.

54. Bouillé, 220–222, 225–226.

4. Our Good City of Paris

1. Mercier, 34, 108, 328. Much of the following is based on this source.

2. Mercier, 34; Tulard, 33–35, 44–49; Roche, chap. 1; Godechot, 67–70, 83.

3. Thompson, 100–101, 118–119.

4. See esp. Censer, chap. 2.

5. Mercier, 70.

6. Short, 20: 585; Mercier, 402; Andress, 177.

7. Boutier and Boutry, 40.

8. Mathiez, 4–10.

9. See in particular Mathiez; Bourdin; Monnier, 4–6.

10. See esp. Burstin, "Une Révolution à l'oeuvre," parts 2 and 3; and Kaplan, *La fin des corporations,* chaps. 13–15.

11. Burstin, "La loi Le Chapelier"; Andress, 122–135.

12. Burstin, "Une Révolution à l'oeuvre"; Andress, chaps. 2–4; Pisani, 1: 191–199; Tackett, *Religion, Revolution, and Regional Culture,* 354.

13. Godechot, 245–48; Burstin, "La Révolution à l'oeuvre," 287–289, 293–295; Carrot, 1: 41, 69–71.

14. Andress, 110–111; Burstin, "Une Révolution à l'oeuvre," 254; Gower, 82.

15. Miles, 1: 209; Gower, 80; Short, 20: 348; Guittard de Floriban, 45.

16. Gaultier de Biauzat, letter of January 29; *Ami du peuple,* February 14 and March 10 (kindly indicated to me by Jeremy Popkin); also Legendre, letter of February 2; Ruault, 221, 233–234; Vernier, letter of May 1; Colson, 192.

17. *AP* 27: 370–372; Aimond, *Enigme,* 52–53; *L'orateur du peuple,* vol. 6, no. 45 (ca. June 20); *L'ami du peuple,* June 21 (published before the king's flight was known).

18. AN D XXIX bis 38, dos. 389; Bimbenet, 14–15, 17, 35–36, 44.

19. Lacroix, 1–2; Leclercq, 582–583.

20. Leclercq, 581; Faulcon, 421; Thibaudeau, 139–140; Colson, 194; Ferrières, 360.

21. Bimbenet, 14, 35–36; Ruault, 246; Panon Desbassayns, 186; Leclercq, 581.

22. Lacroix, 4; Oelsner, 18; *Chronique de Paris,* no. 173, June 22; *Le babillard,* no. 18, June 22; Leclercq, 585.

23. Mousset, 273; Short, 20: 562; *Le babillard,* no. 18, June 22; Oelsner, 38.

24. Lacroix, 1–2, 5, 11.

25. Lacroix, 3, 14–15, 22, 25, 179; Bourdin, 241; Panon Desbassayns, 186.

26. Lacroix, 1–2, 5, 7, 13, 22, 53, 141–142, 185; Charavay, ix; Burstin, "La Révolution à l'oeuvre," 256–257; Genty, 105; Bourdin, 241–244; *Le patriote français,* no. 683, June 22; Mathiez, 51, 64.

27. Bourdin, 235–237; Guittard de Floriban, 34; Short, 19: 635; Gower, 71; Censer, 111–115.

28. Oelsner, 21.

29. *Chronique de Paris,* no. 173, June 22; *Journal de Perlet,* no. 692, June 28.

30. Leclercq, 672–676; *Chronique de Paris,* no. 173, June 22; Roland, 2: 316; Ruault, 246–247; Dumont, 222.

31. AN D XXIX bis 35, dos. 365; *Le patriote français*, no. 683, June 22; Short, 20: 585; *Chronique de Paris*, no. 173, June 22; Mathiez, 51; Mousset, 273.

32. Oelsner, 21; *Chronique de Paris*, no. 173, June 22.

33. Leclercq, 675–76; Duprat, 146–188; Hunt, *Family Romance*, 50–51.

34. *AP* 27: 24–26; Panon Desbassayns, 188; *Chronique de Paris*, no. 174, June 23; Rabaut Saint-Etienne, "Correspondance," 265; Gaultier de Biauzat, 2: 370–371.

35. Lacroix, 49–50, 100; Burstin, 257–258; Panon Desbassayns, 189; McManners, 2: 122–123.

36. Lindet, 286; *Chronique de Paris*, no. 175, June 24; *AP* 27: 444; Thibaudeau, 150–151.

37. *AP* 27: 448, 453–454; Reinhard, 119–120.

38. *AP* 27: 453–454; Lindet, 286; Faulcon, 433; Thibaudeau, 149–151; Roland, 2: 309; Guittard de Floriban, 65; *Journal de Perlet*, no. 689, June 25; Oelsner, 21–22.

39. Roland, 2: 309.

40. Burstin, "Une révolution à l'oeuvre," 257.

41. Ruault, 248.

42. Aulard, *Histoire politique*, 84–89, 105–111; Mathiez, 34–41; Morris, 2: 168; Hesse, 83–98; Pegg, 435; Louis-Philippe, 16.

43. Roland, 2: 316; Ruault, 246–247; Panon Desbassayns, 186; Oelsner, 21; Lombard-Taradeau, 361; Lindet, 293; Lacroix, 46; *Chronique de Paris*, no. 173, June 22.

44. Roland, 2: 302.

45. *Le patriote français*, no. 683, June 22; Mathiez, 85–86; Pegg, 435–445; Whaley, 35–37; Bourdin, 245–248; Kates, 157–164; Baker, 304–305.

46. Mathiez, 47.

47. Mathiez, 48–50; *Le babillard*, nos. 19 and 21, June 23 and 25; Lacroix, 96–97, 117; Bourdin, 241–242.

48. Guittard de Floriban, 65; Bourdin, 259–260; Mathiez, 51, 53–54, 123–125; *Le babillard*, no. 21, June 25.

49. Mathiez, 87; Roland, 2: 322, 325; Braesch, 193–195.

50. Rudé, 83; Mathiez, 86, 233, 328; *Chronique de Paris*, no. 180, June 29; *Le babillard*, nos. 23 and 25–26, July 5 and 8–9; *Journal de Perlet*, no. 700, July 6; Guittard de Floriban, 68.

51. Mathiez, 86–87; Bourdin, 260.

52. Short, 20: 585; Bourdin, 260; Ruault, 250; Mathiez, 88; Roland, 2: 329; *Chronique de Paris*, no. 197, July 16; Gower, 109.

53. Mathiez, 95, 96–97, 100, 108.

54. Ibid., 109.

55. *Le babillard,* no. 32, July 15; *AP* 27: 589–595; Lacroix, 285; Panon Desbassayns, 201; *Journal de Perlet,* no. 710, July 16.

56. Lacroix, 309–310; *Chronique de Paris,* no. 195, July 14; *Les Révolutions de Paris,* July 13–14, 1791.

57. Lacroix, 324–328, 344–345; Guittard de Floriban, 72; Panon Desbassayns, 201.

58. Ruault, 251; Guittard de Floriban, 72; Gower, 106.

59. Mathiez, 110; Lacroix, 345–348; Roland, 2: 327n.

60. Lacroix, 350; Mathiez, 112–115.

5. The Fathers of the Nation

1. For this and the following paragraph, see Tackett, *Becoming a Revolutionary,* chaps. 1–4.

2. Maupetit, 21 (1905): 213–214; Geoffroy, letter of June 19, 1791; Périsse Du Luc, letter of September 12, 1790; Vernier, letter of December 6, 1790; Tackett, "The Constituent Assembly," 162–169.

3. Campmas, letter of August 24, 1790; Lafayette, 3: 175.

4. Tackett, "The Constituent Assembly," 164; Michon, chap. 8.

5. Basquiat de Mugriet, letter of May 31, 1791.

6. Mousset, 255–256; Feuillet de Conches, 2: 48–49; Gower, 79; Michon, chap. 8.

7. Thibaudeau, 143; Gaultier de Biauzat, 2: 367; *AP* 27: 358; Lombard-Taradeau, 360; Toulongeon, 2: 2n.

8. *AP* 27: 369–372; Maupetit, 22 (1906): 475; Faulcon, 423. See also Carrot, 1: 73.

9. Lafayette, 3: 75–76.

10. *AP* 27: 359, esp. speech by Camus; Faulcon, 429–430; Lévis, 5 (1929): 273.

11. *AP* 27: 410–412; Geoffroy, letter of June 22; Toulongeon, 2: 2n and 8n; Thibaudeau, 146–147; Roland, 2: 307.

12. Thibaudeau, 153; *AP* 27: 359.

13. *AP* 27: 363, 365–366, 369, 386, 521; Gower, 96.

14. *AP* 27: 360, 423.

15. *AP* 27: 478; Faulcon, 422; Maupetit, 22 (1906): 475; Rochambeau, 1: 380; Dumas, 1: 486–487; Geoffroy, letter of June 22; Basquiat de Mugriet, letter of June 24; Thibaudeau, 141.

16. *AP* 27: 394–395, 400.

17. *AP* 27: 362; Faulcon, 427; *AP* 27: 370; Fricaud, letter of June 24; Thibaudeau, 153; Lévis, 5 (1929): 272; Ferrières, 362.

18. *AP* 27: 365, 386; Faulcon, 424.

19. Basquiat de Mugriet, letter of June 24; Fricaud, letter of June 24; Lepoutre,

431, 487; Ménard de La Groye, 395; Durand, letter of June 26; Gantheret, letter of June 24; Faulcon, 440–442; Pétion, 191; Bouchette, 600–601.

20. Lafayette, 3:99; Ferrières, 368; Lindet, 287; Durand, letter of July 3; Lafayette, 3: 100.

21. Ferrières, 361; Gaultier de Biauzat, 2: 370; Rabaut Saint-Etienne, "Correspondance," 265; *AP* 27: 24–26.

22. Legendre, 70–71.

23. Gaultier de Biauzat, 2: 384; Gantheret, undated letter (July 1791); Thibaudeau, 161–162.

24. *AP* 27: 517, 538.

25. *AP* 27: 520–521, 536–543, 617–618.

26. Lindet, 289; *AP* 27: 543–544, 552–553; Lafayette, 3: 95.

27. The Constitutional Committee and the Committees on Research, Reports, Military Affairs, Diplomatic Affairs, Criminal Affairs, and Constitutional Revision: *AP* 32: 545–570. These committees included most of the leaders of the moderates in the Assembly, but relatively few of the radicals.

28. Legendre, letter of July 2; Morris, 2: 211; Roger, 74. The official judicial inquest began only on July 11: Bimbenet, 3.

29. Lindet, 293.

30. *AP* 27: 602–660; Bouillé, 252–253.

31. *AP* 27: 565; AD Aisnes, L 12 and L 78.

32. Irland de Bazôges, letter of June 29; Lévis, 5 (1929): 276; Vaudreuil, letter to his constituency: AN D XXIX bis 36 (1), dos. 368; *AP* 28: 91–98.

33. Walter, 97; Tackett, "Conspiracy Obsession," 704–706.

34. *Les révolutions de France et de Brabant,* no. 82.

35. Aulard, *Jacobins,* 2: 533–538; Bouchette, 599; Lafayette, 3: 84; Gaultier de Biauzat, 2: 369; also Faulcon, 430; and Roland, 2: 304.

36. Aulard, *Jacobins,* 2: 554–626.

37. See *AP* 28: 231–336.

38. This and the following pages are based on the *AP* for July 13–16: 28: 231–247, 255–271, 316–336, 377–378.

39. See *AP* 8: 642.

40. *AP* 28: 245, 258; Arnaud, 241. Vadier had spoken only six times previously.

41. *AP* 28: 326, 362.

42. *AP* 28: 260–261, 317–318.

43. *AP* 28: 330.

44. See Gaultier's speech in Aulard, *Jacobins,* 3: 15.

45. Thibaudeau, 167. Marie-Jeanne Roland thought that about forty deputies had opposed the committees' bill on July 15: Roland, 2: 328.

46. See, for example, Gaultier de Biauzat, 2: 381–382; Basquiat de Mugriet, letters of July 9 and 10; Roger, 75–76; Thibaudeau, 161–162; Dubois, 373–375; Maupetit, 22 (1906): 480–482.

47. Arriveur in Dubois, 373; Faulcon, 443–444.

48. Faulcon, 443–444; Gantheret, undated letter (July 1791); also Durand, letter of July 17.

49. Gantheret, undated letter (July 1791); Durand, letter of July 17; Lindet, 297–298.

50. *Le babillard*, no. 34, July 17; Panon Desbassayns, 202; Ruault, 249. Also *Journal de Perlet*, no. 711, July 17; Roland, 2: 331–332; Morris, 2: 219–220.

51. Mathiez, 116–120; Lacroix, 386–387, 391; Aulard, *Jacobins*, 3: 16; Roland, 2: 331–332; *Chronique de Paris*, no. 197, July 15.

52. Aulard, *Jacobins*, 3: 15–18; Mathiez, 122–128, 340–343; Lacroix, 392, 394–395; Bourdin, 277; Braesch, 142 (1923): 201–202, 143 (1923): 10–13; Roland, 2: 333–334; *Révolutions de Paris*, no. 113.

53. Thibaudeau, 162; Gaultier de Biauzat, 2: 386; Legendre, letters of July 16 and 18; Gouvion to Bailly, July 15: BN Ms. Fr. 11697.

54. *AP*, 28: 363–364, 372; Lacroix, 367.

55. Mathiez, 125–127, 129–130, 344–345; *Le babillard*, no. 35, July 18; Roland, 2: 334.

56. Lacroix, 399; *Le babillard*, no. 35, July 18; Roland, 2: 334.

57. Mathiez, 136–144, 269–270, 345–347; Guittard de Floriban, 73–74; Ruault, 258; *Chronique de Paris*, no. 199, July 17; AN F[7] 3688[1] (Seine).

58. Mathiez, 131–136; Lacroix, 431–432.

59. Braesch, 143 (1923): 36–39; Lacroix, 432; Mathiez, 136–138; Rudé, 90–91.

60. *AP*, 28: 380; Lacroix, 402; Mathiez, 138.

61. *AP*, 28: 399–401.

62. Lacroix, 403–407; *AP*, 28: 399–401; Mathiez, 274, 279–281, 350.

63. Guittard de Floriban, 73–74; Alexandre, 140–141; Ruault, 253–54; *AP* 28: 399–401; Lacroix, 407; Mathiez, 144–148, 274–282.

64. Guittard de Floriban, 74; *AP* 28: 401; Lacroix, 432; Ruault, 253–254; Roland, 2: 337, 339; Carrot, 1: 82; Mathiez, 148, 269–270; Burstin, "Une Révolution à l'oeuvre," 258.

65. Guittard de Floriban, 74.

6. Fear and Repression in the Provinces

1. Lindet, 290.

2. *AP* 27: 359; also AD Marne, 1 L 329.

3. AD Ardennes, L 78; AD Aube, L 315; AD Aisne, L 605; AN D XXIX bis 36 (2), dos. 378.

4. AD Meuse, L 2188*; AD Aisne, L 605; AD Ardennes, L 12; AD Vosges, L 479; Fischbach, 110–111; *AP* 27: 662–663; David, 25.

5. Most of what follows is based on AN C 124–131, AN D XXIX bis 33–38, and a variety of local monographs. See also Reinhard, 81–82, 432; and Arbellot and Lepetit, 71.

6. AN C 126 (2) (Huningues). The news traveled the 312 miles from Paris to Lyon in about fifty-eight hours, or 5.4 miles per hour.

7. AN C 124 (2), dos. 404B (Aumont).

8. For example, the town of Dole: AN D XXIX bis 35, dos. 366.

9. AN C 124 (2), dos. 404B (Auxerre); Gaugain, 1: 239–240; Roux, 443–445.

10. Brégail, 97–98; Baumont, 74; AN D XXIX bis 36 (1), dos. 368 and 370; Bruneau, 160–161.

11. Schneider, 19. See also Wahl, 381–382; AN D XXIX bis 36 (1), dos. 369 (Beauvais); D XXIX bis 35, dos. 361 (Argentan).

12. See Legendre, letter of June 13, 1791; and Bouchette, 632.

13. AN D XXIX bis 35, dos. 366; D XXIX bis 36, dos. 374.

14. AC Saint-Quentin, I D 3; Baumont, 74–75; Lecesne, 1: 160; Fischbach, 67.

15. AN C 126 (2).

16. AN D XXIX bis 36 (2), dos. 378; C 130 (1) (Tours), C 126 (2) (Grèves-de-Tallon); Sol, 2: 82–83.

17. Tackett, *Becoming a Revolutionary*, 147–148, 152–154, 277; Hunt, *Politics, Culture, and Class*, 21, 27; Langlois, 2: 389–393.

18. *AP* 27: 359.

19. AC Mézières, BB 23, deliberations of June 22; AN D XXIX bis 35, dos. 366.

20. Fischbach, 124; Vidal, 1: 204–205, 214; Rouvière, 360–361; AD Gironde, 3 L 10; AN D XXIX bis 35, dos. 366; D XXIX bis 36, dos. 377; F^7 3682^{18} (Morbihan).

21. For example, Biernawski, 146; AN D XXIX bis 36 (2), dos. 373.

22. See the reports of the commissioners Dresch and L'Enfant, sent by the department of Meuse to inspect the frontier fortresses: AD Meuse, L 386.

23. AN C 130 (Sedan); also *AP* 27: 662; AD Meuse, L 386; AD Meurthe-et-Moselle, L 212; AD Ardennes, L 78.

24. See, notably, the fears of Varennes itself: Lesort, 12.

25. Bimbenet, 240–248; also Bouillé, 258; and Bouillé fils, 122–129.

26. AD Meuse, L 385–386 and E Dépôt 407, 1 B 1; Fournel, 336–337; Pionnier, 111–112.

27. AD Meuse, L 385–386; Lesort, 15, 17; AN D XXIX bis 36 (1), dos. 368 (Baudonvilliers).

28. AD Marne, 1 L 329; Buirette, 552–554.

29. AD Marne, 1 L 329; and inquest into the riot, AD Marne, 10 L 220.

30. AD Marne, 1 L 329; AD Haute-Marne, L 274; AD Ardennes, L 78; AD Aube, L 315; AD Aisne, L 605; Pionnier, 110; Fischbach, 113–114.

31. Letter from deputies Le Carlier and L'Eleu, June 25: AD Aisne, L 605.

32. Gower, 104; AD Gironde, 12 L 13; *AP* 27: 686; AN C 127 (1) (Mont-de-Marsans), C 128 (2) (Orthez and Pau), C 129 (2) (Saint-Sever).

33. AN C 128 (2), dos. 433 (Noirmoutier); Biernawski, 148; AN F[7] 3682[18] (Morbihan).

34. Binet, 119–120; Gower, 103; *AP* 27: 663; AN F[7] 3682[18] (Morbihan); Panon Desbassayns, 195; AD Gironde, 12 L 13; AN D XXIX bis 35, dos. 366 (Mayenne).

35. AD Aisne, L 605; AD Meuse, L 385; also the reactions in Troyes and Nancy: AD Aube, L 315; and AD Meurthe-et-Moselle, L 1239.

36. Kaplan, *The Famine Plot Persuasion*, 1–2, 62; Tackett, "Conspiracy Obsession," 695–699.

37. Gauville, 46.

38. See, notably, AN D XXIX bis 37, dos. 382.

39. See esp. AN D XXIX bis 33, dos. 345.

40. AD Aisne, L 604 and L 198; Tackett, *Religion, Revolution, and Regional Culture*, 276–279.

41. AN C 130 (2), dos. 455 (Vienne).

42. Brégail, 97–98; also Millot, 200; and AN D XXIX bis 36 (1), dos. 369 (Beauvais).

43. *AP* 27: 362.

44. For example, Bouvier, 100–101; Gaugain, 2: 239–240; AN D XXIX bis 35, dos. 361 (Argentan).

45. Sol, 2: 80–81; Fischbach, 200–204.

46. AN F[7] 3682[18] (Morbihan); Binet, 116.

47. Pastoors, 1: 91; also Fischbach, 67, 73–74, 121–122; AD Meuse, L 385; AD Ardennes, L 78; Rochambeau, 1: 383; Fougeray Du Coudrey, 111; David, 25.

48. Wahl, 395; David, 25; AN C 125 (2) (Cuxac).

49. For example, deliberations of Sézanne, AD Marne, 1 L 329.

50. See, for example, AN D XXIX bis 35, dos. 365.

51. Dupuy, 200–205; also AN D XXIX bis 36 (1), dos. 367 (Landerneau) and dos. 369–370 (Rochefort).

52. AN D XXIX bis 34, dos. 349 (Cahors).

53. *AP* 8: 273–275, 278–279; 17: 695–696. See also Shapiro, 48–55.

54. Deliberations of June 25, AC Pont-à-Mousson, 1 D 4.

55. AN D XXIX bis 35, dos. 366 (Boiscommun); also D XXIX bis 35, dos. 365 (Longwy); D XXIX bis 38, dos. 389 (Geneva); D XXIX bis 35, dos. 361 (Auxonne) and dos. 362 (Boulogne-sur-Mer).

56. AN D XXIX bis 35, dos. 364 and 367 (Cahors); AD Aisne, L 605; AN D XXIX bis 36 (2), dos. 376 (Senlis) and 373 (Painbeuf).

57. Rouvière, 367–369; AD Aisne, L 604 (Soissons, June 24); AN D XXIX bis 36 (1), dos. 367; AD Meuse, L 386; Louis-Philippe, 43–47; Henwood and Monange, 102.

58. AN D XXIX bis 36 (2), dos. 375 (Neufchâtel); D XXIX bis 33, dos. 344 (Neuf-Brisach).

59. AN D XXIX bis 35, dos. 363; and D XXIX bis 36 (2), dos. 373 (Saint-Cyr-sur-Char). Also the inspection of a chateau near Fuligny: AD Aube, L 315.

60. AN F[7] 3682[7] (Marne); and *AP* 29: 587.

61. Wahl, 387–392; AN D XXIX bis 36 (2), dos. 374; *AP* 29: 422; and Viola, 129–148.

62. Also killed were de Patrys in Brest, the count de Tralong in Brittany, and the count de Dampierre outside Sainte-Menehould. On the last, see Lefebvre, "Le meurtre du comte de Dampierre."

63. AN D XXIX 81 (Varennes).

64. AN C 125 (2) (Chalonne); D XXIX bis 35, dos. 361 (Argentan); D XXIX bis 36 (1), dos. 367 (Landerneau); Binet, 106–107.

65. Tackett, *Religion, Revolution, and Regional Culture*, 276–279; AD Gironde, 12 L 13 (July 2).

66. Bruneau, 161–163; Wahl, 385–386.

67. Dupuy, 200–205; Binet, 116–118; AN D XXIX bis 35, dos. 365 (La Roche-Derrien); F[7] 3682[18] (Morbihan).

68. Dupuy, 201–205; Binet, 116–17; AN D XXIX bis 36 (1), dos. 369–370; F[7] 3682[18] (Morbihan); and D XXIX bis 35, dos. 365.

69. AN D XXIX bis 36 (1), dos. 367.

7. To Judge a King

1. See, for example, Legendre, 71; Geoffroy, letter of June 22.

2. Thelander, 472–475; Goubert, 27–30; Bloch, 224–226.

3. Goubert, 30; Hunt, *Family Romance*, chap. 2.

4. Markoff, 370–375; and *AP* vols. 1–8.

5. Egret, 390–395; Gottschalk and Maddox, 114, 205–206.

6. AN C 104 (1) (Troyes). There are many similar statements in this dossier.

7. Kennedy, 260–261, 266–267; AN C 125 (2) (Coudray).

8. AN C 125 (1) (Châteaurenard); Bruneau, 164; Dubois, 330; Gaugain, 1: 239; Gower, 69. Thanksgiving ceremonies for Louis' recovery are mentioned in virtually every local monograph on the Revolutionary period.

9. I have analyzed only statements drafted in the name of collective bodies.

Letters by individuals have been excluded. Such statements were signed by as few as three or four or as many as several hundred individuals. Most such statements were found in AN C 124–130 (filed in alphabetical order by town or department). This corpus was supplemented by documents identified in selected departmental archives and in printed local studies. The corpus contains a total of 662 statements from 392 communities. The AN series has also been examined by Paul Girault de Coursac in a strongly promonarchist study, "L'opinion publique après Varennes." Girault de Coursac's figures and conclusions are different from mine.

10. Of 72 statements sent during this period, 22 (31 percent) were primarily sympathetic toward the king, 21 (29 percent) were primarily critical of him, 26 (36 percent) made no mention of him, and 3 (4 percent) were ambiguous.
11. AN C 124–130, letters of Privas, Montrichard, Châteauroux, Arras, and Limoges; *Ville de Rouen*, 33. See also AD Haute-Marne, L 274 (Saint-Dizier).
12. AN C 130 (2), dos. 454 (Vendôme).
13. AN C 130 (2) (Toulon); Labroue, 147.
14. Boutier and Boutry, 16 and passim.
15. Miles, 1: 250; Labroue, 152; AD Meuse, L 2188*; AD Gironde, 12 L 13.
16. Connac, 64–65; AN C 130 (1), dos. 449 (Tours).
17. A total of 265 letters were received during this period, of which 116 (44 percent) were sent by Jacobin clubs. Of the 265, 44 (17 percent) revealed sympathy for Louis; 3 (1 percent) were ambiguous.
18. Labroue, 27–28; AN C 125 (1), dos. 406 (Brioude).
19. A total of 155 (58.5 percent) of the 265. Of these, 88 (56 percent) were from Jacobins.
20. AN C 124–130, letters of Lauzun, Vesoul, Condom, Nevers, Dole, Mirambeau, Fécamp, and Le Puy.
21. AN C 124–130, letters of Montfort-l'Amaury, Alès, Toulouse, Niort; Pommeret, 140–141.
22. AN C 129 (2) (Saint-Paul-les-Trois-Châteaux) and C 128 (2) (Nantes).
23. A total of 63 (24 percent) of the 265, of whom 18 (29 percent) were from Jacobin clubs.
24. AN C 124–130, letters of Aix-en-Provence, Marennes, Colmar, Collongues, Castelnaudary, and Crévy.
25. AN C 124–130, letters of La Bassée, Besançon, Mirambeau, ibid.; Millot, 205.
26. Kennedy, 274; AN C 124–130, letters of Le Puy and Alès.
27. A total of 62 (23.5 percent) of the 265 letters. Our list of such radical addresses is certainly incomplete. Michael Kennedy, who examined local

Jacobin archives throughout the country, found over 60 asking that the king be deposed: Kennedy, 273. However, most of the locations are not mentioned by the author, and they have not been counted here.

28. A total of 32 (52 percent) of the 62.
29. AN C 128 (1), dos. 431 (Montauban); Fray-Fournier, 39–40; AN C 128 (2), dos. 433 (Nantes).
30. Legendre, letter of July 10; Wahl, 397–398; Mathiez, 93; Hugueney, 137.
31. AN C 126 (1) (Dole).
32. AN C 129 (2) (Saint-Claud); C 128 (2) (Niort); Lecesne, 1: 158.
33. Roland, 2: 305, 319.
34. *AP* 4: 44–58.
35. Chobaut, 548–551; Duval-Jouve, 1: 177; Peronnet, 142.
36. AN C 128 (1) (Montpellier).
37. Those of Béziers, Pézenas, Perpignan, Bar-le-Duc, and Strasbourg.
38. Chobaut, 554–556; AD Gironde, 12 L 13; AD Meuse, L 2188*; Roux, 364; Fray-Fournier, 39–40; Thibaudeau, 138.
39. AN C 124–130, letters of Belleville and Châteauroux.
40. Of 325 letters received during this period, only 22 (7 percent) were sympathetic to the king; 67 (20.5 percent) condemned him, and 236 (72.5 percent) made no mention of him. The one town describing the kingship as "sacred" was Bourbon-Lancy: AN C 125 (1).
41. AN C 124–130, letters of Etain, Aire, and Alès; Pommeret, 141.
42. AN C 124–130, letters of Abbeville, Montreuil-sur-Mer, and Fontenay-le-Comte.
43. AN C 124–130, letters of Caen, Grenoble, Etampes, and Péronne.
44. AN C 124–130, letters of Castres, Josselin, Pons, and Bourges.
45. A total of 39 (12 percent) of the 325.
46. AN C 124–130, letters of Besançon, Troyes, Argentan, and La Teste.
47. For example, Legendre, letter of July 19; AN C 124–130, letters of Lamballe, Montpellier, Quimper, Mâcon, Périgueux, Charolles, and Saintes.

8. The Months and Years After

1. *AP* 28: 402–405; Lacroix, 441–443; Mathiez, 193–194; Gower, 110.
2. Gower, 108; Andress, 207–208. All the individuals mentioned here managed to flee or hide out from the police. The Committees on Research and Reports were formally combined in mid-July.
3. AN D XXIX bis 31 B, dos. 321; D XXIX bis 33, dos. 348; D XXIX bis 34, dos. 349–350; *AP* 28: 543; Mathiez, 201–205; Reinhard, 153.
4. Gaultier de Biauzat, letter of December 23; Basquiat de Mugriet, letter of

July 19; also *AP* 28: 365; Bouchette, 614; Durand, letter of July 24; Maupetit, 22 (1906): 480; Thibaudeau, 166–167; Lepoutre, 494; Faulcon, 445; Legendre, 73–76; Dubois, 373.

5. Roland, 2: 335; Short, 20: 654–655, 674.

6. Burstin, "Une Révolution à l'oeuvre," 262; Ruault, 254.

7. Burstin, "Une Révolution à l'oeuvre," 258–262; Aulard, *Jacobins*, 3: 25 and following; Reinhard, 283, 301; Tackett, "Les députés de l'Assemblée législative," 142.

8. Rabaut Saint-Etienne, "Correspondance," 269–270; Gaultier de Biauzat, 2: 389; Vernier, letters of August 6 and 23; Bouchette, 623.

9. Sagnac, "Marie-Antoinette et Barnave," 209–213.

10. Thibaudeau, 183–184; Maupetit, 23 (1907): 92. See also Lindet, 310–311; Vernier, letters of August 3 and 15; Legendre, letter of September 3. By September only sixty to seventy people were said to be attending the Feuillant Club; Périsse Du Luc, letter of September 2.

11. Bouchette, 632; Thibaudeau, 200.

12. *AP* 30: 620–621, 635; Sagnac, "Marie-Antoinette et Barnave," 223.

13. *AP* 30: 621, 632–633, 646.

14. Campan, 291–292; Lafayette, 3: 94; Gaultier de Biauzat, 2: 399–400; Roger, 79; Maupetit, 23 (1907): 114–115; Lévis, 5: 284; Colson, 203; Faulcon, 261–263; Short, 21: 106.

15. Legendre, letter of August 31; Vernier, letter of September 19; Thibaudeau, 182–183; Faulcon, 455, 461–463; Lindet, 318; also Gaultier de Biauzat, letter of September 27.

16. Sagnac, "Marie-Antoinette et Barnave," 212–241.

17. Arneth, 185.

18. Girault de Coursac and Girault de Coursac, 263–270. Note, however, that Louis was suspicious of his brothers, and it is uncertain to what extent he would have divulged his full sentiments to them.

19. Sagnac, *La Révolution*, 337; also Price, 445–447.

20. Legendre, letter of September 5, 1791; Lepoutre, 501.

21. Goetz-Bernstein, 29–30, 154–158; Kaiser, 263–270.

22. See esp. Jordan, 72–73, 108–114, 126–136.

23. *AP* 55: 3–5. There were thirty-three articles in the indictment.

24. Lenôtre, 327–349.

25. Lenôtre, 302–307.

26. Söderhjelm, *Fersen et Marie-Antoinette*, 320–322.

Bibliography

The following list includes only those materials cited in the text, not all those consulted.

Primary Sources

MANUSCRIPTS

Archives Nationales

C 124–131: Correspondence received by the Secretariat of the National Assembly.
D XXIX bis 31–38: Correspondence received by the Committee on Research.
F⁷ 3688¹ (Seine): Archives of the Ministry of the Interior.
F⁷ 3682¹⁸ (Morbihan): ibid.

Archives Départmentales

Series L: archives of the Revolutionary period, in the departments of Aisne, Ardennes, Aube, Gironde, Haute-Marne, Marne, Meurthe, Meuse, Moselle, and Vosges.

Other Archives and Libraries

Bailly, Jean-Sylvain. Letters to divers. BN Manuscrits français 11697.
Basquiat de Mugriet, Alexis. Letters to the municipality of Saint-Sever. AC Saint-Sever, II D 31.
Campmas, Jean-François. Letters to his brother. BM Albi, ms. 177.

Durand, Antoine. Letters to the municipality of Cahors. AM Cahors, unclassed box of letters from Revolutionary deputies, held in BM Cahors.

Fricaud, Claude. Letters to Jean-Marie Gelin. Copies in the private archives of Dr. Robert Favre.

Gantheret, Claude. Letters to Pierre Leflaive. Private collection of Françoise Misserey, Dijon.

Gaultier de Biauzat, Jean-François. Letters to the correspondence committee of Clermont-Ferrand. BM Clermont-Ferrand, mss. 788–789.

Geoffroy, Claude-Jean-Baptiste. Letters to Jean-Marie Gelin. Private archives of Dr. Robert Favre.

Irland de Bazôges, Pierre-Marie. Letters to Henri Filleau. AD Deux-Sèvres, Fonds Beauchet-Filleau, unclassed register of "Lettres politiques, 1788–90."

Legendre, Laurent-François. Letters to electors and municipal officials in Brest. AM Brest, Series D, unclassed.

Périsse Du Luc, Jean-André. Letters to J. B. Willermoz. BM Lyon, Ms. F. G. 5430.

Vernier, Théodore. Letters to municipality of Lons-le-Saunier. Copies AC Bletterans, unclassed dossier of "Lettres de Vernier."

NEWSPAPERS

L'ami du peuple
Chronique de Paris
Le babillard
Le patriote français
Journal de Perlet
L'orateur du peuple
Les révolutions de France et de Brabant
Les révolutions de Paris

OTHER PRINTED SOURCES

Alexandre, Charles-Alexis. "Fragments des mémoires de Charles-Alexis Alexandre sur les journées révolutionnaires de 1791 et 1792." Edited by Jacques Godechot. *AHRF* 24 (1952): 113–251.

Almanach de la ville de Lyon. Lyon, 1791.

Archives parlementaires de 1787 à 1860, recueil complet des débats législatifs et politiques des chambres françaises. Première série (1787–1799). Edited by Jérôme Mavidal et al. 82 vols. Paris, 1867–1913.

Arneth, Alfred von, ed. *Marie-Antoinette, Joseph II und Leopold. Ihr Briefwechsel.* Leipzig, 1866.

Aulard, Alphonse, ed. *La société des Jacobins: Recueil de documents pour l'histoire du club des Jacobins de Paris.* 6 vols. Paris, 1889–1897.

Bachaumont, Louis Petit de, et al. *Marie-Antoinette, Louis XVI et la famille royale. Journal anecdotique tiré des mémoires secrets pour servir à l'histoire de la république des lettres, 1763–1782.* Edited by Ludovic Lalanne. Paris, 1866.

Bimbenet, Eugène. "Pièces justificatives." In *Fuite de Louis XVI à Varennes.* 2d ed. Paris, 1868.

Bouchette, François-Joseph. *Lettres de François-Joseph Bouchette (1735–1810).* Edited by Camille Looten. Lille, 1909.

Bouillé, François-Claude-Amour, marquis de. *Mémoires du marquis de Bouillé.* Edited by François Barrière. Paris, 1859.

Bouillé fils, Louis-Joseph-Amour, marquis de. "Le mémoire inédit de M. le marquis de Bouillé (Comte Louis), lieutenant-général, sur le départ de Louis XVI au mois de juin 1791." In *Mémoires sur l'affaire de Varennes.* Paris, 1823, 17–136.

Campan, Jeanne-Louise-Henriette de. *Mémoires sur la vie de Marie-Antoinette.* Edited by François Barrière. Paris, 1855.

Choiseul-Stainville, Claude-Antoine-Gabriel, duc de. *Relations du départ de Louis XVI, le 20 juin 1791.* Paris, 1822.

Colson, Adrien-Joseph. *Lettres d'un bourgeois de Paris à un ami de province, 1788–1793.* Edited by Chantal Plantier-Sanson. Paris, 1993.

Damas, comte Charles de. "Affaire de Varennes: Rapport de M. le comte Charles de Damas." In *Mémoires sur l'affaire de Varennes.* Paris, 1823, 197–241.

Dumas, Mathieu. *Souvenirs du lieutenant-général comte Mathieu Dumas.* Edited by Christian-Léon Dumas. 3 vols. Paris, 1839.

Dumont, Etienne. *Souvenirs sur Mirabeau et sur les deux premières assemblées législatives.* Paris, 1832.

Falloux, Albert de, ed. *Réflexions sur mes entretiens [du futur Louis XVI] avec M. le duc de La Vauguyon.* Paris, 1851.

Faulcon, Félix. *Correspondance.* Vol. 2: *1789–91.* Edited by G. Debien. Poitiers, 1953.

Ferrières, Charles-Elie, marquis de. *Correspondance inédite.* Edited by Henri Carré. Paris, 1932.

Fersen, Axel von. *Le comte de Fersen et la cour de France. Extraits des papiers.* Vol. 1. Edited by Baron R. M. Klinckowström. Paris, 1877.

Feuillet de Conches, Félix-Sébastien, ed. *Louis XVI, Marie-Antoinette, et Madame Elisabeth. Lettres et documents inédits.* 6 vols. Paris, 1864–1873.

Fischbach, Gustave. *La fuite de Louis XVI d'après les archives municipales de Strasbourg.* Strasbourg, 1879.

Gaultier de Biauzat, Jean-François. *Gaultier de Biauzat, député du Tiers état aux*

Etats généraux de 1789. Sa vie et sa correspondance. Edited by Francisque Mège. 2 vols. Clermont-Ferrand, 1890.

Gauville, Louis-Henri-Charles, baron de. *Journal du baron de Gauville*. Edited by Edouard de Barthélemy. Paris, 1864.

Girault de Coursac, Paul, and Pierrette Girault de Coursac, eds. *Louis XVI à la parole*. Paris, 1989.

Goguelat, François de. *Mémoire de M. le baron de Goguelat, lieutenant-général, sur les événements relatifs au voyage de Louis XVI à Varennes*. Paris, 1823.

Gower, Earl George Granville Leveson. *The Despatches of Earl Gower, English Ambassador at Paris, from June 1790 to August 1792*. Edited by Oscar Browning. Cambridge, 1885.

Guittard de Floriban, Nicolas-Célestin. *Journal de Nicolas-Célestin Guittard de Floriban, bourgeois de Paris sous la Révolution, 1791–1796*. Edited by Raymond Aubert. Paris, 1974.

Heidenstam, O. G., ed. *Marie-Antoinette, Fersen, et Barnave. Leur correspondance*. Paris, 1913.

Lacroix, Sigismond, ed. *Actes de la Commune de Paris pendant la Révolution. 2e série*. Vol. 5: *21 juin–31 juillet 1791*. Paris, 1907.

Lafayette, Marie-Joseph-Paul-Yvres-Roch-Gilbert du Motier, marquis de. *Mémoires, correspondance, et manuscrits*. 6 vols. Paris, 1837–38.

Lagache, M. de. "Relations de M. de Lagache, adressées à Louis XVIII." In Marc Bouloiseau, "Deux relations de l'arrestation du roi à Varennes." *AHRF* 44 (1972): 449–455.

Lefebvre, Georges, ed. *Recueil de documents relatifs aux séances des Etats généraux*. Vol. 1, Part 2: *La séance du 23 juin*. Paris, 1962.

Legendre, Laurent-François. "Correspondance de Legendre, député du Tiers de la sénéchaussée de Brest aux Etats généraux et à l'Assemblée constituante (1789–1791)." *RF* 39 (1900): 515–558; 40 (1901): 46–78.

Lepoutre, Pierre-François. *Député-paysan et fermière de Flandre en 1789. La correspondance des Lepoutre*. Edited by Jean-Pierre Jessenne and Edna Hindie Lemay. Villeneuve d'Ascq, 1998.

Lescure, Mathurin de. *Correspondance secrète inédite sur Louis XVI, Marie-Antoinette, la cour et la ville, de 1777 à 1792*. Paris, 1866.

Lévis, Pierre-Marc-Gaston, duc de. "Lettres du duc de Lévis, 1784–1795." Edited by the duc de Lévis-Mirepoix. *La revue de France* 4 (1929): 227–274, 425–444; 5: 258–295, 418–442, 614–649.

Lindet, Thomas. *Correspondance de Thomas Lindet pendant la Constituante et la Législative (1789–92)*. Edited by Amand Montier. Paris, 1899.

Lombard-Taradeau, Jacques-Athanase de. "Lettres (1789–91)." Edited by L. Honoré. *Le Var historique et géographique* 2 (1925–1927): 230–248, 255–278, 322–342, 347–367.

Louis XVIII. *Relation d'un voyage à Bruxelles et à Coblentz en 1791*. Paris, 1823.

Louis-Philippe. *Mémorial des pensées et actions du duc de Chartres . . . écrit par lui-même en 1790 et 1791*. Paris, 1830.

Maupetit, Michel René. "Lettres (1789–91)." Edited by Quéruau-Lamérie. *Bulletin de la Commission historique et archéologique de la Mayenne*, 2d ser., 17 (1901): 302–327, 439–454; 18 (1902): 133–163, 321–33, 447–475; 19 (1903): 205–250, 348–378; 20 (1904): 88–125, 176–203, 358–377, 446–472; 21 (1905): 93–124, 204–223, 325–363, 365–388; 22 (1906): 67–95, 213–239, 349–384, 454–493; 23 (1907): 87–115.

Ménard de La Groye, François-René-Pierre. *Correspondance (1789–1791)*. Edited by Florence Mirouse. Le Mans, 1989.

Mercier, Louis-Sébastien. *Tableau de Paris* (1781). In *Paris le jour, Paris la nuit*. Edited by Michel Delon. Paris, 1990.

Miles, William Augustus. *The Correspondence of William Augustus Miles on the French Revolution, 1789–1817*. Edited by Charles Popham Miles. 2 vols. London, 1890.

Morris, Gouverneur. *A Diary of the French Revolution*. Edited by Beatrix Cary Davenport. 2 vols. Boston, 1939.

Mousset, Albert. *Un témoignage de la Révolution, le comte de Fernan Nuñez, ambassadeur d'Espagne à Paris, 1787–1791*. Paris, 1923.

Moustier, François-Melchoir de. *Relation du voyage de S. M. Louis XVI lors de son départ pour Montmédy et son arrestation à Varennes*. Paris, 1815.

Nicolardot, Louis. *Journal de Louis XVI*. Paris, 1873.

Oelsner, Konrad-Engelbert. *Flucht Verhör und Hinrichtung Ludwigs XVI, nach der Schilderung eines deutschen Beobachters*. Edited by A. Cartellieri. Leipzig, 1911.

Panon Desbassayns, Henri-Paulin. *Voyage à Paris pendant la Révolution (1790–92). Journal inédit d'un habitant de l'Ile Bourbon*. Edited by Jean-Claude de Guillermin des Sagettes. Paris, 1985.

Pétion, Jérôme. "Voyage de Pétion au retour de Varennes." In *Mémoires inédits de Pétion et mémoires de Buzot et de Barbaroux*. Edited by C. A. Dauban. Paris, 1866, 189–204.

Planta de Wildenberg, chevalier de. "Arrestation du roi Louis XVI à Varennes." In Marc Bouloiseau, "Deux relations de l'arrestation du roi à Varennes." *AHRF* 44 (1972): 440–448.

Rabaut Saint-Etienne, Jean-Paul. "Correspondance pendant la Révolution (1789–93)." Edited by Armand Lods. *RF* 35 (1898): 78–89, 157–177, 259–277.

———— *Précis historique de la Révolution française*. Paris, 1792.

Raigecourt, comte Charles de. "Exposé de la conduite de M. le comte Charles de Ragecourt à l'affaire de Varennes." In *Mémoires sur l'affaire de Varennes*. Paris, 1823, 187–195.

Rochambeau, Jean-Baptiste Donatien de Vimeur, comte de. *Mémoires militaires, historiques, et politiques*. 2 vols. Paris, 1824.

Roger, Jean-Pierre. "Lettres du constituant Roger." Edited by R. Rumeau. *RF* 43 (1902): 68–82.

Roland, Marie-Jeanne. *Les lettres de Madame Roland*. Edited by Claude Perroud. 2 vols. Paris, 1901–02.

Ruault, Nicolas. *Gazette d'un Parisien sous la Révolution. Lettres à son frère, 1783–96*. Edited by Christiane Rimbaud and Anne Vassal. Paris, 1976.

Saint-Priest, François-Emmanuel Guignard, comte de. *Mémoires: Règnes de Louis XV et de Louis XVI*. Edited by baron de Barante. 2 vols. Paris, 1929.

Short, William. "Letters." In *The Papers of Thomas Jefferson*. Edited by Julian P. Boyd. Vols. 19–22. Princeton, 1974–1986.

Thibaudeau, Antoine-René-Hyacinthe. *Correspondance inédite*. Edited by H. Carré and Pierre Boissonnade. Paris, 1898.

Thompson, J. M. *English Witnesses of the French Revolution*. Oxford, 1938.

Toulongeon, François-Emmanuel, vicomte de. *Histoire de la France depuis la Révolution*. 7 vols. Paris, 1801.

Tourzel, Louise-Elisabeth de. *Mémoires de Madame la duchesse de Tourzel*. Edited by Jean Chalon. Paris, 1969.

Valory, François-Florent de. "Précis historique du voyage entrepris par S. M. Louis XVI le 21 juin 1791. De l'arrestation de la famille royale à Varennes, et de son retour." In *Mémoires sur l'affaire de Varennes*. Paris, 1823, 243–324.

Ville de Rouen. Analyses des délibérations. Rouen, 1905.

Weber, Joseph. *Mémoires de Weber, frère de lait de Marie-Antoinette, reine de France*. Paris, 1847.

Secondary Sources

Aimond, Charles. *L'énigme de Varennes*. Paris, 1936.

———— *Histoire de la ville de Varennes-en-Argonne*. Bar-le-Duc, 1928.

———— *Histoire religieuse de la Révolution dans le département de la Meuse et le diocèse de Verdun (1789–1802)*. Paris, 1949.

Andress, David. *Massacre at the Champ de Mars: Popular Dissent and Political Culture in the French Revolution*. Woodbridge, England, 2000.

Arbellot, Guy, and Bernard Lepetit. *Atlas de la Révolution française*. Vol. 1: *Routes et communications*. Paris, 1987.

Arnaud, Gaston. *Histoire de la Révolution dans le département de l'Ariège, 1789–1795*. Toulouse, 1904.

Aulard, Alphonse. *Histoire politique de la Révolution française.* 3d ed. Paris, 1905.

Baker, Keith. *Condorcet: From Natural Philosophy to Social Mathematics.* Chicago, 1975.

Baumont, Henri. *Le département de l'Oise pendant la Révolution (1790–1795).* Paris, 1993.

Beauvalet-Boutouyrie, Scarlet. *Dictionnaire démographique des communes de la Meuse, 1800–1982.* Bar-le-Duc, n.d.

Biernawski, Louis. *Un département sous la Révolution française. L'Allier de 1789 à l'an III.* Paris, 1909.

Binet, C. "Les répercussions de la fuite de Louis XVI en Bretagne." *Comité des travaux historiques. Bulletin historique et philologique,* 1911, 93–122.

Bloch, Marc. *The Royal Touch.* New York, 1989.

Bourdin, Isabelle. *Les sociétés populaires à Paris pendant la Révolution.* Paris, 1937.

Boutier, Jean, and Philippe Boutry. *Atlas de la Révolution française.* Vol. 6: *Les sociétés politiques.* Paris, 1992.

Bouvier, Félix. *Les Vosges pendant la Révolution, 1789–1800. Etude historique.* Paris, 1885.

Braesch, Frédéric. "Les pétitions du Champ de Mars." *Revue historique* 142 (1923): 192–209; 143: 1–39, 181–197.

Brégail, M. *Le Gers pendant la Révolution.* Auch, 1934.

Bruneau, Marcel. *Les débuts de la Révolution dans les départements du Cher et de l'Indre.* Paris, 1902.

Buirette, Claude. *Histoire de la ville de Sainte-Menehould et de ses environs.* 2d ed. Sainte-Menehould, 1882.

Burstin, Haim. "La loi Le Chapelier et la conjoncture révolutionnaire." In *Naissance des libertés économiques.* Edited by Alain Plessis. Paris, 1993.

———— "Problèmes du travail à Paris sous la Révolution." *Revue d'histoire moderne et contemporaine* 44 (1997): 650–682.

———— "Une Révolution à l'oeuvre. Le faubourg Saint-Marcel (1789–1794)." Doctoral thesis, University of Paris I, 1999.

Carrot, Georges. *Le maintien de l'ordre en France.* 2 vols. Toulouse, 1984.

Censer, Jack Richard. *Prelude to Power: The Parisian Radical Press, 1789–1791.* Baltimore, 1976.

Charavay, Etienne. *Les assemblées électorales de Paris, 26 août 1791–12 août 1792.* Paris, 1894.

Chobaut, H. "La pétition du club de Montpellier en faveur de la république." *AHRF* 4 (1927): 547–563.

Connac, Emile. *Histoire de la Révolution à Toulouse et dans le département de la Haute-Garonne.* Toulouse, 1901.

David, Philippe. *Un port de l'océan pendant la Révolution. La Rochelle et son district, 1791–1795.* La Rochelle, 1938.

Dubois, Eugène. *Histoire de la Révolution dans l'Ain.* Vol. 1: *La Constituante (1789–1791).* Bourg-en-Bresse, 1931.

Duprat, Annie. *Le roi décapité. Essai sur les imaginaires politiques.* Paris, 1992.

Dupuy, Roger. *La garde nationale et les débuts de la Révolution en Ille-et-Vilaine (1789–mars 1793).* Paris, 1972.

Duval-Jouve, Joseph. *Montpellier pendant la Révolution.* 2 vols. Montpellier, 1879–1881.

Egret, Jean. *Necker, ministre de Louis XVI.* Paris, 1975.

Farge, Arlette. *Dire et mal dire. L'opinion publique au XVIII siècle.* Paris, 1992.

Fougeray Du Coudrey, R. *Granville et ses environs pendant la Révolution.* Granville, 1920.

Fournel, Victor. *L'événement de Varennes.* Paris, 1890.

Fray-Fournier, A. *Le club des Jacobins de Limoges.* Limoges, 1903.

Gaugain, Ferdinand. *Histoire de la Révolution dans la Mayenne.* 4 vols. Laval, 1919–1921.

Genty, Maurice. *Paris, 1789–1795. L'apprentissage de la citoyenneté.* Paris, 1987.

Gillet, P. *Louis XVI et sa famille à Epernay aux retour de Varennes.* Epernay, 1968.

Girault de Coursac, Paul. "L'opinion publique après Varennes." *Découverte,* no. 22 (1978): 3–28; no. 23: 3–26; no. 24: 3–28.

Godechot, Jacques. *La prise de la Bastille.* Paris, 1965.

Goetz-Bernstein, H. A. *La diplomatie de la Gironde. Jacques-Pierre Brissot.* Paris, 1912.

Gottschalk, Louis, and Margaret Maddox. *Lafayette in the French Revolution: From the October Days through the Federation.* Chicago, 1973.

Goubert, Pierre. *L'ancien régime.* Vol. 2: *Les pouvoirs.* Paris, 1973.

Hardman, John. *Louis XVI.* New Haven, 1993.

Hardman, John, and Munro Price, eds. *Louis XVI and the Comte de Vergennes: Correspondence, 1774–1787.* Oxford, 1998.

Henwood, Philippe, and Edmond Monange. *Brest. Un port en Révolution, 1789–1799.* N.p., 1989.

Hesse, Carla. *The Other Enlightenment: How French Women Became Modern.* Princeton, 2001.

Hugueney, Louis. *Les clubs dijonnais sous la Révolution.* Dijon, 1905.

Hunt, Lynn. *The Family Romance of the French Revolution.* Berkeley, 1992.

———— *Politics, Culture, and Class in the French Revolution.* Berkeley, 1984.

Jordan, David P. *The King's Trial: Louis XVI vs. the French Revolution.* Berkeley, 1979.

Kaiser, Thomas. "Who's Afraid of Marie-Antoinette? Diplomacy, Austrophobia, and the Queen." *French History* 14 (2000): 241–271.

Kaplan, Steven L. *The Famine Plot Persuasion in Eighteenth-Century France.* Philadelphia, 1982.

———— *La fin des corporations*. Paris, 2001.

Kates, Gary. *The Cercle Social, the Girondins, and the French Revolution*. Princeton, 1985.

Kennedy, Michael L. *The Jacobin Clubs in the French Revolution: The First Years*. Princeton, 1982.

Klaits, Joseph. *Printed Propaganda under Louis XIV: Absolute Monarchy and Public Opinion*. Princeton, 1976.

Labroue, Henri. *L'esprit public en Dordogne pendant la Révolution*. Paris, 1911.

Langlois, Claude. "Le serment révolutionnaire, 1789–1791: Fondation et exclusion." In *Le serment*. Edited by Raymond Verdier. Vol. 2. Paris, 1991, 389–395.

Laurent, Gustave. "A propos de Drouet." *AHRF* 21 (1949): 247–251.

Lecesne, Edmond. *Arras sous la Révolution*. 2 vols. Arras, 1882–83.

Leclercq, Henri. *La fuite du roi (avril–juillet 1791)*. Paris, 1936.

Lefebvre, Georges. "Le meurtre du comte de Dampierre (22 juin 1791)." In *Etudes sur la Révolution française*. Paris, 1963, 393–405.

———— *La Révolution française. La fuite du roi*. Paris, 1951.

Lenôtre, Georges. *Le drame de Varennes, juin 1791*. Paris, 1905.

Lesort, André. *L'esprit public dans le département de la Meuse au moment de l'arrestation de Louis XVI à Varennes*. Paris, 1908.

Lever, Evelyne. *Louis XVI*. Paris, 1985.

Markoff, John. "Images of the King at the Beginning of the Revolution." In *Revolutionary Demands: A Content Analysis of the Cahiers de Doléances of 1789*. Edited by Gilbert Shapiro and John Markoff. Stanford, 1997, 369–376.

Mathiez, Albert. *Le club des Cordeliers pendant la crise de Varennes*. Paris, 1910.

McManners, John. *Church and Society in Eighteenth-Century France*. 2 vols. Oxford, 1998.

Michon, Georges. *Essai sur l'histoire du parti Feuillant. Adrien Duport*. Paris, 1924.

Millot, Jean. "La fuite à Varennes, conséquences dans l'ordre public et le domaine politique à Besançon." *Académie des sciences, belles-lettres et arts de Besançon. Procès-verbaux et mémoires* 172 (1957): 197–214.

Monnier, Raymonde. "Paris au printemps 1791. Les sociétés fraternelles et le problème de la souveraineté." *AHRF* 64 (1992): 1–16.

Nicolas, Raymond. *L'esprit public et les élections dans le département de la Marne de 1790 à l'an VIII. Essai sur la Révolution française en province*. Châlons-sur-Marne, 1909.

Padover, Saul K. *The Life and Death of Louis XVI*. New York, 1939.

Pastoors, A. *Histoire de la ville de Cambrai pendant la Révolution, 1789–1802*. 2 vols. Cambrai, 1908.

Pegg, Carl Hamilton. "Sentiments républicains dans la presse parisienne lors de la fuite du roi." *AHRF* 11 (1934): 435–445.

Péronnet, Michel. "Le club de Montpellier appelle la république." In *La république en Languedoc et Roussillon, 1792–1958. Colloque de Nîmes, 4 et 5 septembre 1991.* Nîmes, 1993, 139–165.

Pionnier, Edmond. *Essai sur l'histoire de la Révolution à Verdun (1789–1795).* Nancy, 1905.

Pisani, Paul. *L'église de Paris et la Révolution.* 4 vols. Paris, 1908–1911.

Pommeret, Hervé. *L'esprit politique dans le département des Côtes-du-Nord pendant la Révolution: 1789–99.* Saint-Brieuc, 1921.

Price, Munro. "Louis XVI and Gustavus III: Secret Diplomacy and Counter-revolution, 1791–1792." *Historical Journal* 42 (1999): 435–466.

Reinhard, Marcel. *La chute de la royauté.* Paris, 1969.

Roche, Daniel. *The People of Paris: An Essay in Popular Culture in the Eighteenth Century.* Berkeley, 1987.

Rouvière, François. *Histoire de la Révolution française dans le département du Gard.* Vol. 1. Nîmes, 1887.

Roux, marquis Marie de. *La Révolution à Poitiers et dans la Vienne.* Paris, 1910.

Rudé, George. *The Crowd in the French Revolution.* New York, 1959.

Sagnac, Philippe. "L'état des esprits en France à l'époque de Varennes (juin–juillet 1791)." *Revue de l'histoire moderne* 12 (1909): 149–175.

——— "Marie-Antoinette et Barnave d'après leur correspondance secrète." *RF*, n.s., 3 (1935): 207–241.

——— *La Révolution (1789–1792).* Paris, 1920.

Schneider, René. *Au lendemain de Varennes. Un épisode de la Révolution en Moselle.* Metz, 1989.

Shapiro, Barry M. *Revolutionary Justice in Paris, 1789–1890.* Cambridge, 1993.

Söderhjelm, Alma. *Correspondance secrète. Marie-Antoinette et Barnave.* Paris, 1934.

——— *Fersen et Marie-Antoinette.* Paris, 1930.

Sol, Eugène. *La Révolution en Quercy.* 4 vols. Paris, 1926.

Tackett, Timothy. *Becoming a Revolutionary: The Deputies of the French National Assembly and the Emergence of a Revolutionary Culture.* Princeton, 1996.

——— "Conspiracy Obsession in a Time of Revolution: French Elites and the Origins of the Terror: 1789–1792." *American Historical Review* 105 (2000): 691–713.

——— "The Constituent Assembly in the Second Year of the French Revolution." In *Revolution, Society, and the Politics of Memory.* Edited by Michael Adcock et al. Melbourne, 1996, 162–169.

——— "Les députés de l'Assemblée législative, 1791–92." In *Pour la Révolu-*

tion française. En hommage à Claude Mazauric. Edited by Christine Le Bozec and Eric Wauters. Rouen, 1998, 139–144.

———— *Religion, Revolution, and Regional Culture.* Princeton, 1987.

Thelander, Dorothy R. "Mother Goose and Her Goslings: The France of Louis XIV as Seen through the Fairy Tale." *Journal of Modern History* 54 (1982): 467–496.

Tulard, Jean. *Nouvelle histoire de Paris. La Révolution.* Paris, 1789.

Van Kley, Dale K. *The Religious Origins of the French Revolution: From Calvin to the Civil Constitution, 1560–1791.* New Haven, 1996.

Vast, Albert. *Sur le chemin de Varennes. Vieux souvenirs du 21 juin 1791 d'après de nouveaux documents et les relations de témoins oculaires.* Paris, 1907.

Vidal, Pierre. *Histoire de la Révolution française dans le département des Pyrénées-Orientales.* 3 vols. Perpignan, 1885–1888.

Viola, Paolo. *Il trono vuoto. La transizione della sovranità nella rivoluzione francese.* Turin, 1989.

Wahl, Maurice. *Les premières années de la Révolution à Lyon, 1788–1792.* Paris, 1894.

Walter, Gérard. *Histoire des Jacobins.* Paris, 1946.

Whaley, Leigh. "The Varennes Crisis and the Division amongst the Radicals in the French Revolution." *Modern and Contemporary France* 38 (1989): 34–44.

Wick, Daniel L. *A Conspiracy of Well-Intentioned Men: The Society of Thirty and the French Revolution.* New York, 1987.

Zweig, Stefan. *Marie-Antoinette: The Portrait of an Average Woman.* New York, 1933.

Index

mercenaries, 4, 14–15, 17–18, 21, 47,
53, 59, 65, 67, 68–71, 75, 77–78, 86,
87, 161, 162
Mercier, Louis-Sébastien, 90, 92
Mercure nationale, 109
Mercy-Argenteuil, François, count de
(Austrian ambassador), 36, 39, 55–
56, 87, 212
Méthains, abbé, 13
Metz, 20, 46, 50, 53, 68, 152, 161, 163
Meuse, department, 12, 15, 162
Meuse, river, 20, 68, 161, 162
Mézières, 159
Miles, William Augustus, 96, 187
militias. *See* national guards
ministers, 34–36, 42, 54, 102, 117, 127,
128, 132
Mirabeau, Gabriel-Jean-Honoré,
count de, 39, 40
Monarchy Club, 42, 95
monarchy, 8, 29, 38, 39, 41, 56, 82,
108–112, 113, 116, 118, 130, 131,
133, 134, 138, 139, 158, 179, 180–
184, 192, 193–198, 199–200, 201,
207, 221
money, paper, 72, 73, 94
Montauban, 193
Montblainville, 19
Montesquieu, Charles de Secondat,
baron de, 199
Montfaucon, 9, 19
Montmartre, 83
Montmédy, 3, 8, 50, 54, 55, 63, 68, 69,
85, 133, 160, 219
Montmirail, 51, 66, 81
Montmorillon, 155
Montpellier, 172, 196–197, 201
Morris, Gouverneur, 133
Moselle, 163
Moulins, 152
Moustier, François-Melchoir de, 58,

59, 62, 63, 65, 66, 75–76, 79. *See
also* bodyguards
Muguet de Nanthou, Hyacinthe-
François-Félix, 137, 141

Nancy, 152
Nancy, mutiny of, 14, 50, 69
Nantes, 153, 175, 189, 193
Napoleon, 218
National Assembly, 4, 21, 23, 24, 36,
37, 41, 45, 49, 54, 79, 87, 91, 95,
100, 104, 119–150, 153, 164, 167,
173, 177, 179, 186, 191, 201, 210,
219–223; correspondence, 10, 120,
130, 134, 139, 141, 154–155, 156,
166, 179, 183, 184–185, 198, 204;
decrees of, 12, 23, 67, 82, 94–95,
100, 114, 115, 126–127, 141, 144,
151–152, 155, 158–159, 165, 168,
170, 171, 175, 176, 198, 201, 202,
203, 204, 207; representatives on
mission, 81–85, 128; popular image
of, 84, 105–108, 114, 118, 122, 139,
143, 144, 147, 150, 175, 190, 198–
202, 205, 221; attitudes towards
Paris crowds, 93, 122, 124, 128,
144–145, 147; hall, 106, 113, 120,
140; petitions presented to, 111–
112, 113, 114, 118, 143, 144, 146,
149, 186, 187, 197, 200, 204, 222;
reaction to king's flight, 114, 118,
124–142, 194; oaths taken by deputies, 120, 126, 157; factions, 121,
126, 207; attitudes towards king,
124, 125, 129–130, 133, 136–137,
138–139, 140, 142; assumes executive powers, 126–127, 132, 134, 135;
oaths and affirmations of allegiance to, 127, 128, 157, 185, 190,
199
national guards: in Varennes, 4, 8, 11–

12, 13, 14; involvement in arrest of
king, 5, 16–20, 23, 24, 70, 74, 75,
78–79, 80, 81, 82; uniforms, 11, 96,
98, 106, 109; creation of, 11–12; appearance in parades and celebrations, 12, 39, 117, 118, 208; and local defense, 14, 70, 128, 159–160,
161, 162–163, 164, 170; reaction of
Parisian guards to king's flight, 23,
98, 99, 100, 106; insubordination
and opposition to king, 37, 44, 49,
57, 118, 122, 147, 215, 220; and control of popular unrest in Paris, 42–
43, 83, 84, 95–96, 113, 144, 145,
146, 148–150, 203, 205; reaction of
provincial guards to king's flight,
71, 156, 157, 179, 185, 188, 192, 195,
196; and repression in provinces,
168, 170, 172, 173–174, 175, 176–
177, 204
nationalism, 11, 87, 158, 215
Necker, Jacques, 35, 36
Neuville, Madame de, 5, 37, 47, 48,
59, 60, 63, 66, 82, 132
newspapers, 32, 66, 91–92, 97, 99,
101, 102, 104, 105, 109, 111, 115–
116, 122, 152, 185, 186, 203. *See also*
journalists
Night of August 4 (1789), 120
Niort, 196
nobility, 10, 11, 15, 18, 36, 44–45, 54,
69, 87, 95, 97, 107, 119, 135, 165,
169–170, 171, 173, 174, 175–177,
195, 205, 221, 222–223
Normandy, 175
Notre Dame, 88, 101, 116

oath, ecclesiastical, 13, 41, 95, 122,
220
Oath, Tennis Court, 120, 158, 191
oaths, patriotic, 12, 106–107, 156–158,

168, 189, 190. *See also* National As-
sembly, oaths and affirmations of
allegiance to
October Days, 37, 42, 58, 60, 108, 120
Oelsner, Konrad-Engelbert, 99, 101
Oise, 163
Orléans, 171, 194
Orléans, duke d', 194

Paine, Thomas, 111
Palais Royal, 143, 144
panics, 13–14, 79–80, 128, 150, 161–
164, 222. *See also* Great Fear
Panon Desbassayns, Henri-Paulin,
118, 143
Paris, 8, 21, 57, 88–118, 205; western
suburbs, 59, 88–89; eastern suburbs, 61–62, 84, 89, 107, 112; population's reaction to king's flight,
83–85, 97–118, 142–150, 222; general description, 88–89; population,
89–90; *map,* 90; politicization of
the population, 90–93, 113; political associations, 92–94; sections,
94, 100–101, 107, 112, 117, 152, 186;
municipal government, 94, 95–96,
98, 100–101, 114, 115, 116–117,
147–148
parish clergy, 13, 95, 105, 119, 167
Parlement, 88, 91
passive citizens, 93, 100
patriotic clubs, 12, 53, 86, 92–94, 121,
152, 156, 185, 186, 187, 188, 194,
197, 204. *See also* fraternal societies
Pau, 164
Périgueux, 202
Perpignan, 153
Pétion de Villeneuve, Jérôme, 40, 82,
83, 85, 114, 123, 124, 133, 138, 144,
196, 205, 206, 207, 217
Petit, Monsieur, 171, 173